The Ties That Bind:
African-American Consciousness of Africa

By

Bernard Makhosezwe Magubane

Africa World Press, Inc.

P.O. Box 1892
Trenton, New Jersey 08607

AFRICA WORLD PRESS, INC.
P.O. Box 1892
TRENTON, NEW JERSEY 08607

First Printing 1987
Second Printing 1989

Copyright ©Bernard Magubane

Typeset by TypeHouse of Pennington

Cover design by Adjoa Jackson-Burrowes

Library of Congress Catalog Card Number: 86-70980

ISBN: 0-86543-036-5 Cloth
       0-86543-037-3 Paper

Dedicated To Our Grandchildren:
Nomzamo
Nosizwe
Thulani
And Many More To Come

Contents

Preface

Using the phrase Afro-American* Consciousness of Africa this study will seek to explore the historical significance of the relationship of black Americans to Africa. I make no pretense to presenting a history of American blacks' opinions about Africa. The purpose is to interpret some facts that I assume most people already know—at least in outline. The theme of this study, the Afro-American's consciousness of Africa, is nothing but the interpretation of the black man's responses to certain cultural and historical premises, established by his captors, and upon which black self-contempt was built. Looking at the image of Africa given by his captors we are able to throw some light on the sources of the black man's self-contempt. It is on this thesis that the Afro-American did not reject his background; he rejected instead the negative image imposed on his motherland by his captors.

It was the poet Countee Cullen, who in his poem *Heritage* asked the poignant question:

> What is Africa to me
> Copper sun or scarlet sea,
> Jungle star or jungle track,
> Strong bronzed men, or regal black
> Women from whose loins I sprang
> When the birds of Eden sang?
> *One three centuries removed*
> *From the scenes his fathers loved*
> *Spicy grove, cinnamon tree*
> *What is Africa to me?*[1]

*The terms Afro-American and black are used throughout the text. The word Negro, because it has come to have pejorative implications, is used only where it refers to official terminology or documentation.

Many decades after the question was posed, the answer to the meaning and significance of Africa to the Afro-American still remains unsettled. Various writers concerned with the problems of identity in the Afro-American community still have not provided us with a consensual view about the ways in which the African background affects the identity problems of black people in America. On the contrary there is a host of diverse opinions often marked by contradictory thoughts that dispute whether Africa has anything to do with the Afro-American's self-conceptions or his conception by the white society.

An examination of Western European and American literature, motion pictures, cartoons and even casual conversations reveals the fact that in the Western world, Africa and its people are still viewed as a land of primitive childhood, if not a country of wild animals and wild people. This deeply-imbedded stereotype was bound in one way or another to stimulate black thinking about Africa. In almost every case, assumptions about Afro-American inferiority begin by associating him with the continent of Africa and African people who were assumed to have certain genetic defects which the black man in America inherited.

The denigration of Africa was functionally related to the defense of imperialist interest and the rationalizations of slavery and oppression of the descendants of Africa in their lands of captivity. Afro-American concerns about Africa and desire for its redemption were, in a sense, testimony to the fact that blacks could neither hope in America (for they knew both its origins and its moment), nor could they love America and love their bleeding forefathers as well.[2] If, therefore, pride and prejudice about Africa means anything, they can only mean the underlying historical process of alienation of a people in relationship to world historical developments, in particular Europe's defamation and prostitutions of Africa during the era of capitalism and imperialism. The African was enslaved and disgraced and a racial ideology of white supremacy emerged as the scientifically-cloaked foundation for the power lust, and to justify the new world order and its socioeconomic system.

To understand the nature and the evolution of the American black's ambivalence in his consciousness of Africa, certain factors, including the context from which any feeling about Africa on the part of the black emerged, must be spelled out. The black man's economic enslavement and pillage were supported by pseudo philosophical, sociological and psychological ideas that assigned a subaltern place to Africa and its people in the general world history. The assumptions of the white world about Africa and the black man evoked in every black man a complex of emotional responses and a distinct psychology about himself and his relations to Africa. An historical understanding of white assumptions about Africa clarifies the birth, continuity and meaning of the black man's self-hatred, lowered self-esteem and estrangement from anything African. It also explains the constant self-discovery that has been part of the black experience: colored, Negro and now black and Afro-American.

Lacking control on the political and economic plane by virtue of enslavement and incorporation into the developing capitalist civilization, black folks invariably lacked autonomy and control of their historical and cultural destiny. Any possibility of interfering in the society of their captors and of the capitalist civilization was made impossible. Formed as a negation of their civilization, their sufferings were made hopeless by the most cruel ideological persecution. The thrust of racism from the onset was to inspire self-contempt and self-hatred. As Ribeiro put it, "Even the most enlightened strata among extra-European peoples learned to view themselves and their fellow men as a subhumanity destined to a subaltern role."[3]

The combination of various factors—enslavement, denigration and contempt of Africa (and all it stood for), exploitation and white definitions of the black and his role in world history—created severe problems of identity. Was it possible for the black man to accept white definitions of the African character and to retain his integrity and self-identity? Ruth F. Baird sums up the thoughts that have given rise to the Africa problematic discussed in this work; in her poem *Nemesis* she writes:

> You snatched me from my land,
> Branded my body with your irons,
> And my soul with the slave name "Negro"
> (How devilish clever to spell it upper
>   case
> and keep me always lower!)

As long as white hegemony over Africa in particular, and the world in general, remained as an unchallenged world order, the black man could not have a true identity with himself or with his African kith and kin. The aversion to Africa on the part of the blacks should be treated as an historical error, not a personal or individual one. Viewed from that angle we see that the historical conception of Africa during the epoch of white supremacy must be defined and elaborated. It was the stereotypes created by whites which made any organic assimilation of the African cultural history by most blacks almost impossible. Slavery brought the African into the New World in a violent and traumatic manner. It cut him off from all traditional human ties of kin and nation and even his own cosmology. Insofar as it was possible he was prevented from creating new ties, except to his master, and in consequence his descendents behave in ways even more alienated. This was the basis that led eventually to the rejection of the African past and even to the name Afro-American.

The result was the development among black people of what Ribeiro calls a spurious self-image, constructed to find a new place in the world of white supremacy. The name Negro became a new description given to the black man in America, a new identity divorced from Africa. The new description was tantamount, however, to an acceptance of compulsory deculturation.[4]

This book then presents an interpretation and analysis of the phenomenon of ambivalence so persistent in the Afro-American consciousness of Africa. Today a wide range of black opinion has accepted Pan-Africanism and Africa and many are consciously making an effective attempt to create "more links with Africa." The right of blacks to be culturally independent is now accepted, at least verbally, without question. But this was not always the case. The present study is offered as an exploration in the field of social identity as it effects people in diaspora. The identity of every people is shaped in the environment, it is a legacy of historical forces.

Any study of black identity must obviously begin with the image of Africa in the Western world. Was Africa a dark savage continent when the black man was enslaved? The first chapter deals with the ideological issues in the deformed African image, and the second is a concept analysis of the stereotypes about Africa. The third chapter deals with the ideas of racism and how these ideas always began by identifying black inferiority with African backwardness. The fourth chapter deals with the genesis of Africanism in the Afro-American community. The fifth chapter deals with Garvey's "Back-to-Africa" movement as an exercise in self-discovery or self-legitimation. This exercise was to be more materially expressed in Pan-Africanism, dealt with in the sixth chapter. The seventh chapter deals with the Italian assault on Ethiopia and how this was perceived as another white man's assault of black people. This incident awakened the Pan-African consciousness to a new level. The eighth chapter deals with African independence and nationhood after World War II, and the change this brought about in the Afro-American's identity and self-respect. The ninth chapter deals with racism in South Africa and the Afro-American response and the tenth chapter is a summarization of the arguments.

Among the many friends who helped in this study I would like to express special thanks to Leo Kuper and John Horton, my dissertation committee advisors. Even more I would like to thank Professor Donald Scott Jr. and M. Wade Keller who helped materially. For special indulgence and assistance beyond the call of duty, I would like to say a word of thanks to

Anthony Ngubo who read the draft and Roy Bryce Laporte with whom I discussed many of the ideas now expressed in this work. None of these good folks is in any way responsible for what is contained in this exercise, I alone am responsible for any errors of fact or interpretation. Last but not least I would like to thank the Research Foundation of the University of Connecticut for typing the draft revision of the manuscript.

Notes

[1]Countee Cullen, *On These I Stand*, Harper and Row, New York, 1927.

[2]Vincent Harding, "Beyond Chaos: Black History and the Search for New Land," *Amistad*, A Vintage Periodical, February 1970, p. 285.

[3]Darcy Ribeiro, *The Americas and Civilization*, E.P. Dutton and Company, New York, 1972, p. 74.

[4]*Ibid.*, p. 24.

CHAPTER ONE

Afro-American Consciousness of Africa: Some Theoretical Issues

The colored people are not yet known, even to their most professed friends among the white Americans, for the reason that politicians, religionists and abolitionists have each and all, at different times, presumed to think for, dictate to, and know better what suited colored people than they knew themselves; and consequently, there has been no other knowledge of them obtained, than that which has been obtained through these mediums. Their history, past, present, and future, has been written by them, who, for reasons well known . . . are not their representatives, and therefore, do not properly nor fairly represent their wants and claims among their fellows. Of these impressions, we intend disabusing the public mind and correcting the false impressions of all classes upon this great subject. A moral and mental, is as obnoxious as a physical servitude, and not to be tolerated; as the one may, eventually, lead to the other . . . .

—Martin R. Delany, 1852

One of the persistent themes in the Afro-American's efforts for full citizenship in American society is one form or another of black nationalism. However, black nationalism is for most people difficult to conceive, let alone to accept as reality. It is for them the kind of truth which is too terrible to be believed; it leads nowhere but to despair; it subverts hope, the ultimate pillar of the social order. The fact that black nationalism lacks a territorial base is a further complication because the American black has no felt relationship to Western history even though he has been part of it for over three centuries. His nationalism springs from a never-never land, according to its critics, and leads nowhere. He cannot invoke the Judeo-Christian past as the structure of his present. What Willbald said about the Germans and their history could be applied to the Afro-American and Western history:

It is quite correct that we Germans have no connections with the history of our people—but what is the reason for this? It is because this history has been *without results*, because we are unable to look upon ourselves as products of its organic development like the English and the French, for example; because what we needs must call our history is the history not of our *life*, but of our *illness* which has still to reach its crisis.[1] (Emphasis in the original)

The only other alternative is to invoke the African past, yet all references to black inferiority are associated with that past. Therefore what holds true for the black in his lack of identification with the Judeo-Christian past also holds true for his African past. The Afro-American dilemma is explained as follows by Drake:

> In America, this "African descent" is considered to be the only really socially relevant fact about Negroes, and some states actually define a Negro as "anyone with an ascertainable trace of Negro blood." Whether those who are defined as "American Negroes" like it or not, history and the peculiar evaluations of American society have linked them with the fate of Africa and its peoples. This is a reality to which Negroes in the United States have always had to adjust.[2]

The African past is not clear and easily accessible to the American black without extensive learning; it is not part of his daily folklore.[3] The black child only comes in contact with the negative aspect of it in school, and the masses cannot be said to find themselves at home in it. They are obliged to halt before it, as before some alien and unintelligible world. Thus DuBois could write:

> The spell of Africa is upon me. The ancient witchery of her medicine is burning my drowsy, dreamy blood. This is not a country, it is a world— a universe of itself and for itself, a thing Different, Immense, Menacing, Alluring. It is a great black bosom where the Spirit longs to die . . . . Africa is the Spiritual Frontier of humankind.[4]

The American black, because he had been denied a natural evolution in American society, has a perpetual question about who he is. DuBois and others found themselves retreating into mysticism in the face of this problem. Richard Wright expressed the dilemma in these words:

> The Negro American is the only American in America who says: "I want to be an American." More-or-less all other Americans are born

Americans and take their Americanism for granted. Hence the American Negro's effort to be an American is a self-conscious thing. America is something outside him and he wishes to become part of that America. But, since color easily marks him off from being an ordinary American, and since he lives amidst social conditions pregnant with racism he becomes an American who is not accepted as an American, hence a kind of negative American.[5]

The loss of identity implied in what Wright is saying ultimately leads the individual to a state of alienation both from himself and from the larger society. He is then constantly preoccupied with the seeking of the self, and black nationalism in its search for roots becomes inextricably conscious of, even though ambivalent about, Africa. But to recognize this still leaves the crucial question unanswered: Is black nationalism legitimate in a nation which is described as a melting pot?

Formal freedom granted to the blacks more than 100 years ago did not lead to social integration but to social rejection. This confronted the generation of freed blacks after emancipation with the acute problem of not belonging. Their plight was that they were formally free and equal under the Constitution, particularly in the North, but deprived of a place in the world which could make their opinion significant and their actions effective. DuBois noted:

It is doubtful if there is another group of twelve million people in the midst of modern cultured land who are so widely inhibited and mentally confined as the American Negro. Within the colored race the philosophy of salvation has by the pressure of caste been curiously twisted and distorted. Shall they use the torch and dynamite? Shall they go North, of fight it out in the South? Shall they segregate themselves even more than they are now, in states, towns, cities, or sections. Shall they leave the country? Are they Americans or foreigners? Shall they stand and sing "My Country 'Tis of Thee"? Shall they marry and rear children and save and buy homes, or deliberately commit race suicide?[6]

It is the nature of this experience and the vicarious role Africa played in the black's historical plight that are the focus of our interest. As Hannah Arendt pointed out: "Something much more fundamental than freedom and justice, which are the rights of citizens, is at stake when belonging to the community into which one is born is no longer a matter of course, and not belonging no longer a matter of choice."[7] Did this "not belonging" instead of leading to a gradual lessening of ethnic and spiritual consciousness of Africa, not nurture and keep it alive? The more blacks were excluded from rights in any form, the more they tended to look for reintegration into their own Afro-American community: hence, Africa became an ideology of pride and prejudice.

What accounts for the American blacks' ambivalent motivational structure with regard to his historical past? The sociologist Parsons has written that "where there is historically no longer any attachment to the object—the attitude is not alienation but indifference.[8] But the black has not been able to develop an indifferent or neutral attitude toward his historical past. In the first place, the African past was converted into what sociologists call a negative reference stereotype, toward which the black was "dependently hostile rather than simply indifferent."[9] But even this rejection did not lead to eradication of his African origin. There was a constant pressure on him to find a socially significant identity through Africa.

Explaining the historical nature of what he called compulsive alienation, Parsons stated that a situation may have both conformative and alienative facets; i.e., the individual is subject not only to a strain in his relation with the dominant group, but also to an internal conflict in his own need disposition system.[10] Richard Wright put the problem more succinctly: "I stand, therefore, mentally and emotionally in both directions, being claimed by a negative identification, and being excluded by a feeling of repulsion on the other."[11] It is indeed, quite understandable that to a people denied acceptance for racial reasons, being black and of African origin should appear as a disability of which they would fain rid themselves.

Since emancipation the black man has stood for the purest form of social integration, because of all groups in the United States, the "American Negro" (as the name suggests) has been unquestionably interwoven with the history of American society. Alone among all the groups, blacks joined the stream of American history as slaves; and while this condition facilitated their acceptance of the norms of the dominant group, they are the one group that has suffered total social rejection, except in formal constitutional terms. Speaking to the slaves themselves, a black abolitionist said:

> Slavery has fixed a deep gulf between you and us, and while it shuts out from you the relief and consolation which your friends would willingly render, it afflicts and persecutes you with a fierceness which we might not expect to see in the fiends of hell.[12]

The denial of social equality placed the American black in the same status position as his putative brother in colonized Africa. The emergence of African states into nationhood with their diplomatic missions in the

United States, put into even sharper focus the question of social exclusion of the American black, and re-emphasized the bonds which united the African and the Afro-American. Part of this bond was the place they were assigned in the developing capitalist system. Their common role as the ultimate exploited class denied them social acceptance. Theoretically the blacks were part of the world proletariat, in the sense that they were an exploited class of cheap laborers, but in practice they were not recognized by the world proletariat to any great extent. They became the source of superprofits, the victims of physical oppression, social ostracism, economic exclusion and personal hatred. They were, in the words of DuBois, a part of

> that dark and vast sea of human labor in China and India, the South Seas and all Africa; in the West Indies and Central America and in the United States—that great majority of mankind, on whose bent and broken backs rest today the founding stones of modern industry, [that] shares a common destiny; it is despised and rejected by race and color, paid a wage below the level of decent living; driven, beaten, prisoned and enslaved in all but name; spawning the world's raw material and luxury—cotton, wool, coffee, tea, cocoa, palm oil, fibers, spices, rubber, silks, lumber, copper, gold, diamonds, leather—how shall we end the list and where? All these are gathered up at prices lowest of the low; manufactured, transformed and transported at fabulous gain; and the resultant wealth is distributed and displayed and made the basis of world power and universal dominion and armed arrogance in London and Paris, Berlin and Rome, New York and Rio de Janeiro.[13]

Events follow one another; events also give rise to one another. But those events that seem to follow one another so naturally do not always stand in a cause and effect relationship. Social exclusion and reduction to second-class citizenship followed the emancipation of the American black; and his efforts at integration coincided with hegemonic dominance of the white world over the nonwhite world.

The historical image of the American black and his attitude toward Africa are sociological facts that cannot be understood independently of the main currents of Western historical images of the nonwhite and their images and attitudes toward Africa. After all, slavery had rudely cut off the American black from Africa and plunged him into a racked and famished world where he was to fashion unaided a new image. Sharing the same territory in what was called a white, Protestant, Anglo-Saxon country, his perpetual alien status received added historical and sociological significance.

This perpetual alien status of the black man was actually brought about by circumstances which were peculiar to the American and the Anglo-Saxon world of the post-Civil War era. In the spirit of Anglo-Saxon theory, the black could not be integrated as a social equal. Anglo-Saxon exclusiveness and dominance left no place for black folks except servitude and second-class citizenship.

Contemporary literature on the black in this period of great agitation for equality, has taken the view that the black rejected his past and thus rejected himself; that he tried to be more white than the whites themselves. This may be symptomatic of the terrible spiritual and psychological crisis brought on by the pressure of the white world, which refused to accept the black on the basis of his humanity because of the color of his skin. But this is only one side of the picture; the larger part is made up of yeoman struggles against concepts of black inferiority and specifically against the image of the depravity of Africa and its people. The historical development of this struggle in the era of universal prejudice against Africa and its people is one of the greatest human efforts of all time. No doubt hesitancy did occur and it would be miraculous if it did not —but Afro-American thought on Africa remained steadfast in its insistence that its people were not the stepsons of the human race.

One of the cardinal theses of the sociology of knowledge is that knowledge is socially conditioned; and one must study the social conditions that formed the world of the blacks if one is to understand their ambivalence and identity crisis. As one sociologist put it:

A man's condition in life is, for better or worse, his fate; his soul cannot escape its imprint. Many features in a work of art are rightly ascribed to the author's personality; but this personality in and by itself clashes with circumstances.[14]

Human beings are anchored to reality and purpose by a sense of *who they are*. History acquaints the child with the stirring epics from the distant and romantic past. What happens to people who are assumed to have no historical past? Identity, broadly understood, involves the individual as he exists in his society. Man must know who he is; he must be able to sense himself as the center of his own being and not as a masquerader.

This self-identity grows out of a number of factors, some social, and others psychological, which are manifestations of social and structural influences. Still other factors entering into the development of identity are philosophical; that is, they involve an existential outlook on the world. The sociological, psychological, and philosophical factors that enter into the American blacks' growth of identity change as the black situation changes. Hence, there is a need to study the phenomenon of identity historically.

Weber, in *Ethnic Segregation and Caste*, has put forth a tentative hypothesis of the way in which the sense of dignity in a negatively privileged group takes a specific direction:

> The sense of dignity that characterizes positively privileged status groups is naturally related to their "being" which does not transcend itself; that is, it is to their "beauty" and excellence. Their kingdom is "of this world." They live for the present and by exploiting the great past. The sense of dignity of the negatively privileged strata naturally refers to a future lying beyond the present whether it is of this life or of another. In other words it must be nurtured by a belief in a providential "mission" and by a belief in a specific honor before God.[15]

The quest for dignity and identity has for many years received a classic exemplification in the blacks of the United States. "Ethiopia shall rise again and spread her wing and rule . . ." has been a constant cry for Africa and its redemption, and has created the belief that only then shall the blacks in the United States regain their dignity. The dialectical relationship between the blacks in the United States and Africa, in the quest for identity, was a sociological development in their struggle for emancipation.

Many sociologists have already decided that black nationalism is illegitimate and they study what is called the Negro problem in terms of the nature of prejudice—the black's position in American society being conceived as a dilemma in the consciousness of white Americans. Alternatively, academic sociological research has busied itself with finding whether black people in America retain any traits of their African origin beyond their physical characteristics. Both points of view have led to sterility. The ultimate result is to focus on ways to minimize prejudice by reducing what is seen as the "repulsive" aspect of the victim of discrimination. These theoretical positions have not come to grips with the recurrent and dialectical reality of black nationalism and consciousness of Africa, except to dismiss them as aberrations. Every aberration (if nationalism and African consciousness are false) has its moment of truth; and race relations theory cannot sweep it under the rug and pretend it does not exist simply because it happens to contradict the assumptions and the folklore of dominant groups. The danger of this has been recognized by John Horton:

The result could be a rather costly misunderstanding: the Negro may not recognize himself in the sociological story: worse he may not even learn to accept it.[16]

This sociological point of view suggests that we are all to a greater or lesser extent prisoners of our culture, and that it is difficult for some sociologists to break through the middle-class way of looking at the problem. Myrdal stated the position of those scholars who reject black assumptions as irrelevant:

The Negro's life and, consequently, also his opinions on the Negro problem are, in the main, to be considered as secondary reactions to more primary pressures from the side of the dominant white majority.[17]

This position, besides having a disarming effect on the black's efforts toward self-emancipation, has a fatal methodological flaw: it ignores certain aspects of reality by dismissing them as illegitimate. One cannot ignore the fact that the blacks taken collectively, as Richard Wright pointed out, "are not simply twelve million people. In reality they constitute a separate nation, shunned and stripped and held captive within their nation, devoid of political, social, economic and property rights."[18] The fact that at the present time efforts are still being made to integrate blacks into the mainstream of American society has not yet altered this reality. "After three-and-one-half centuries in residence the Negro does not feel at home."[19]

Fixed theories about the Negro problem, laying fixed stress on fixed categories, have become too much infused with ideologies of what ought to be. They cannot adequately explain the persistency and legitimacy of nationalism and Black Zionist movements which, to me, attest to the fact that the American black may have a self-determining identity. Horton suggested that terms like "moral dilemma," "pluralism," "assimilation," and "integration" all describe motives for desirable action: "They are definitions placed on human action, not the action itself independent of social values." He went on to state, "Seeing the lower-class Negro within a white liberal vocabulary may be realistic politics, but it is not very accurate sociology."[20]

The other issue arising from fixed categories is that the dialectical relationship between the class position of the black and expressions of black nationalism cannot be understood, let alone be interpreted anew. If such understanding does not take place, belief in the class character of societies, where class conflict is not immediately intelligible as such to the actors, becomes as much a faith as the expectation that whites will someday decide to live in accordance with the American Creed. Although there have been white workers who, as a class, have identified with the black struggle for full social and economic equality, it must be acknowledged that the bulk of the white proletariat has shown itself hostile to the demands of the black. An understanding of nationalistic expressions among blacks will give new dimensions to the issue of class where it is overlaid by nationality. The way out, of course, is to overcome the old theoretical positions by considering those phenomena which until now have not been explained by the accepted theoretical assumptions. This means correcting the ahistorical approach of most studies. It also means an examination of any social question within definite historical limits, and understanding the peculiarities that distinguish a particular phase from others within the same political period.[21] Black nationalism is an expression of the black's historical position of marginality as a national class. According to Lenin the actual condition of the workers in the oppressor and oppressed nations is not the same. Economically, the worker in the oppressor nations receives services due to the exploitation of the oppressed nation. Politically, compared with the workers of the oppressed nations, the workers from the oppressor nations occupy a privileged position in many spheres of political life. Ideologically, they are taught at school and in life disdain and contempt for the workers of the oppressed nation.

While acknowledging the legitimacy and validity of black nationalistic aspirations, I accept nevertheless the self-evident fact that the American black is an American. But for the black to feel complete Americanness implies in my opinion an abrupt realization of economic and social truths; in Ellison's phrase "not an exchange of pathologies, but a change of the basis of society."[22] If the black is alienated from the larger society and from himself, it is historically the result of economic exploitation and of a veritable will to dehumanize him. The alienation of the black man cannot be understood only in psychological terms nor simply as an expression of individual consciousness. It was the historical plight of the black man when he came into contact with (and was conquered and enslaved by) the white world. Society, unlike biochemical processes, does not escape human influences. In fact, man is what society succeeds in being.

The reality of blacks in America demands, I feel, a total understanding. The historical, the objective and the subjective factors must be brought forth, dissected and understood. What have been the historical responses of black people when confronted with the civilization of the whites? Could the blacks have been integrated fully into Anglo-American society during the period of imperialism? What were the assumptions of imperialism? Why did the second bourgeois democratic revolution (the Civil War and Reconstruction) while abolishing chattel slavery, stop short of carrying through the land revolution and guaranteeing full citizenship rights for the black freedman? One reason why the continued subordination of blacks remained a cardinal principal of American society is provided by DuBois:

> Just as Europe lurched forward to a new realization of beauty, a new freedom of thought and religious belief, a new demand for laborers to do their work and enjoy its fruits, uncurbed greed rose to seize and monopolize the uncounted treasures of the fruit of labor. Labor was degraded, humanity was despised, the theory of "race" arose. There came a new realization of universal labor: mankind was of two sorts— the superior and the inferior; the inferior toiled for the superior and the superior were the real men, the inferior, halfmen or less. Among the white lords of creation there were lower classes resembling the inferior darker folk. Where possible they were raised to equality with the master class. But no equality was possible or desirable for the "darkies."[23]

The sentiments of African consciousness have shown an historical persistence and resilience that have been strengthened by recent events in Africa and Asia. Black nationalism, historically speaking, was one of the most powerful and important political forces ever to arise among American blacks. Its singular importance rests not in the measure to which it was or was not embraced, nor in a catalogue of victories or defeats which may be associated with its energies. Its greatness lies in the simple fact that it corresponds with the objective and subjective conditions of the times in which it was born. Furthermore, it associated the emancipation of the black in America with the liberation of the African in Africa, and with other peoples of color who were subjects of colonialism and imperialism.[24]

The study of black nationalism in its dialectical relationship with African consciousness should explore the empirically and theoretically determined thought of blacks in a single worldwide system, and better still in the structure of worldwide society; and should try to reveal the thought of the Afro-American as the ideology of the black man in the epoch of Western imperialism. The historical reality of capitalist imperialism attempted to expel the black man from history with its insistence upon his innate and immutable inferiority. Black nationalism and African consciousness (whether negative or positive) have a direct relevance to the Afro-American's identity, and they make up one continuous history with his misfortunes in the New World.

That is why any study of black nationalism must examine white assumptions about the black and about Africa in the period of imperialism.

This approach acknowledges the fact that racial theory, as a theory of biological inequality among people, has deep roots; but recognizes also that it reached its height at the time of the colonial expansion of European capitalistic powers. The image of Africa portrayed during the period of imperialist colonial conquest made it impossible for the Afro-American to have a positive identity either about himself or about his African background. How could he have positive reactions to an image which was deliberately stereotyped and made negative? The black abolitionist Garnet understood the depth of this crime:

> By an almost common consent, the modern world seems determined to pilfer Africa of glory. It were not enough that her children have been scattered over the globe, clothed in garments of shame—humiliated and oppressed—but her merciless foes weary themselves in plundering the tombs of our revered sires, and in obliterating their worthy deeds, which were inscribed by fame upon the pages of ancient history.[25]

An historical understanding of white assumptions clarifies the birth, continuity, and meaning of self-hatred and lowered self-esteem. Charles S. Johnson summarized in 1923 the attitudes prevalent in American society and their consequences for blacks as follows:

> They cannot escape being assailed on every hand from early childhood to the end of their lives with a pervading intimation of their own inferiority. From the beginning they are saturated in a tradition of their own incompetence . . . They grew up in the system not only inferior to the other race, but to their own potential selves. They are in the midst of an advanced social system, definite culture influences, but denied full participation. They many never escape the insistent implications of their status and race.[26]

Was it possible for the black to accept white definitions and to live by their world view? Why did the dominant thinking about the black in the Western world denigrate him? We can learn about groups from "philosophies" because they are a way of thinking about life. We have also to accept the fact that we live in a world impregnated with racial thinking and stereotypes. This racism has conditioned the thinking of most black people as well as most white people. Using the categories "white people" as opposed to "black people," I am not unaware of the existence and the labors of that tiny minority of whites who opposed and fought against racism. Their numbers were too few to influence the course of history. The best they could do was to temper and ameliorate the worst excesses of racist practices.

The history of black people in the United States is not merely a two hundred year narration of slavery, racial discrimination and self-pity. It is also the history of the never-ending struggle for freedom and human dignity. In the struggle they held high the banner of Africa and its place in history. Against all odds, black faith in Africa's greatness was not paralyzed.

Apart from a negligible minority, Afro-Americans have not sought the solution to black-white relationships in obliterating their own blackness. According to DuBois, "Its full solution will lie in the creation of a democracy in which the black man will be free to define himself for what he is and, within the larger framework of that democracy, for what he desires to do."[27] There needs to be no dichotomy between black consciousness and living in coexistence with other groups. This of course does raise the whole question of the meaning of integratión as a solution to black disabilities. If integration does not confront the economic disabilities of black powerlessness, it will remain an anomaly, if not an attempt to maintain the status quo. In terms of past experiences, what may be of greatest significance for the future is the way in which the lower-class black perceives the issues and responds to his condition. Black nationalism has its greatest appeal among lower-class blacks; whether integration succeeds or fails will be decided to a large extent by the way in which the lower-class black reacts; or by what is done to him. But as DuBois pointed out the mental frustration of the poor cannot indefinitely continue:

Some day it may burst in fire and blood. Who will be to blame? And where the greater cost? Black folk, after all, have little to lose, but civilization has all.

This the American black man knows: his fight here is a fight to the finish. Either he dies or wins. If he wins it will be by no subterfuge or evasion of amalgamation. He will enter modern civilization here in America as a blackman, on terms of perfect and unlimited equality with any whiteman, or he will enter not at all. Either extermination of root and branch, or absolute equality. There can be no compromise. This is the last battle of the West.[28]

Notes

[1]Quoted in Georg Lukacs, *The Historical Novel*, Beacon Press, Boston, 1963, p. 67.
[2]St. Clair Drake, "Hide my Face? On Pan-Africanism and Negritude," in *Soon, One Morning: New Writings by American Negroes, 1940-1962*, selected and

edited with an introduction and biographical notes, by Herbert Hill, Alfred A. Knopf, New York, 1963, p. 78.

[3] Such periodicals as *Negro History Bulletin* are poor attempts to make up for this deficiency published by the Association for the Study of Negro Life and History, Washington, D.C.

[4] Quoted in Bernard Fonlon, "The Passing of a Great African," *Freedomways* 5(1), 1965, p. 198.

[5] Richard Wright, *White Man Listen*, Doubleday, New York, 1964, p. 16.

[6] W.E.B. DuBois, *Black Reconstruction in America, 1860-1880*, Median Books, New York, 1964, p. 703.

[7] Hannah Arendt, *The Origins of Totalitarianism*, Meridian Books, New York, 1962, p. 296.

[8] Talcott Parsons, *The Social System*, The Free Press, Glencoe, 1951, p. 254.

[9] Robert Merton, *Social Theory and Social Structure*, The Free Press, Glencoe, 1961, p. 205.

[10] Parsons, *op. cit.*, p. 254.

[11] Wright, *op. cit.*, p. 49.

[12] Henry Highland Garnet, "An Address to the Slaves of the United States of America" (1843), *Black Nationalism in America*, edited by John H. Bracey Jr., August Meier, and Elliott Rudwick, the Bobbs-Merrill Company, New York, 1970, p. 67.

[13] DuBois, *Black Reconstruction*, pp. 15-16.

[14] Warner Stark, *The Sociology of Knowledge*, Routledge and Kegan Paul, London, 1958, p. 26.

[15] H.H. Gerth and C. Wright Mills, *From Max Weber*, Routledge and Kegan Paul, London, 1952, p. 190.

[16] John Horton, "Order and Conflict Theories of Social Problems and Competing Ideologies," *The American Journal of Sociology*, Vol. 71, No. 6, May 1966, p. 701. I.F. Stone, quoted in the same article, made the same observations: "But ours is an age in which, in a manner late Victorian liberal and Marxist optimists had thought obsolete, the ancient divisive forces of nationalism and tribalism have demonstrated a furious vitality. It would be a mistake to dismiss their recurrence among Negroes as a passing aberration. In an age of decolonization, it may be fruitful to regard the problem of the American Negro as a unique case of colonialism, an instance of internal imperialism, an underdeveloped people in our very midst."

[17] Quoted in Horton, *op. cit.*, p. 711.

[18] Quoted in Herbert Hill, *Soon, One Morning*, New Writings by American Negroes, Alfred A. Knopf, New York, 1963, p. 5.

[19] Stone, Quoted in Horton, *op. cit.*, p. 701.

[20] Horton, *op. cit.*, p. 173. Oscar Handlin observed similarly: "It is the ultimate of integration to deny the separateness of the Negro and therefore to inhibit him from creating communal institutions which can help him cope with his problems ... To confuse segregation, the function of which is to establish Negro inferiority, with the awareness of separate identity, the function of which is to generate the power for voluntary action, hopelessly confuses the struggle for equality. As long as common

memories, experience and interests make the Negro a group, they will find it advantageous to organize and act as such. And the society will be better able to accommodate them as equal on those terms than it could under the pretense that integration could wipe out the past." "The Goals of Integration," *Daedalus*, Vol. 95, No. 1, Winter 1966.

[21]Thus in this study I shall deal with specific manifestations of consciousness of Africa, but this must not be misinterpreted as suggesting that these are autonomous events unconnected with others; rather, they should be understood as different strands making up one piece of cloth.

[22]Ralph Ellison, *Shadow and Act*, Random House, New York, 1966, p. 315.

[23]W.E.B. DuBois, *The World and Africa*, New World Paperback, 1965, New York, p. 19.

[24]Commenting on the role of American blacks, W.E.B. DuBois stated: "American Negroes have even crossed the waters and held three Pan-African Congresses to arouse black men through the world to work for modern democractic development. Thus the emancipation of the Negro slaves in America becomes through his own determined effort simply one step toward the emancipation of all men," W.E.B. DuBois, *The Gift of Black Folk: Negroes in the Making of America*, Washington Square Press, New York, 1970, p. 140.

[25]Henry Highland Garnet, *op. cit.*, p. 115.

[26]Charles S. Johnson, "Public Opinion and the Negro," in *Proceedings of the National Conference in Social Work, 1923*, Chicago, 1924.

[27]DuBois, *Black Reconstruction, op. cit.*, p. 304.

[28]*Ibid.*, p. 703.

CHAPTER TWO
The Image of Africa and
the Afro-American

The genesis of many a nation is nothing to be proud of, a discomforting knowledge which natural historians, acting as mental hygienists, comfortably conceal from literate minds. Yet who would think of reminding the British, at every turn, that their ancestors practiced cannibalism long after other European peoples had forgotten this particular cuisine? Or why would anyone constantly remind the Australians that their pedigree originated in penal colonies?

—The Minority of One, Nov., 1965

The theme of this chapter is twofold: the nature and meaning of white hegemony, and the image of Africa to which blacks in the Western world were exposed, particularly during the era of imperialism. This image was of particular import in the development of the black's self-image. White ideas about blacks did not arise in a vacuum, but had certain economic and political determinants. There was no agreement among Westerners about the validity of these ideas. In fact, we can distinguish three types of views which arose independently, but which coalesced in determining the dominant attitudes. These were the views of academicians, popular views and the views of decision-makers.

Ideas never burst onto the scene full-blown. They have a long and variegated history. I cannot attempt in the pages that follow to present a total picture of white ideas about blacks. I shall try to outline the general framework in which these ideas occurred, particularly those economic and political transformations that took place throughout the Western world as a result of its colonial and imperial expansion. To take one example: in literature the blacks for a long time inspired American writers. The significant thing for us is the way these writers have portrayed the black man as a character—a fascinating subject which can only be indicated here. DuBois wrote that, in the days of Shakespeare and long afterward,

15

... the black man of fiction was a man, a brave, fine, if withal overtrustful and impulsive, hero. In science he was different but equal, cunning in an unusual but mighty possibilities [sic]. Then with the slave trade he suddenly became a clown and dropped from sight. He emerged slowly beginning about 1830 as a dull stupid but contented slave, capable of dog-like devotion, superstitious and incapable of education. Then, in the abolition controversy he became a victim, a man of sorrows, a fugitive chased by bloodhounds, a beautiful raped octoroon, a crucified Uncle Tom, but a lay figure, objectively pitiable but seldom subjectively conceived. Suddenly a change came after Reconstruction. The black man was either a faithful "Befoh de Wah" darky worshipping lordly white folk, or a frolicking ape, or a villain, a sullen scoundrel, a violator of womanhood, a low thief and mis-birthed monster. He was subnormal and congenitally incapable. He was represented as an unfit survival of Darwinian natural selection. Philanthropy and religion stood powerless before his pigmy brain and underdeveloped morals. In a "thousand years"? Perhaps. But at present, an upper beast.[1]

The changing images of the black man described by DuBois were not accidental. They were the result of ideologies which justified and made legitimate white rule over blacks and white exploitation of foreign lands. They were part of a hegemonic superstructure which created crises of personal identity and destiny among many darker peoples of the world. It was precisely this that created the beginnings of common outlooks and efforts among certain black intellectuals to comprehend their own existence as something historically determined and conditioned. It made them see their plight as the universal tragedy of colonized people. The redemption of Africa through American black migration, Pan-Africanism and/or Garveyism were results of this increasing consciousness of the historical character of colonialism and imperialism. As a part of white hegemonic dominance, the Afro-American was never made to appear either in fiction or in the science of white writers (with a few exceptions) as a human being reacting to human situations and problems.

THE NATURE AND MEANING OF WHITE HEGEMONY

Mark Twain once said that when a country enslaves a people, the first necessity is to make the world feel that the people enslaved are subhuman. The next effort is to make his fellow countrymen believe that the enslaved man is inferior; and then, the worst cut of all is to make that man believe himself inferior. White hegemony attempted this in various forms. Some national historians, sociologists and anthropologists, while acting as mental hygienists for the white community by telling it that its values were highly desirable, constantly told the black man that God and Nature made a mistake when it came to creating him. It was this constantly whispered theme that made the black experience the totality of what Hannah Arendt called the "abstract nakedness of being human and nothing but human."[2] When the black man was enslaved he became subjected both physically and ideologically to the white world. This state of affairs underlies the problem of identity.

There are few human conditions more frightening than amnesia—a state in which a person is cut off from his own reality; or, from another perspective, when reality is such that he cannot possibly identify with it. The individual finds himself drifting aimlessly, his actions without meaning or purpose. When an amnesia victim turns to some authority in his predicament, it is to get help in finding out who he is. Later I shall show how American blacks went back to the study of African history in order to find out where they came from and who they were.

Identity is rooted in a social order, and this is true both in the cognitive or substantive sense of who and what a person is, and in the evaluative sense of how he is effectively regarded by his fellows and how he feels about himself. A person's self-feeling derives from his place in the social order, and from his ability to conduct himself according to the role relation attaching thereto.[3] From the moment the black was abducted from the African continent until the time he was proclaimed free, to the point when he was finally degraded to second-class citizenship, he has always retained a marginal and tenuous relationship to the American social structure, and has never experienced self-determination.

Identity is not a static state; it is a dynamic process that changes through time as an individual acquires abilities and accumulates a record of achievements and failures. In the process of development it is important for individuals or people to believe that undesirable features of their identities are capable of alteration. Success in the effort at self-improvement is as much dependent on the individual or group, as on the attitudes of others in the surrounding world. The American black has lived in a hostile world which insisted on degrading all his efforts. When he attempted to revive his African cultural past, it was called a survival, and when he tried to assimilate the culture of his environment, he was regarded as engaging in an impertinent masquerade. The greatest human damage was inflicted on the black man when he was regarded as a species that was called a Negro, with all the derogatory connotations of this term.

C. Van Woodward, in describing American attitudes toward history, throws some light on the importance of historical image. He writes, "Americans no less than other people have expected too much of history. They have made too many demands upon it, and put it into too many questionable uses. In fact, it is probable that Americans have for certain reasons made more exorbitant demands upon history than have other peoples."[4]

Woodward may have stated the case too strongly, but he does point to an important sociological fact about a people's history. History serves as a source of the folklore, myth and legend that seem so essential to the spiritual comfort of a people, both in terms of who they are and where they are going. European peoples, even though they sprang from barbarian tribes that destroyed the Roman Empire and sank the continent into what is called the Dark Ages, never tire of reminding the world of their Greco-Roman heritage. They trace their political institutions to the "Glory that was Greece" and the "Splendor that was Rome."

Americans experience a certain ambivalence in regard to their own history. They would like to identify themselves with progress unencumbered by tradition and, indeed, their history falls within the historic era of the age of discovery, exploration and settlement. When they won their independence they self-consciously severed their ties with European history and created a specifically New World tradition. Later, those Northern European and Mediterranean immigrants who cast their lot with the Anglo-Americans as willingly accepted the new-born myths and traditions. Nevertheless, as Lloyd Louis remarks, the Americans soon discovered "that having banished King George, they had lost King Arthur, and along with him a host of patron saints and familiar deities."[5] It may be appropriate to mention here an interesting, if anomalous, situation. The United States boasts proudly of its origin in the overthrow of monarchy, yet the American public is strongly attracted to royalty, and probably no other country can boast of as many sheets, beds, cigarettes, pots and pans, automobiles, telephones, and even foods that are "royal," "regal," "imperial" or "princely."

It was into this social situation that the blacks were emancipated. Having neither made a choice to throw in their lot with the Anglo-Americans, nor to come to America in search of freedom, they have in the process of being rejected become myth-hungry and legend-starved.

The American black more than any other nonwhite group has, because of his particular situatic·, been the most thoroughly conditioned by the prejudices of past history. Indeed, it would be no exaggeration to say that the traditions of the dead generations weigh on him like a nightmare. The reality of the hegemony of one group over another is a cultural tissue of great variety and subtlety, extending all the way from the education of the young to the naming of streets, bridges and universities, and may involve a whole ideological superstructure that explains and justifies people's beliefs and creates mental blocks in regard to other beliefs. I shall pursue this point in my next chapter.

The black man has been subjected to a hegemonic system which according to Truman Nelson is "buttressed and concealed, as it were, by the best, the kindest, and the most advanced consciousness the country can produce."[6] It portrays itself as the ultimate in human development—political, economic, social, and sometimes even moral and cultural. The idealism that was created by whites—the white man's burden—became the protective armor of most whites, in effect assuming the features of a natural landscape.

The black man, by contrast, was the representative of that order of humanity that was barbaric, ignorant, superstitious and sometimes even evil. His inferiority appeared as the incarnation of inevitable, timeless tradition, and the authority over him appeared equally timeless by traditional and legitimate existence. It was the naturalness of white supremacy which the black had to try to debunk and negate, and as DuBois pointed out: "The facing of so vast a prejudice could not but bring the inevitable self-questioning, self-disparagement, and lowering of ideals which ever accompany repression and breed in an atmosphere of contempt and hate."[7]

It should be quite obvious then, that the problem of identity among blacks in the United States is in the words of Hannah Arendt, a "total social and historical phenomenon";[8] a structure, cultural and social as much as it is economic and demographic, and one that becomes intelligible only in relation to the structural system that sustains it. Richard Wright illustrated the nature of this feeling by borrowing the "Frog Perspective" concept from Neitzche which:

.... describes someone looking from below upwards, a sense of someone who feels lower than others. The concept of distance involved here is not physical, it is psychological. It involves a situation in which, for moral and social reasons, a person or a group feels there is another person or group above it. Yet physically, they all live on the same general material plane. A certain degree of hate combined with love (ambivalence) is always involved in this looking from below upward, and the object against which the subject is measuring himself undergoes constant change. He loves the object because he would like to resemble it, he hates the object because his chances of resembling it are remote, slight.[9]

For a long time blacks in the United States have depended on the whites for definition and measurement of what is called progress and acculturation. During slavery and after emancipation the blacks were told that nowhere else would they be so highly regarded as in America, and that they must struggle and plead within the framework of that charitable outlook. For instance, it was William H. Henry, the president of an elite American college, who said in an inaugural address:

> As regards the African race there is little to lament (about slavery) in comparison with the great benefits conferred on the slaves. From a state of barbarism, it raised the race into a state of civilization, to which no other barbarous people ever attained in so short a time. The late African slave is now rated by our government as a superior to the American Indian, and to the natives of the celestial empire of China, and is entrusted with the highest privilege of an American civilization. [10]

One may not begrudge the college president his extreme ethnocentrism, but one does regret that so many other American intellectuals of the late 19th century, succumbing to the prejudices of their time, provided the rationalization for a governmental system which preserved most Southern states in official wretchedness. [11] DuBois lamented with justification that:

> This is the modern paradox of Sin before which the Puritan stands openmouthed and mute. A group, a nation or a race, commits murder and rape, steals and destroys, yet no individual is guilty, no one is to blame, no one can be punished. The Black world squirms beneath the feet of the White in impotent fury or sullen hate. [12]

Many obvious wrongs were committed against the black, yet they have been obscured in apologetics like that of the college president. Thus, the betrayal of the blacks after the Civil War (1877) was given moral legitimation on the grounds that the black was inefficient and corrupt. The moralistic rationale that the American black was better off than his counterpart in Africa has become an ideology of absolution and a classical psychological bulwark against the pangs of conscience which might have resulted from the betrayal and ill-treatment of blacks over the years. [13]

> T's but a poor relief they gain,
> Who change the place but keep the pain.

The crux of the Negro problem in the United States is that when the black was abducted from Africa he was deprived of a place in the world from which to make his opinions significant and his actions effective. Hannah Arendt pointed out that:

> something much more fundamental than freedom and justice, which are the rights of citizens, is at stake, when belonging to the community into which one is born is no longer a matter of course, and not belonging a matter of choice, or when one is placed in a situation where, unless he commits a crime, his treatment by others does not depend on what he does and does not do. This extremity, and nothing else, is the situation of people deprived of human rights. They are deprived not of the right to freedom, but of the right to action, not of the right to think whatever they please but of the right to opinion.[14]

The state of affairs so perceptively described by Arendt created in the Negro a feeling of *not to have*. "BUT *NOT TO HAVE*," wrote Karl Marx,

> is not a mere category, it is a most disconsolate reality; today a man who has nothing is nothing, for he is cut off from existence in general, and still more from human existence, for the condition of having nothing is a complete reality of the dehumanized, a very positive *TO HAVE*, a HAVING of hunger, of cold, of disease, of crime, of disabusement, of all inhumanity and monstrosity.[15]

A person, a group of persons or a national minority subject to complete dominance by another group may become, as we have said, the victim of amnesia, or its identity may become a caricature of the dominant group. The black population of the United States has experienced many movements of political protest cloaked in religious symbolism, and due to their limitations these movements produced long periods of withdrawal, manifesting themselves even in the rejection of their African background and self. That the failure of emancipation, coinciding with the hegemonic dominance of Africa by Europe, contributed its own moral and psychological despondency cannot be doubted. Perry Anderson defined hegemony as:

> the complete dominance of one social block over another, but not simply by means of force or wealth but by a total social authority whose ultimate sanction and expression is a profound cultural supremacy. This imperative order not merely sets limits to action and aims of the subordinate block, it structures the vision of itself and the world,

imposing contingent historical fact as the necessary coordinate of social life. The hegemonic class is the primary determinant of consciousness, character, and customs throughout society.[16]

The nature of the attitudes held by whites about the black and Africa from this point of view provides a critical point of departure for understanding certain manifestations of black behavior, and the whole process of alienation and ambivalent attitudes toward black cultural roots. Saunders Redding stated at the first American Negro Writers Congress held in Paris in 1956 that "a people's ultimate purpose is to use their gift to develop their awareness of themselves; a people's relation to their culture is the same as a relation of a child to a mother's breast." But the blacks' relation both to American culture and African culture had been that of a stepchild to its adopted parents. The rule of the whites over the nonwhites had for so long been tranquil and unchallenged, that for some it appeared as immutably perfect and sacrosanct. It could not be challenged; all that was necessary was to assimilate others into it on its own terms, and at its own rate of adjustment. Characteristic expressions describing acceptance of this attitude on the part of some blacks even today are: "We are rising," or "We are making it" and "We are integrating."

I shall attempt in the next chapter to sketch the images of the black which were a direct consequence of white hegemony. I shall distinguish between white concepts which made the black feel inferior, thus stripping him of identity, and those ideas which meant that when the black looked at Africa he saw nothing but his own depraved state, thus conditioning him to accept his present station with all its hardships.

THE BLACK IMAGE

The Atlantic slave trade, the crux of the Euro-American slave system, was the largest forced transportation of labor power from one part of the globe to another in the world's history, and for the African, one of the greatest unnatural disasters of all time. It lasted approximately 250 years and estimates put the total figures of Africans transported as high as 40 million. How could such cruelty and evil go on for such a long time? As it was evil in every respect, whoever profited from it was corrupted by it, even many of those who eventually came to oppose it. The long-range consequences of the system were devasting. Europe in general, and America and Africa in particular, are to this day suffering from that period of their history, and will go on suffering for a long time. The legacy of slavery and degradation of Africa weighs like a curse on America.

During the 200 years of the triangular trade the degradation of anything black went hand in hand with the depiction of Africa as nothing but a place of unredeemable savagery. It can be said without fear of contradiction that ever since the African set foot on the shores of the New World his status as a human being has been, at best, probationary. For a long time he was told that he was enslaved because he was less than human: inherently inferior, mentally primitive and emotionally underdeveloped. One need only read (to quote one example) the article on the Negro in the 1791 *Encyclopedia Britannica* which presented a list of alleged racial characteristics including treachery, lying, cruelty, impudence, intemperance, and a penchant for stealing, debauchery, and profanity. Blacks were said to be " . . . strangers to every sentiment of compassion and an example of man when left to himself."[17] One could quote innumerable examples of studies concerned with black pathology which focus on the supposed defects of the victim, as if these and not the racist structure of American society were the cause of all the woes that the American black experiences.

In geography text books, races have been described in conformity with the program of the current propaganda, thus engendering in the white race a hate for the black, and in the blacks a contempt for themselves. Stereotyped illustrations further degraded the black by depicting him as a savage with a ring through his nose, while his yellow brother was depicted as a poet of distinction, his brown brother as a fine prince, and his red brother as a proud warrior. The black invariably stood at the bottom of the social ladder.[18]

It thus happens that the black's racial pride is even further humiliated when he tries to contemplate the great drama of world history and the role played by different continents in the history of civilization. He finds himself accorded no honorable part in the performance. The tendency is to glorify the white races and debase the black. The effect upon the spirit of the black is deplorably oppressive; he must forever dwell upon a picture in which all worthwhile traits and deeds are ascribed to the white races and none to his. The question then is: in the Western world, where can he derive spirit and inspiration?[19]

Before I attempt to answer the question posed above, let me look at some of the conceptions of Africa and the black in history held and propagated by the dominant interests.[20] There is no doubt that the history of Africa and the black man has until recently remained a vast lacuna in the story of mankind. After the distortions of the past by racist historians, anthropologists and other social scientists, the black's incorporation into the destinies of universal history had to await the incorporation of Africa and the African into world politics. It was Hegel who made the classic statement on the black man's role in history:

Africa proper, as far as history goes back, remained for all purposes of connection with the rest of the world, shut up. It was the gold land compressed within itself—the land of childhood, which lying beyond the day of self-conscious history, is enveloped in the dark mantle of night . . . The peculiarly African character is difficult to comprehend, for the very reason that in reference to it we must quite give up the principle that accompanies all our ideas—the category of universality. In Negro life the characteristic point is the fact that consciousness has not yet reached the realization of any substantial objective existence— as for example, God or Law, in which the interest of man's volition is involved, and in which he realizes his own being . . .

The Negro, as already observed, exhibits the natural man in his completely wild, untamed state. We must lay aside all thought of reverence and morality—all we call feeling—if we would rightly comprehend him; there is nothing in this type of character. The copies and the circumstantial accounts of missionaries completely confirm this, and Mohammedanism appears to be the only thing which in any way brings the Negro within the range of culture . . .

Another characteristic fact in reference to the Negro is slavery. Negroes are enslaved by Europeans and sold to America. Bad as this may be, their lot in their own land is even worse, since there a slavery quite as absolute exists, for it is the essential principle of slavery that man has not yet attained a consciousness of his freedom, and consequently sinks down to a mere Thing—an object of no value. Among Negroes moral sentiments are quite weak, or more strictly speaking, non-existent . . .

And with characteristic foresight of what was to happen in the next hundred years, Hegel concluded that:

At this point we leave Africa, not to mention it again. For it is no historical part of the world, it has no moment or development to exhibit. Historical moment in it—that is in its Northern part belongs to the Asiatic or European world. Carthage displayed there an important transitory phase of civilization, but as the Phoenician colony, it belongs to Asia. Egypt will be considered in reference to the passage of the human mind from the Eastern to the Western phase, but it does not belong to African Spirit. What we properly understand by Africa is the unhistorical and underdeveloped spirit, still involved in the conditions of mere nature, and which had to be presented here only as the threshold of World History.[21]

I have quoted Hegel at such length because he seems to have anticipated most of the arguments that were to be used later by racist and imperialist intellectuals. Hegel was a philosopher of great repute and his influence on European thought is still felt today, regardless of the validity of his writings. His description of Africa and the sources of his data do not require extensive scrutiny to reveal that they violate even the method of philosophy. He made no attempt to describe Africa as it was, but simply drew sweeping conclusions from the writings of travelers and missionaries.

Transcendental philosophy has been described as a kind of poetry, and the human tragedy that has been the consequence of some of its assumptions led Barrows Dunham to observe: "First the philosopher, then the politico, then the commentator, and then—oh Lord."[2] The Southern populist Tom Watson, in an editoral attack on Booker T. Washington, wrote in 1905:

What does civilization owe to the Negro?
Nothing!
Nothing!!
Nothing!!![23]

L.S.B. Leakey's remark as late as 1961 that

In every country that one visits, and where one is drawn into conversation about Africa, the question is regularly asked by people who should know better: "But what has Africa contributed to world progress? . . . not the wheel, not writing, not mathematics, not art . . . not this, not that, and not the other thing."[24]

Both these statements reflects the prejudice that informs most Westerners against Africa. This prejudice severely inhibits most people from giving the credit that is due Africa. All this stems from the cultural rigidities of earlier white supremacist indoctrinations.

The notion that the black has not contributed anything to the progress of civilization dominates the era of imperialism. DuBois cited as typical a book published in Philadelphia in 1866, which attempted to prove in its lengthy introduction that the black is a species different from the rest of mankind:

Let us take, for illustration, the White and Black races supposed by many to represent the two extremes of the scale of gradation. The whole history of the former shows an uninterrupted progress, that of the latter, monotonous stagnation. To the one man owes the most valuable discoveries in the domain of thought and their practical application; to the other it owes nothing. For ages plunged in the darkest gloom of barbarism, there is not one ray of even temporary or borrowed improvement to cheer the dismal picture of its history or inspire the hope of the disheartened philanthropist.[25]

History forces man to face himself in the mirror of events. History is man's autobiography and his biography. As man continues to live, history and all the ideologies of whose genesis it is the record, continue to unfold. It unfolds in the present in our actions, as we move and live in the real society of today. From the time Africans were enslaved to the time the African continent was collectively dismembered by the Europeans, the Western-educated African to a large extent has looked at himself through the eyes of Europe. His achievements have been attributed to Europeans. The imperialist world has looked at Africa not in terms of what it was but:

through the eyes of human sentiment and dividends. This has led to the invention of all sorts of arguments based upon estimates of "physical phenomena" as conceived by phrenology and physiognomy, using signs to describe every part of man—from the heel to the skull—to prove the mental and moral inferiority of the Negro.[26]

As a result of contact and the conquest of black peoples by the Europeans, the Anglo-Saxons have consistently refused to look themselves in the eye. Their history has been the history of self-praise and adulation. It was in reaction to this arrogance by the bards of the Anglo-Saxon myth that Edward Blyden made this comment:

The whole of the rest of mankind doesn't hold the European, in view of his past history, in such unqualified admiration, as to admit without serious questions that he has the right to embody in terse phrases and parade in titles of books, pamphlets, and addresses his contempt for other races . . . The African now coming forward through education and culture cannot have unlimited respect for all the qualities of the European races, a people with a passion for taking away the countries of others and dignifying robbery as conquest, and whose systematic cruelty has been shown for ages in chaining, buying and selling other races. The intelligent Negro feels that the part of the oppressors, that the part of the man-sellers and man-stealers is far more contemptible than the part of the man stolen or sold.[27]

The function of positively portraying European history while negatively portraying that of the black is quite obvious. It justified white dominance and rule, not in terms of its sheer military superiority, but in terms of its cultural supremacy. The historian, the ethnologist and the sociologist became self-appointed prosecutors, accusing on behalf of the past, and admonishing on behalf of the future. As Nkrumah put it: "Their accusations and admonishings have been set in a rigid framework of presuppositions, both about the nature of the good men and about the nature of the good society, in such a way that these presuppositions serve as intimations of an implicit ideology."[28] The denial to the African of a particular history also was the denial to him of a place in universal history. For surely if Africans had been allowed their history some of the notions about the Dark Continent would not have been held and some of the discoveries of the black man would not have been shrouded in hermetic mysticism.

The black, sharing the same soil with the white people in the United States, was taught to admire the Hebrews, the Greeks, the Romans, and the Gentiles, but to despise the Africans. In most American schools the black was studied as a problem or dismissed as of little or no consequence. Because of their particular bias, the schools became a questionable factor in the life of this despised people. It was Carter Woodson who observed that "to handicap a student by teaching him that his black face is a curse and that his struggle to change his condition is hopeless, is the worst sort of lynching."[29] Why not, it begins to be felt, exploit, enslave or exterminate a class that everyone is taught to regard as inferior? The status of the black was justly fixed as that of an inferior. Teachers of black children in the first schools after emancipation did not proclaim and did not have to proclaim any such doctrine, for the content of their curricula justified these inferences.

Furthermore, particular ways of looking at the world lead to particular ways of attempting to control it. The image of "darkest Africa" and of the African as a "child of nature" can be thought of as an expression of geographic ignorance or of mental arrogance current among certain circles in 19th century Europe. But it was also an expression of a great moral cynicism, which was reflected in the way its people and natural resources were treated. Joseph Conrad wrote:

> This talk was the talk of sordid buccaneers: it was reckless without hardihood, greedy with audacity, and cruel without courage; there was not an atom of foresight or serious intention . . . and they did not seem aware that things are wanted for the work of the world. To tear the treasure out of the barrels of the land was their desire, with no more

moral purpose at the back of it than there was in a burglar breaking into a safe.[30]

Stereotyped thinking about Africa grew in intensity and viciousness with the growth of imperialism. It became historically linked with the defense of imperialist interests. It changed only when the African people reasserted their independence.[31] Therefore it appears to be the transformation of political and social structures of African societies, rather than good will or the dissemination of knowledge about Africa, that became a primary variable in affecting the ideological thought about Africa.

Human knowledge, as we shall try to show in the next chapter, is a social fact. It becomes affected by the habits and practices of a lifetime which, if they continue being practiced, end by producing a philosophical rationale. The desire to exploit the African, whether in Africa or abroad, produced erroneous theories about his capabilities. These theories, because of the particular socioeconomic needs of Europe and America, soon became dogmatic truths. Thus error, instead of being simply error, was compounded by certain interests to produce very complex prejudices. In the 19th century, almost any negative idea about Africa and about the black and his way of life seemed to suffice, provided it was specious enough. When one reads about the Congo massacres under King Leopold II of Belgium, or when one reads about the activities of the lynch mobs in the United States during the latter part of the 19th century (1880-1900), the image of Africa and all the stereotypes about the Africans become understandable, not as proper descriptions of Africa, but as another of the dark deeds that Africans experienced at the hands of some white peoples. These deeds led Mark Twain to remark, "There are many amusing things in the world, among them the white man's notion that he is less savage than other savages."[32]

The early accounts of Africa in the 15th and 16th centuries, though not complimentary, were not mendacious. They emphasized the unique and the exotic, but they never doubted the humanity of the Africans. The slave trade with its cruelties necessitated the emphasis on the so-called degradation of the Africans; enslavement, according to this view, was a better state because it was supposed to have rescued the African from darkness and brought him to a state of enlightenment. The imperialist expansion of the 19th century diverted attention from the slave trade and focused it on Africa itself. During this period of imperialism a new type of relationship between Europe and Africa emerged, replacing an earlier relationship whereby Africans were sent as slaves to the New World to work in the plantations. The new relationship was expressed by a European writer in epigramatic rhetoric:

The eighteenth century stole the black man from his country, the nineteenth century steals his country from him.[33]

Just as the stealing of men was disguised in humanitarian and philanthropic terms, the taking away of their country was put in soothing terms and described as the white man's burden.

The new ideological image of the role of the Europeans in Africa had begun to take shape by the 1880s. This change came at a time when the coincidence of certain factors made an extremely depraved image of Africa and the African almost inevitable. The slave trade had been abolished because of moral, economic and technological factors; the Darwinian theory with its emphasis on natural selection and survival of the fittest was being misread and widely misapplied; and in Berlin, in 1884, collective imperialism and individual plunder became the official policy of European powers, and led to the partition of Africa. The new relationship that was being fashioned with Africa, and which was to virtually enslave the African in his homeland, was related to the new economic transformation in the Western world.

I may point out that the growing consciousness of the dignity of the human soul was, before the end of the 19th century, once again brought face to face with a new system of cruelty to man—imperialism. And it was ironic that the abolition of formal slavery was followed in both Africa and America, insofar as the treatment of the African people was concerned, by an informal slavery even more debasing. The new slavery had a remarkable effect both in England and America, countries which had, after the emancipation of the slaves, experienced a new wave of humanitarianism. Imperialism drowned pious zeal, chivalrous enthusiasm and humdrum sentimentalism in the chill waters of selfish calculation. As a biographer of Marx pointed out: "It has degraded personal dignity to the level of exchange value, and in the place of countless, dearly-bought chartered freedom, it has set up one solitary unscrupulous freedom—freedom of trade."[34]

To be sure, history does not follow a straight course; it meanders—twisting, turning, zigzagging. As a result, the relationship between Africa and the West has many nuances, and one can view as a genuine concern the impulse to uplift and civilize the backward races of mankind, and thus can regret the unfortunate and unanticipated results of these humanistic attempts. One can also look at it in terms of the requirements of European industry. The dramatic changes in the productive relations of Europe demanded changes in European relations with the colonial world. We know that after the abolition of the slave trade in the 1830s, British interest in West Africa began to taper off and reached its lowest point in 1865. However it rose again with the rise of the new era of imperialism, and between 1880 and 1890 the Western world entered fully into the scramble for Africa, or what we might rightly call collective colonialism. The image of Africa and the African changed drastically as we will try to show below.

In America there were significant developments with regard to the treatment of black people. The Civil War was fought between 1860 and 1865. The Emancipation Proclamation came in 1863. Between 1868 and 1876 there were important attempts through Reconstruction to integrate blacks into the American society. The attempts to make black people full-fledged American citizens saw the creation of the Freedmen's Bureau in 1865 as a war measure, which was contrived to provide material and economic aid in order to facilitate the blacks' adjustment. In 1866, the Civil Rights Act was passed. It declared that all persons born in the United States, except untaxed Indians, were entitled to equality of treatment before the law, any "statute to the contrary notwithstanding." The main features of this act were incorporated into the 14th Amendment in 1868, which also bestowed citizenship upon all persons born or naturalized in the United States and subject to its jurisdiction. No state was to take action that would violate the rights that this section sought to protect.

The second section, in substance, gave the states the choice between granting suffrage to all adult male citizens, or suffering a reduction in the House of Representatives and in the electoral colleges proportional to the number denied the vote. The third section barred from federal and state office many of the most important pre-Civil War Southerners. This amendment was adopted while the Southern states were under military rule established by the Great Reconstruction Acts of 1867. In accordance with these laws, blacks were given the right to vote and to sit in the state constitutional conventions. The 15th Amendment of 1870 declared that this right to vote could not be abridged or denied by the United States or any one state on account of race, color, or previous condition of servitude. Finally, the Civil Rights Act of 1875 prohibited individuals from discriminating against blacks in public places and on public carriers.

This was the state of the blacks' legal emancipation when the Hayes-Tilden Compromise of 1877 was signed. It provided for the withdrawal of Federal troops from the South. The significance of this compromise was that during the following years the black was gradually and forcibly reduced to a second-class citizen, a state of affairs that by the turn of the century was accepted by the presidency, the Supreme Court, Congress, and all other major institutions of the nation. Frederick Douglass, realizing the critical turn of events, asked in 1899, "Whether American justice, American liberty, American civilization, American law, and American Christianity could be made to include and protect alike, forever, all American citizens in the rights which have been guaranteed to them by the organic and fundamental laws of the land."[35]

Logan has described the period 1877-1901 as the nadir in the American black's quest for equal rights. Henry Arthur Callis, a physician born in 1886, termed the first decade of the 20th century "a low, rugged plateau," and John Hope Franklin states in 1961 that, "For the American Negro the last decades of the 19th century were more critical than the Reconstruction years of 1868 to 1876."[36]

I have taken this excursion to investigate America's attempt to integrate the black folk into the mainstream of American society, because I feel that its failure and particularly its coincidence with the era of imperial expansion, is significant in terms of our analysis.

W.E.B. DuBois remarked that the history of the last two decades of the 19th and the early part of this century

> may be epitomized in one word—Empire, the domination of White Europe over Black Africa and Yellow Asia, through political power built on the economic control of labor, income and ideas. The echo of this industrial imperialism in America was the expulsion of the Black men from the American democracy, their subjection to caste control and wage slavery.[37]

Philip C. Curtin's book, *Image of Africa*, divides the 19th century into two periods: the years before 1850, the "period of limited missionary and commercial penetration" which also coincided with the era of humanitarianism; and the three decades from about 1850 to about 1880 which mark what he calls a transition from humanitarianism to the era of imperialism.[38] However, this neat categorization of people and events, while convenient, may be something less than accurate. The ideology which made imperialism a viable concept in the second period was at least seminally present in the first. The good intentions of the spiritually exalted Quakers, Methodists, altruists and humanitarian reformers are not in doubt. But humanitarians were human beings, not saints, and as such were subject to many of the prejudices and emotional responses of their time. Therefore, it is not surprising that most of the evangelical activists spent more time trying to cultivate the natural resources of West Africa than they did the African himself.[39] Their abundant energies were devoted more to the extinction of idleness in particular than of evil in general. For these compulsive improvers, the end of indolence was the beginning of salvation. Their goal and purpose was to instill in the African the same kind of work ethic which permeated the processes of the Industrial Revolution in the West and which so admirably served the development of capitalism there. The humanitarianism of the 19th century tended to push even further the 17th century colonial formula of "sowing spirituals and reaping temporals."

During the period of transition from humanitarianism to imperialism in Europe, the government and the people of the United States, according to Logan, "were not prodded by an effective criticism." The war scare of 1875 put Europe on the razor's edge on the eve of the end of Reconstruction; and the scramble for Africa began almost immediately thereafter.

> Leopold II of Belgium organized the International Association for Exploration and Civilization of Central Africa in 1876, the year of the Hayes-Tilden election. Belgium, Britain and France, soon to be followed by Germany and Italy, carried the "blessings" of white civilization to Africa. They were not likely at the same time to condemn the restoration of White supremacy in the South.[40]

After wiping out the Indian frontier in 1878, the United States began its imperialistic adventures in the Pacific and Caribbean. This brought under the jurisdiction of the United States some eight million people of the colored races—"A varied assortment of inferior races," as The Nation described them, "which of course could not be allowed to vote." As America shouldered the white man's burden, she took up at the same time many of what are called the Southern attitudes on the subject of race. "If the stronger and the cleverer race," said the editor of The Atlantic Monthly, "is free to impose its will upon the 'new-caught sullen people' on the other side of the globe, why not in South Carolina and Mississippi?" The Boston Evening Transcript of January 14, 1899, admitted that Southern race policy was "now the policy of the administration of the very party which carried the country into and through the Civil War to free the slave." The New York Times of May 10, 1900, commented editorially that "Northern men . . . no longer denounce the suppression of the Negro vote (in the South) as it used to be denounced in the Reconstruction days. The necessity of it under the supreme law of self-preservation is candidly recognized."[41]

The white supremacists in the South thoroughly grasped and expanded the implications of the new imperialism for their domestic policies. "No Republican leader," declared Senator Tillman of South Carolina, "not even Governor Roosevelt will now dare to wear the bloody shirt and preach a crusade against the South's treatment of the Negro. The North has the bloody shirt of its own. Many of them have been made into shrouds for murdered Filipinos, done to [sic] because they were fighting for liberty."

And the junior Senator from South Carolina, John J. McLanom, thanked Senator George F. Hoar of Massachusetts "for his complete announcement of the divine right of the Caucasian to govern the inferior races," a position which "most amply vindicated the South."[42]

The body of knowledge about Africa, which existed in Europe at the turn of the century and which influenced the attitudes of white peoples toward American blacks and Africans, transcended what a particular European country thought at a particular time, and fashioned the history of the relations between white people and black people. It is therefore not surprising that European imperial ideas about Africans affected the blacks in the United States. Those ideas suited the treatment of the black people in the high noon of imperialism, and helped to shape the future of the black-white relationship. The rise of the Anglo-Saxon mystique both in England and in America further rationalized the rule of the whites over the blacks.

The understanding of this fact will show that the tragedy of emancipation was not that it was immature, but that it was premature. Its maximum fervor and insurgency preceded by a few years the rise of imperialism and the complete hegemonic dominance of the entire non-white world by the whites. As a consequence, the American black had to pay the price of having been the forerunner of black emancipation. The rise of militant imperialism fostered in the whites the deepest contempt for blacks. Any idea on the part of the black man that he was an equal of the whites was brutally suppressed. One finds that among blacks in the United States the desire to return to Africa increased proportionately to their persecution and exclusion from American institutions.[43] Early efforts at building an African consciousness to combat Anglo-Saxonism failed with disastrous consequences for the masses of black folks who were in a state of amnesia and withdrawal.

The distinctive effect of imperialism was to associate Anglo-Saxonism with innate qualities of excellence in intelligence, beauty and the right to rule other races. Its reverse effect on the black was to degrade his color, and the physical subordination that had been imposed by force came to be associated with the black's innate qualities. Theodore Roosevelt stated in 1895, "A perfectly stupid race can never rise to a very high plane; the Negro, for instance, has been kept down as much by lack of intellectual development as anything else." Slavery had thrown the black folks into a distorted and famished milieu and imperialism finally expelled him from the history of mankind. Its success in conquering the non-white world became a sociological ceiling on the black's rights and human respect. The celebration of Anglo-Saxon excellence, omnipotence and omnipresence mesmerized some black folks and led them to a passive acceptance of the inferiority of the black race, and sometimes to a sickly striving to become black Anglo-Saxons. Having lost their nerve, they finally ended by losing their identity.

"The dawn of the twentieth century," wrote DuBois, "found white Europe master of the world, and the white peoples almost universally recognized as the rulers for whose benefit the rest of the world existed. Never before in the history of civilization had self-worship of a people's accomplishment attained the heights that the worship of white Europe by Europeans reached."[44] The late Victorian era and the high point of imperialism were to weld the whites together,[45] wherever they were, into a single social bloc, in control of the darker races of the earth. Thus the former Dutch colonials in South Africa, who to all intents and purposes had become a white tribe in South Africa, were in 1910 given equal political power with their English conquerors and the African, despite his professions of loyalty to the English crown, was given only token representation. Some black intellectuals in the United States and in the West Indies, with a few Africans who understood the Western idiom and the white dominance of the world, fought passionately and unaided. They called the first Pan-African Congress in 1900, and the second in 1919, which was dismissed by the *Chicago Tribune* of January 1919 as an "Ethiopian Utopia." The important assumption of these attempts was that the problems of the American black must be thought of and settled with continual reference to the problems of West Indian blacks, the problems of the French and English blacks and, above all, the problems of the Africans in Africa. This was the thought behind the Pan-African movement in all its various manifestations.[46]

It is customary to explain European commentators on Africa by saying that in the 19th century they were too ethnocentric, looking at everything in terms of Europe's conceptions, and never making an effort to abandon their social milieu in order to gain a perspective on African norms and customs. Such explanations assume that if these commentators had made the effort, they would have realized that the African social matrix and values were equally valid and legitimate. This, of course, supposes that they even remotely had the desire to understand African cultures and is contradicted by the fact that a sincere effort at understanding would naturally have undermined their supremacist assumptions.

We cannot speculate as to what would have happened had such and such been the case; we can only judge the Europeans' intentions and their attitudes toward Africa from the disparity between what they professed and what they did. Individuals trying to save the world by means of some innate wisdom will often develop a philosophy around it in order to guide their actions. Ideals thereby give eyes to practice and inform philosophy.

European travellers, imperial anthropologists and some missionaries wished not only to inform, but also to please their audiences. Unfortunately they created images of Africa which made the predatory activities of imperialists look humanitarian when compared to the "depraved" state of the African.

Throughout the last quarter of the 19th century and the first two decades of the 20th, we find that this state of affairs with few exceptions generally held true. The images of the African tended to coincide with colonial and imperial interests. Hannah Arendt correctly pointed out:

> Imperialism would have necessitated the invention of racism as the only possible explanation and excuse for its deeds, even if no race thinking had ever existed in the civilized world.[47]

In 19th century literature on Africans, one finds that such aspects of African culture as religion and art were of little interest to imperial anthropologists who dismissed them as pagan errors. But such practices as human sacrifice, judicial ordeals and polygamy were described in detail and with relish. The reporting of this period stressed precisely those aspects of African life that were known to be unfamiliar in the Western world, and were likely to cause horror. The contextual meaning of the customs and the fact that these practices were not uniquely African but could be found in most other societies at some stage of historical development were ignored. I find it difficult to agree with Curtin who writes:

> The love of the extraordinary was partly the reflection of a much older European interest in the exotic—an interest blending genuine intellectual curiosity with a libidinous fascination for description of other people who break with impunity the taboos of one's own society.[48]

It was unfortunate that the Europeans' love of the extraordinary brought misery to the Africans, and made easy the consciences of those who were not so much interested in the exotic as they were in the gold in Africa's bowels. For these natural resources could only be obtained through the sweat of African labor.

Negative stereotyping of the African produced among American blacks disconcerting feelings. An interesting but revealing attitude toward Africa was the dispute over the name by which a company to exploit the Johannesburg gold mines was to be called. The South African magnate Oppenheimer, suggested the name "African-American," but an American representative to the company could not accept that name because

"African-American would suggest on this side our dark-skinned countrymen and probably result in ridicule."[49] Primitive African art and music had many admirers in the West, but the social milieu which produced it filled these connoisseurs with shame and revulsion. St. Clair Drake wrote: "They can accept phychologically Benin art, but not its 'customs.' The American Negroes, because of their subjection to Western values, have been defensive and ambivalent when discussing Africa and African societies."[50]

One can begin to understand this defensiveness when one reads some of the horror stories about African barbarism in both official and journalistic dispatches of the 19th century. Stanley, who went in search of Livingstone, wrote a book in 1874 describing a military campaign against the Ashanti. In his book he quoted at length a letter from Sir Garnet Wolesley to the Secretary of State for the colonies, declaring of the Ashanti that "no more utterly atrocious government existed on the face of the earth." He further went on to state about these people that their capital was a charnel house, their religion a combination of cruelty and treachery, their policy the natural outcome of their religion. Stanley wrote of the customs which involve human sacrifice, pointing out that, "a thousand slaves, offenders and others" were executed annually "to swell the terrible death role of the Kumasi Golgotha." He describes the execution spot in grisly detail, and speaks of how good it was that the King had been dethroned and human sacrifice ended. Almost as an afterthought he wrote, "King Coffee (Kofi) is too rich a neighbor to be left alone in all his riches, with his tons of gold dust and accumulation of wealth to himself." He was sure that Britain could better organize the energies of the Ashanti people who he said had been traitors.[51]

The Afro-American child from his cradle to his grave had to be inflicted with the knowledge that all people of color, and in particular Africans, his forebears, were in varying stages of savagery and barbarism due to geography, environment, race and even providence. Imperialists, missionaries and social anthropologists seem to agree that there was such a thing as the white man's burden; that the white man had a civilizing mission toward those who were half-savages, and that these same people were inherently a lesser breed without the law. Africa, as we have pointed out, was a special case; it was the most savage and the most barbaric of the black areas. It was Joseph Conrad who in his inimitable style expressed this feeling graphically: "We were wanderers on a prehistoric earth, on an earth that wore the aspect of the unknown planet. We could have fancied ourselves the first men taking possession of an accursed inheritance to be subdued at the cost of profound anguish and excessive toil."[52]

Carter G. Woodson was well aware of the implication of this type of treatment of everything connected with the black folk. It is an implication that must be taken into account by those who seem to think that education is a formula for the solution of the Negro problem:

> The so-called modern education, with all its defects, however, does for others so much more good than it does the Negro, because it has been worked out in conformity to the needs of those who have enslaved and oppressed weaker peoples. For example, the philosophy and ethics resulting from our educational system have justified slavery, peonage, segregation and lynching. The oppressor has the right to exploit, to handicap and kill the oppressed.[53]

George Lamming, the West Indian writer, seems to agree with Woodson when he points out the dilemma that has inhibited the West Indian intelligence in pursuit of what he calls "total liberation"—"At this level of intellectual discovery, Africa has remained a blank." He points out further the difference between a white American's return to Europe and the West Indian's first projection of an Africa in his head. "The American's experience of English tombs and French kitchens, however tasteless and dirty, often begins as an abstraction that purifies. Not so with the black man of the Caribbean and Africa." He indicates why this is so:

> His [the West Indian's] education did not provide him with any reading to rummage through as a guide to lost kingdoms, of the names and places which give geography a human significance. He knows (Africa) through rumor and myth, which is made sinister by a foreign tutelage, and becomes, through the gradual conditioning of his education, identified with fear: fear of that continent as a world beyond human intervention. Part product of that world, and living still under the shadow of its past disfigurement, he appears reluctant to acknowledge his share of the legacy which is part of his heritage.[54]

White hegemonic views about Africa and about its inhabitants did not allow the black man in diaspora to have his prehistory percolate unimpeded through vital layers of the black man's consciousness. Until this happens no one can say for sure what the "true" meaning and import of Africa is for the black man's identity in America. But it is this dilemma, this aura of uncertainty, that has fertilized the black imagination about Africa. The dilemma involves ambivalence, embarrassment and a sense of possibility.

Notes

[1]W.E.B. DuBois, *The Gift of Black Folk, the Negroes in the Making of America*, with introduction by Truman Nelson, Washington Square Press, New York, 1970, p. 162.

[2]Arendt, *The Origins of Totalitarianism*, p. 299.

[3]For a fuller discussion see Ward H. Goodenough, *Cooperation in Change: An Anthropological Approach to Community Development*, Russell Sage Foundation, New York, 1963.

[4]C. Van Woodward, *American Attitudes Toward History, an inaugural lecture delivered before the University of Oxford on 22 February, 1955*, Clarendon Press, Oxford, 1955.

[5]*Ibid.*, p. 2.

[6]Truman Nelson, "W.E.B. DuBois as a Prophet," *Freedomways*, Vol. 5, No. 1, Winter 1965, p. 50.

[&]W.E.B. DuBois, *The Souls of Black Folk*, Fawcett Publications, Greenwich, Connecticut, 1961, p. 21.

[8]Hannah Arendt, *Origins of Totalitarianism*, Meridian Books, New York, 1962, p. 299.

[9]Wright, *White Man, Listen!*, p. 6.

[10]Quoted in *Freedomways*, Vol. 5, No. 1, Winter 1965, p. 49. In reaction to this brand of hypocrisy David Walker, in his *Appeal to the Colored Citizens of the World, 1829-1830*, wrote: "Now I appeal to heaven and to earth, particularly to the Americans themselves who cease not to declare that our condition is not hard, and that we are comparatively satisfied to rest in wretchedness and misery, under them and their children. Not indeed to show me a colored President, a Governor, a Legislator, a Mayor, or an Attorney at the Bar—but to show me a man of color who holds the low office of a Constable, or one who sits in a Juror Box, even on a case of one of his wretched brethren, throughout this great Republic! . . . I ask those people who treat us so *well*, Oh! I ask them where is the most barren spot of land which they have given? Israel had the most fertile land in all Egypt."

[11]For a good discussion on this point see Charles H. Wesley's, "The Concept of Negro Inferiority in American Thought," *Journal of Negro History*, Vol. 25, No. 4, 1940, pp. 540-41.

[12]W.E.B. DuBois, *Dusk of Dawn: An Essay Toward an Autobiography of a Race Concept*, Harcourt, Brace and Company, New York, 1940, p. 96.

[13]Frederick Douglass observed: "In the hurry and confusion of the hour and the eager desire to have the union restored there was more care for the sublime superstructure of the Republic than for the solid foundation upon which it could alone be upheld. To the freed men was given the machinery of liberty, but there was denied them the steam to put it into motion. They were given the uniform of soldiers, but no arms, they were called citizens but left almost slaves. The older master class was not deprived of the power of life and death which was the soul of the relation of

master and slave." Frederick Douglass, *Selection from his Writings*, editor, Philip S. Foner, International Publisher, 1945, p. 82.

[14]Arendt, *The Origins of Totalitarianism*, p. 296.

[15]Karl Marx and Frederick Engels, *The Holy Family*, Foreign Language Publishing House, Moscow, 1956, p. 59.

[16]Perry Anderson, "The Origins of the Present Crisis," *New Left Review*, Vol. 23, 1964, pp. 26-35. Max Weber made the same point: "Strata in solid possession of social honor and power usually tend to fashion their status legend in such a way as to claim a special intrinsic quality of their own, usually a quality of blood; their sense of dignity feeds on their sense of actual or alleged being," Gerth and Mills, *op. cit.*, p. 276.

[17]A classic work on slavery in the Old South: "The Negro is improvident, will not lay up in summer for the wants of winter, will not accumulate in youth for the exigencies of age. He would become an insufferable burden to society. Society has a right to prevent this and can only do this by subjecting him to domestic slavery." George Fitzburgh and H.R. Helper, editors, *Ante-Bellum: Three Classic Writings on Slavery in the Old South*, p. 89.

[18]Carter Woodson, *The Mis-Education of the Negro*, Associated Publishers, Washington, D.C., 1933, p. 11.

[19]Kelly Miller, Quoted in *The Negro in Our History*, by Carter G. Woodson, Associated Publishers, Inc., Washington, D.C., 1966, p. xxviii.

[20]I am well aware that other notions about Africa and the black did exist, but here I am interested in those ideas which exercised considerable influence upon most white people in their attitudes toward black people, i.e., those ideas which tended to harmonize with tendencies of the time. These are the ideas upon which have been built pernicious forms of racial arrogance. Even "humanitarians," especially in the 19th century, were "racists" in the sense that they attributed certain characteristics to certain skin colors. They may have believed that these were not inherent but would be "removed" over a period of time. This in itself, however, meant they were willing to treat blacks differently.

[21]G.W.F. Hegel, *The Philosophy of History*, Daner Publications, Inc., 1956, pp. 91-99.

[22]Burrows Dunham, *The Giant in Chains*, Little, Brown and Company, Boston, 1963, p. 80.

[23]Thomas F. Gossett, *Race: The History of an Idea in America*, Shocken Books, New York, 1965. p. 253.

[24]L.S.B. Leakey, *The Progress and Evolution of Man in Africa*, Oxford University Press, New York, 1961, p. 1.

[25]Quoted in W.E.B. DuBois, "Review of American Dilemma," by Gunnar Myrdal, *Phylon*, Vol. 5, No. 2, p. 118.

[26]Woodson, *The Negro in Our History*, p. 1.

[27]E.W. Blyden, *Christianity, Islam, and the Negro Race*, W.B. Wittingham and Company, London, 1917 (originally published in 1888), p. 160.

[28]Kwame Nkrumah, *Consciencism: Philosophy, and Ideology for Decolonization*, Monthly Review Press, New York, 1970, p. 64.

[29]Woodson, *The Negro in Our History*, p. 3.

[30]Joseph Conrad, *The Heart of Darkness*, New American Library, New York, 1963, p. 69.

[31]This does not deny the contributions made by voices of protest within the European societies. For instance, the Races Congress held in London in 1910 articulated this protest. Communism, Fabianism, Socialism and the labor movements did not accept the imperialist ideas.

[32]Mark Twain, *King Leopold's Soliloquy*, Seven Seas Publishers, Berlin, 1963, p. 14.

[33]Mark Twain, *ibid.*

[34]Otto Ruhle, *Karl Marx—His Life and Work*, New House Library, New York, 1943, p. 3.

[35]For a fuller discussion see W.F. Logan, *The Betrayal of the Negro*, Macmillan, New York, 1965, Chapter V.

[36]Cited *Ibid.*

[37]Quoted in *Freedomways*, Vol. 5, No. 1, 1965, p. 168.

[38]Philip C. Curtin, *Image of Africa*, University of Wisconsin Press, Madison, 1964, p. vi.

[39]Michael Banton has observed: "To rouse interest and support among church people, missionary bodies glamorized the work of their agents and described the native life in horrifying terms. The reports of administrators, merchants, and missionaries brought home to the public the technological backwardness of the colonial peoples, and, as civilization was often equated with machines and material benefits, this reinforced the image of the colored man as uncivilized." *White and Coloured*, Rutgers University Press, New Brunswick, New Jersey, 1960, p. 69. I recommend the reading of Chapter IV in Banton's book as complementary to the present discussion since it makes a similar survey of changing conceptions of the colored man.

[40]Logan, *op. cit.*, p. 21.

[41]Cf. C. Van Woodward, *The Strange Career of Jim Crow*, Oxford University Press, Chapter I.

[42]*Ibid.*, see also W.F. Logan, *op. cit.*

[43]I discuss this in Chapters III, IV and V.

[44]W.E.B. DuBois, *The World and Africa*, International Publishers, New York, 1965, p. 26.

[45]Wherever whites have settled among non-white societies they have become a privileged group. In places like France where many Negro artists exiled themselves, they were such an infinitesimal minority that no direct discrimination was practiced against them.

[46]W.E.B. DuBois, "Pan-Africa and the New Radical Philosophy," *Crisis*, Vol. 40, No. 11, November, 1933, p. 247.

[47]Hannah Arendt, *The Burden of Our Times*, Secker and Warburg, London, 1950, p. 180.

[48]Curtin, *op. cit.*, p. 24.

[49]Quoted in Theodore Gregory, *Ernest Oppenheimer and the Economic Development of Southern Africa*, Oxford University Press, New York, 1962, p. 88.

[50]*Africa: Seen by American Negro Scholars*, Presence Africaine, New York, 1963, pp. 11-31.

[51]Quoted in *Africa: Seen by American Negro Scholars*, pp. 11-13.

[52]Conrad, *op. cit.*, p. 105.

[53]Woodson, *The Mis-Education of the Negro*, p. xii.

[54]Quoted in *African Forum*, Vol. 1, No. 4, p. 33.

CHAPTER THREE
Racism and
The Afro-American's Self-Image

Social life is essentially practical. All mysteries which misled theory to mysticism find their rational solution in human practice and in the comprehension of this practice.

—Karl Marx

The American black's conception of himself and his identity cannot be fully appreciated without a continual reference to the popular image Africa enjoyed in the white world. And there is no gainsaying the fact that one group's view of another is never simply an outcome of popular fancies and myths. The white's dominant conception of the African has been powerfully influenced by certain intellectual ideas, current in Europe at different epochs, about man's relation to man and the nature of society. A Marxist historian noted the difference between ancient and modern myths:

> In our more secular era, "scientific" myths have greater influence. These myths fall into historical, anatomical, anthropological, and psychological categories, all strongly reinforced by the misreading of Darwinism to justify political backwardness, moral ferocity, avid acquisitiveness, and social injustice, and especially because of the biological base of Darwinism, the subordination of the Black, exactly on the grounds of natural, i.e., biological, inferiority.[1]

The black having been part of the Western world since the 16th century has been partially conditioned by the concepts which white people have had about him and the place they have assigned him. He also has been treated in accordance with the assumptions of these views. Therefore, to look at some of the ideas about blacks current in America in the second half of the 19th century is to acknowledge that any phase of intellectual history tells us what men have at different times known and believed about themselves and their destiny and about others; the use they have made, in

43

service of their interests and aspirations, of this knowledge; and the underlying presumptions which have made their knowledge seem to them relevant and their beliefs to be true.[2]

Thus when black folks were enslaved, and when Africa was dismembered, the fact that it became such a lucrative enterprise produced a host of apologists, for as Michael Banton pointed out: "The merchant's profits benefit a large section of the nation and forge a chain of vested interest."[3] These imperial apologists will form the central thesis of this chapter. What Frank H. Hankins observed about the anthro-sociological contribution of the late 19th century is extremely relevant:

If they had deceived themselves only, little harm would have resulted. But they greatly strengthened doctrines upon which have been based pernicious forms of racial arrogance in Germany, England and the United States. They assisted in the inflation of the Teutonic chauvinists and Pan-Germanists, they lent aid and comfort to Anglo-Saxon imperialists, they gave a sense of moral righteousness to the spirit of racial intolerance.[4]

The intellectual and emotional investment of the Western world in trying to prove that humanity was divided into superior (white) and inferior (black) races and the degrading conditions they forced black folks to live under is unique in human experience. Why and how? Alexis de Tocqueville in his celebrated book, *Democracy in America*, provided a partial answer:

When the Europeans choose their slaves from a race differing from their own, which many . . . considered as inferior to the other races of mankind and which they all repelled with horror from any notion of intimate connection, they must have believed that slavery would last forever; since there is no intermediate state, which can be durable, between the excessive inequality and complete equality which originates in independence. The Europeans did imperfectly feel this truth, but without acknowledging it even to themselves. Whenever they have had to do with Negroes, their conduct has either been directed by their interests and their pride or by their compassion. They first violated every right of humanity by their treatment of the Negroes, and they afterwards informed him that those rights were precious and inviolable. They affected to open their ranks to the slaves but the Negroes who attempted to penetrate into the community were driven back with scorn, and they have uncautiously and involuntarily been led to admit of freedom instead of slavery, without knowing the courage to be wholly iniquitous or wholly just.[5]

In the United States, racism became institutionalized. European thought and practice assigned blacks third-class status; that is, to claim any right to survive, blacks had to serve the interest of whites who considered themselves the lords of humanity.

The economics of slavery could not have persisted over an extended period as just a set of shrewd market-oriented operations. Elaboration of a whole *culture of control*, with political, ideological and social formulations, was necessary to maintain dominance over black slaves and to keep non-slaveholding whites in line. Given that white Europeans were subjugating African blacks, the culture of control became largely structured around a color-oriented racialism. "Slavery could not exist if the Negro were not a man set apart; he simply had to be different if slavery were to exist at all."[6]

Once the distinctiveness of the African *vis-a-vis* the whites was established in the ideology of slavery, the transplanted black population in the United States had to be socialized to accept their inferior new status. Thus, they were subjected to a twofold process as the full-fledged system of control evolved. Initially this process took the form of systematic deculturation which, according to Ribeiro, operates in those special situations where a subject people is forced to abandon its own culture and adopt new ways of thinking and behaving by being removed from its culture context through impressment, enslavement or transplantation. Deculturation is almost always a stage preceding and prerequisite to acculturation. The defamation of Africa and the ideology of black inferiority were part of the process of deculturation. According to Ribeiro: "The detribalization of the Negro and his fusion into the neo-American societies constitute one of the most prodigious population movements and the most dramatic process of deculturation in history".[7]

Since the extreme form of alienation attendant upon existence in this cultural vacuum demanded some sort of alleviation, a second stage, that of acculturation, was set in motion. Acculturation in a situation of dominance and subjugation, however, is a one-way process, and not a mutual interchange of ideas, values and culture traits. It was necessary to the economic interests of the dominant group that the Africans renounce their ethnic patterns of socio-cultural thought and behavior, but it was equally necessary that they become indoctrinated with values and thought patterns congruent with their new roles. Christianity functioned as the instrument through which this was accomplished.[8] Conversion of the slaves to Christianity represented, if only symbolically, the incorporation of enslaved Africans into the mental and cultural universe of the whites. It thus had the value of initiating the process of disciplinary adaptation to Western cultural norms. Perry Anderson's conclusions about the role of Christianity in colonial Africa are equally applicable to the American setting:

Conversion also has an important psychological function within the white community. Confronted with the fathomless alterity of the African population, its opaque and menial presence outside the familiar, regulated universe of white society, an immense fear often seizes the white settler . . . In a situation of extreme insecurity, organized religion, intent on converting the African, reassures.

Christianity in a slave situation is a domestication of the slave population. Objectively, Anderson observed, it frees the white of his terror of the black by including him in the same canon as himself.

At the same time, it has a crucial additional interest for any colonizer. It represents an ideal *arrested threshold of acculturation* for the native (slave). A colonial (slave) system needs a subject population with a certain minimal level of Europeanization, for the purpose of order and exploitation.

The most attractive feature of the Christian religion for the slave must have been the hope for the Messiah, the prospect of a kingdom of universal happiness, but this could not be extricated from the doctrine of servility which gave fresh support to the slavery system. Christianity raised the obedience of the slave to a moral duty, something to be performed with gladness for future rewards. It is interesting to note that many leaders of the black community who were educated in Christian missionary institutions were also instrumental in the rise of movements of rebellion. The apparent paradox becomes explicable when one takes into consideration the shameless brutality of the system of oppression, its structural contradictions and the contradictory elements within traditional Christianity itself. In his *Foundations of Christianity*, Kautsky noted:

Just as the human rights of the American Declaration of Independence made peace with slavery, so did the all-embracing brotherhood of love of neighbor and equality of all before the God of the Messianic community.[9]

By exposing the African to what was formally a central but, in fact, a peripheral and profoundly castrating area of white culture, the slave owners were able to provide the slaves with efficient means to defuse their anger. By adopting the Christian view of the world and themselves, they were able to place themselves once more in a defined context and thus to relieve the extremity of their condition. In doing so, however, they were forced to replace one form of alienation with another, for the concepts which they adopted had been devised to justify their own subjugation. This new form of alienation has characterized the black experience in America until the present day.

The concept of "pure knowledge" and value neutrality has fallen on evil days. Knowledge and consciousness of social factors are *immanent*, both in terms of the process of cognition, and as a final result of this process. That is, knowledge is man's contact with reality, and the ground of his attempted control over it. Any social production to which human effort is directed, and which brings man into direct contact with nature, does not merely influence cognition and serve, with respect to it, as one of the external factors, it is the foundation of knowledge, its real impelling force, the final source of any heuristic interest.[10] The horizon of human curiosity is historically determined.

Since the first contact between Africans and white people, the latter's ideas about blacks have been determined by the role they wanted the African to play in the production process. From mercantilist to the slave and imperialist epoch, the image of the black has assumed different characteristics which have been reflected in ideological thought. Marx wrote in his *The Eighteenth Brumaire of Louis Bonaparte*, how the ideologists reproduce at the level of theory, that reality which the rank and file member encounters in his daily life, and which in the final analysis dictates to him a given course of behavior, given strivings and moral standards. The social reality of the dominant strata is justified by its own ideology which these groups readily accept, while rejecting the one reflecting the objective interests of the subordinate groups.[11]

At the level of ideology, there is what the functional sociologists call interest articulation and expectations of a group or a class, determined basically by its real position in the social structure. This takes the form of a more or less complete picture of the "desired society," in plans of social organization—a social utopia that is at the core of an entire system of corresponding ideological concepts. But society is characterized further by definite, objective tendencies not dependent in the slightest upon these projects of the desired and the essentials developed by ideologists of various social groups. Social thought to be plausible must take into account these objective developments.

The criterion of truth, therefore, has to do with the comparison of two perspectives: the "project" advanced by a given social group, and the real tendency of objective historical development. Ideologies reflect, above all, objective factors. And the very nature of the distortion of truth in the ideology of the exploitating classes is also objectively determined.

According to Bernard Crick: "If a nation wishes to deny that a large number of its subject inhabitants can ever attain national status and citizenship, it needs a justification which transcends theoretical categories of nationalism. . . So racialism then becomes a theory by which one nation can oppress other nations."[12] In the long history of the white man's attempt to ossify the black's station in life, several theories have been expounded. Slavery, peonage and abortive types of apprenticeship have had their day. Along with these practices, and in justification of them, there developed a corpus of assumptions, like Anglo-Saxon superiority and African inferiority, white supremacy and black subordination.

All the theories of white hegemony have certain assumptions underlying them, whether they are absolute or evolutionary. The fundamental assumptions of such theories are the denial of change, and the rationalization and petrification of the status quo. Even if we grant that evolutionist theory was initially characterized by a belief in progress, its obverse side was to create a new beatitude in the national religions of the West: Might is Right. Professor L. Langer, an authority on this period, concluded that "the prevalence of evolutionary teaching was perhaps crucial. It not only justified competition and struggle, but it introduced an element of ruthlessness and immorality that was so characteristic of the whole movement."[13] Add to this the other assumption associated with evolution, which makes change so slow and imperceptible as in fact to deny it. Modern sociological theory, in particular, functionalism, is an inheritor of this tradition and has been burdened with trying to reassure itself that within its equilibrating system change is feasible.

In America, according to Howard Zinn, the emphasis has been placed on ideological heritage rather than on material circumstances, and change has meant the gradual realization of what is called the American dream, "which explains rigidity more than it explains change."[14] This is why the Negro problem is sometimes called a moral dilemma, the faltering of American ideals.

The implications of de-emphasizing change were explained by Burrows Dunham in this fashion: "Suppose then, you abolish change; you abolish time with it. Time being gone, what about space? Space without time would have no locomotion in it, it would be a dead solid like a cannon ball."[15] The theories which were current in the 19th century to explain the position of the black had the effect of setting him outside history and time; he could not be improved nor his circumstances changed because change would ruin him. It is not difficult to see that this affection for permanence expressed a complacent and smug satisfaction with the existing society. The white supremacists' theories were tied to a particular epoch of historical development, and as that epoch began to show contradictions between reality and theory, some of the metaphysical assumptions degenerated into reactionary ideologies.

We have touched above on the assertion that knowledge is a social fact and that any theory of methods needs to take account of it. Society affects knowledge in two ways: it limits or enlarges the range of the chances for new discoveries, and it conditions the observer as to what he will perceive. The scholastics who rejected the plain sensory evidence of Galileo's experiments were, no doubt, the victims of a moribund social structure. Error is just error; compounded with a social lag, it becomes prejudice.

Slavery provided more than the ideological roots for segregation. And insofar as the black's status was fixed and proclaimed by enslavement, there was no occasion to resort to segregation in order to establish his caste and his subordination. The Civil War and the Emancipation Proclamation initiated a new phase. This was the period of the black as a legally free individual, theoretically equal to the whites. Earlier there had been free blacks in both North and South and it was, according to C. Van Woodward, in the treatment accorded these people in both North and South that the ante-bellum period came nearest to foreshadowing segregation. "Denied full rights and privileges of citizens, deprived of equality in the Courts, and restricted in their freedom of assembly and freedom of movement, the free Negro shared many of the deprivations of the slave. In addition, measures of ostracism were levelled at members of this class to emphasize their status."[16]

The next critical phase of Afro-American history began after 1877 with the withdrawal of federal troops from the South. The federal government abandoned its wardship over the black folks. It did this by not enforcing sections of the Constitution, the various amendments that guaranteed the freed man his civil and political rights. There was after 1877 an acquiescence by the rest of the country to the South's demand that the whole problem be left to the disposition of the dominant southern white people. C. Van Woodward observed:

What the new status of the Negro would be was not at once apparent, nor were the Southern white people themselves so united on that subject at first as has been generally assumed. The determination of the Negroes' "place" took shape gradually under the influence of economic and political conflicts among divided white people—conflicts that were eventually resolved in part at the expense of the Negro. In the early years of the twentieth century, it was becoming clear that the Negro would be effectively disfranchised throughout the South, that he would be firmly relegated to the lower rungs of the economic ladder, and that neither equality nor aspirations for equality in any department of life were for him.[17]

The economic and political conflicts which assigned the black folk to a position of a second-class citizenship also took place at the theoretical and ideological level. The social and philosophical theories of the period 1850-1940, all seem to have conspired to create illusions in most white people of Europe and America, who must have believed that their supremacy over the black people would extend to eternity. The objective development of past history was either completely missed or ignored; and where it was not missed, attempts were made to make sure that its future course fulfilled this projected state. Thus, in order to further make the whites' position immutable a whole superstructure of Jim Crow laws was enacted to help enforce what was considered God's law of nature. And these laws were always predicated on the assumption that they were the final settlement. One racist even called the presence of the Afro-American "the happiest conjunction that ever had occurred in human affairs since it made inescapably obvious the superiority and relative equality of whites compared with inferior blacks." It made possible "a new civilization based on foundations of everlasting truth"—on the "natural" distinctions of race instead of the "artificial" distinctions of class.[18]

An analysis of race thinking which aims at being casual cannot take consciousness as being prior and write the sociology of this time in terms of man's desires and ideals. True history is made partly by the conscious activities of men, but it must include consciousness as historically conditioned, an outcome of the development of economic production and the division of labor.[19] Race thinking has its roots deep in the history of mankind, but racism as we know it now only emerged as a cohesive system of thought in most Western societies during the second half of the 19th century. More explicitly, racism became an ideology during the imperialistic era. Prior to this period, people were conscious of their own racial kind. thus, we have had the notion of the chosen race, especially favored by God, for a long time. Even the notion of one's own social group as exclusively human has been characteristic of mankind, while most people have associated esthetic standards of human beauty with their own kind. There is, for instance, a story of the North American Indians which has it that both the black and the white man were created before God mastered his technique. In baking the first man, God cooked him too long and he emerged black. The white man, also a culinary failure, had not been baked enough. It was only in the third attempt that God was able to produce the properly golden brown Indian.[20]

Any of these views may be described as "racist" but they need to be kept separate from the full-blown pseudo-scientific racism which dominated much of Europe in the period 1840-1940. The difference lies in the fact that science, a body of knowledge rationally derived from empirical observations, supported the proposition that race, in particular skin color, was the principal determinant of attitudes, endowments, capabilities and even inherent tendencies among human beings. From now on, these theories seemed to say, race would determine the course and the fortunes of human history. The 19th century could, without exaggeration, be described as a period of exhaustive (and, as it turned out, futile) search for the criterion to define race differences. "The leading characters . . . of various races of mankind are," as one European racialist put it, "simply representations of the development of the highest or Caucasian type.[21]

In his history of American racism, Thomas F. Gossett posed the following question: "When the evidence began to be overwhelming that none of their systems worked, why did the anthropologists not consider the possibility that there are no 'hierarchies' of race?" He then answered himself: "Some of them were bold enough to come to exactly this conclusion, but for others the idea of race was so real that no amount of failure could convince them that it might be an illusion."[22] It is interesting to read the admission of defeat in this pursuit for a racial character by a French anthropologist, Topinord, who wrote in 1879: "Race in the present state of things, is an abstract conception, a notion of continuity in discontinuity, of unity in diversity. It is the rehabilitation of a real, but directly unattainable thing."[23] And Wesley Powell, Director of the Bureau of Ethnology of the Smithsonian Institute in the 1880s flatly declared that "there was no science of ethnology," by which he meant the determination of race differences.[24] But many anthropologists hoped that a method of determining and classifying races might still be found, and racists in general were hardly daunted at all by the failure of the anthropologists.

PROVING THE BLACKS INFERIOR:
A SYNOPTIC LOOK AT RACE THEORIES[25]

During the period of slavery two theories of race—the monogenic and the polygenic, vied for acceptance. The attempt to classify the races of mankind both quantitatively and qualitatively dominated the scene until the publication of *The Origin of Species*. In almost every system of classification the African occupied the lowest rung of the human ladder. Some natural scientists, in fact, argued that he was closer to the orangutan than to the Caucasian. Monogenesis was essentially an ideological version of the orthodox Christian view that God had created man in His image at a specific point in time. In order to account for variations among the offspring of Adam and Eve, monogenists went so far as to explain Negroid features and color in terms of environmental conditioning. Although they did believe that Africans had degenerated from the pure stock of Adam, they held out some hope for the regeneration of the black race in the near future.

Polygenists, on the other hand, proved less charitable. They insisted that each race had been created separately and distinctly from that of Adam and his descendants. This view was contrary to Biblical authority and it denied that Africans were even potentially equal to caucasians. Most 18th century rationalists drew a causal connection between racial and cultural inferiority. Polygenists subscribed to a rigid hierarchical view of races and cultures, and they equated dark pigmentation with vices and character defects.

Another doctrine was that of Darwin, which concluded that man is related not only to man, but to animal life as well; that the existence of lower races shows clearly that gradual differences alone separate man and beast, and that a powerful struggle for existence dominates all living things. Darwinism was especially strengthened by the fact that it followed the path of the old might-right doctrine. It was generally believed that history would reveal the gradual emergence of the white race as the victor in the struggle for survival since it seemed to be obviously so much better equipped to subjugate people of other colors. This in itself was considered an indication of inherent superiority and thus a mandate for domination.

Darwinism succeeded because it provided on the basis of inheritance the ideological weapons of race, as well as class rule. It could be used for, as well as against, race discrimination. The doctrine of the survival of the fittest, with the implications that the top layer of society was the fittest, suited the imperialist struggle to submerge the world under its regime; and it died when the conquest doctrine died, namely, at the moment when the ruling classes in England or the English domination of the colonial possessions were no longer absolutely secure, and when it became highly doubtful whether those who were fittest today would still be the strongest tomorrow.

The Darwinian theory destroyed the monogenist/polygenist controversy concerning man's origin and nature. It made these controversies seem absurd to a point of quaintness. But Darwin destroyed the basis of older racism, only to replace it with a more up-to-date rationale, within which nearly all the older arguments and conclusions about race superiority could find a place.[26]

Darwinism was put at the service of the imperial urge; for, as is well known, the method of playing any game follows from the nature of the thing to be done. For example, the nature of the game called golf is such that you cannot play it with rackets and skates. Imperialism as a distinctive economic game had its own inherent philosophy and practice. The imperialists' system, according to Perry Anderson, "sets a premium on a patrician political style as a pure system of alien domination; it always, within the limits of safety, seeks to maximize the existential differences between the ruling and ruled, to create a magical and impassable gulf between two fixed essences."[27]

It must not be assumed that we are saying that Darwinism was the primary source of the belligerent ideology and dogmatic racism of the late 19th century; it became a new instrument in the hands of the theorists of race and race struggle. At about this time there arose both in America and England the Anglo-Saxon mythomania, which whether pacific or belligerent became a dominant abstract rationale for the imperialism of both countries. Hosmer, who wrote the *Short History of the Anglo-Saxon Freedom*, believed that the English-speaking race would grow in enormous numbers and spread over the New World of Africa and Australia. "The primacy of the world," he concluded, will be with us. English institutions, English speech, English thought, [are] to become the main features of the political, social and intellectual life of mankind. Thus [will] the survival of the fittest be written large in the world's political future."[28]

It is quite obvious that the rise of social Darwinism, with its doctrine of evolution, offered the best rationale for the *status quo* in 19th century Europe and the white-dominated dependencies. It harmonized perfectly with the philosophy of the ruling class on the one hand and white hegemony of the non-white world on the other. Whatever was, was because it had to be, because it ought to be. The American jurist John Burgess was thus expressing the general mood of the times when he wrote:

I do not think that Asia and Africa can ever receive political organizations in any way. The national state is . . . the most modern and complete solution of the whole problem of political organization which the world has yet produced, and the fact that it is the creation of the Teutonic political genius stamps the Teutonic nations as political nations *par excellence*, and authorizes them, in the economy of the world, to assume the leadership in the establishment and administration of states. The teutonic nations can never regard the exercise of the political power as a right of man. With them, this power must be based upon the capacity to discharge political duty, and they themselves are the best organs which have as yet appeared to determine when and where this capacity exists.[29]

The ignorance of the unsophisticated may lead to bizarre or terrifying conceptions of the world; but the ignorance of men like Burgess, reinforced and confirmed by the misuse of science, has, through their potential influence, a perniciousness infinitely beyond the most cruel expressions of the merely uninformed.

Can we assume that most of the intellectuals, whose racial views dominated the end of the 19th century were sycophants of imperialism? Of course we cannot. Fundamentally, the white supremacy idea is related to the basic rationalization that exploiters used for their system even before racism was concocted: the poor are poor because they are no good. Among the apologists of such ideas were those who were actually interested in expanding the area of knowledge for its own sake and not in the interests of the status quo, but who failed to examine critically those traditions which were absorbed at the maternal knee. For the most part, white supremacy was spared criticism and as such became a lure for facts which were later observed, and which became entrapped in this whole superstructure. By dint of rationalizing, we can get a whole philosophy out of one of these persistent fossils, and since fundamentally we never look at things in any other way, this philosophy will seem to us to work.[30]

Thomas F. Gossett has observed that: "If there is one conviction which unites modern liberals, it is a resistance to the idea of race. We need to understand that liberalism only recently acquired this conviction. The liberals of the latter part of the 19th century were frequently not, it is painfully clear, liberals on the subject of race. Part of the reason why racism flourished so mightily in this period is that it had no really effective opposition, where one might have expected it, since it also flourished among liberals.[31]

What Gossett noted was also observed by Karl Marx during this same period of history. "Upon the different forms of property, upon the social conditions of existence, rises an entire superstructure of distinct and peculiarly formed sentiments, illusions, modes of thought and views of life. The entire class creates and forms them out of its material foundations and out of the corresponding social relations."[32] The process by which the ideological superstructure arises takes place unconsciously. As it assumes a certain naturalness and compels respect from the society in which it grows, individuals who grow under the influence of education and environments may be filled with the most sincere, most elevated attitudes to the views and forms of social existence which arose historically on the basis of more or less narrow class interests. For instance, among 19th century sociologists we see a contradiction between a passion for democracy and an addiction to race theories. We shall presently examine the theories of Ward, Cooley and Sumner, all of whom accepted in varying degrees the prevailing racial theories.

ANTHROPOLOGY AND SOCIOLOGY IN THE 19th AND EARLY PART OF THE 20th CENTURY

What we have called imperialist anthropology arose towards the end of the 19th century, with Herbert Spencer as one of its founding fathers and chief exponents. The studies which were carried out by Spencer and his followers in the field of anthropology have one thing in common. They studied primitive societies not to find out their nature or what they were like, but what they thought they ought to be like. They sought to find in these primitive societies traces of those forms of behavior through which their own societies had passed. They seem to have been determined, however unconsciously, to superimpose their own ideas of the evolutionary sequences upon that of the primitive societies. As Calverton observed in his history of the science of anthropology:

> A whole state of mind was at work here, and not merely an error in scientific approach. A state of mind fostered by the enormous material advance of the 19th century civilization, and the new ideological armament which it had already begun to perfect. This state of mind made it impossible for the anthropologists of the day to use the facts as they were or to interpret them except in the caricatured forms of current prejudices. They studied primitive man as we would a puzzle, shifting facts in every way, out of all sequence and context, in order to find solutions. They were anxious to find universal evolutionary laws, which would explain the rise of man from the crudities of primitivism to the refinements of 19th century civilization.[33]

Thus it is that, between 1880 and 1920 at least, American thought lacks any perception of the black as a human being with potentialities for self-determination. Most of the people who wrote about the blacks accepted without question the idea that intelligence and temperament were racially determined and unalterable. They concluded, therefore, that the failure of Reconstruction, the low educational status of the black, his high statistics of crime, disease, and poverty were simply the inevitable consequence of his heredity. Professor Paul B. Baringer of the University of Virginia told the Southern Education Association in 1900: "the Negro race is essentially a race of peasant farmers and laborers . . . as a source of cheap labor for a warm climate, he is beyond competition; everywhere else, he is a foredoomed failure, and as he knows this, he despises his own color. Let us go back to the old rule of the South," urged Baringer, "and be done forever with frauds of an educational suffrage." Southern sentiment in 1904 suggested to Carl Schurz "a striking resemblance to the pro-slavery arguments . . . heard before the Civil War, and they brought forth . . . with the same assertion the Negro's predestination for serfdom the same certainty that he will not work," without physical compulsion, the same contemptuous rejection of black education as a thing that will only unfit him for work.[34]

This prjudice was not just limited to blacks in America, it included all the non-white peoples. Josiah Royce, the distinguished American philosopher, believed that white races should benevolently take charge of the affairs of "natives" of underdeveloped countries. He suggested certain patterns of conduct for the Americans in their relation with the Philippines. He asked them to emulate the British in their colonial administration:

> The Englishman, in his official and government dealings with the backward peoples, has a great way of being superior, without very often publicly saying he is superior. You well know that in dealing as an individual with other individuals, trouble is seldom made by the fact that you are actually the superior of another man in any respect. The trouble comes when you tell the other man, too stridently, that you are his superior. Be my superior quietly, simply showing your superiority in your deeds and very likely I shall love you for the fact of your superiority. For we all love our leaders. But tell me I am your inferior and then, perhaps, I may grow boyish and may throw stones. Well, it is so with races. Grant them that yours is the superior race. Then you can afford to say little about the subject in your public dealings with the backward races. Superiority is best shown by good deeds and by few boasts.[35]

One cannot be so ungenerous as to doubt Royce's sincerity, intellect and kindly soul. But he seems to be unaware that the deference which was given him in the academic environment hardly applies in the nightmare of everyday living. Royce seems to have been the victim of the archaic and moribund racial theories of his time. He accepted *prima facie* the assertions of superiority. Royce failed to comprehend the civilization of his time; a civilization which, in the words of Engels, "achieved things of which gentile society was not even remotely capable. But it achieved them by setting in motion the lowest instincts and passions in man and developing them at the expense of all his other abilities. From its first day to this, sheer greed was the driving spirit of civilization; wealth and again wealth and once more wealth, wealth not of society, but of the single scurvy individual—here was its one and final aim."[36]

The attitude of "taking things for granted" becomes more startling in the case of sociologist William Graham Sumner, who discussed folk traditions and mores in his book *Folkways* (1907). Sumner, writing at a time when the statutes of the American South were replete with the most ingenious structure of racial legislation and discrimination, maintained that legislation cannot change folkways. According to his description, folkways are "uniform and universal in the group, imperative and invariable." On another occasion Sumner declared that to talk about reforming "a system" was like "talking of making a man of sixty into something else than what his life has made him." And further, he states: "A man may curse his fate because he is born to an inferior race, but he will get no answer from heaven for imprecations.[37]

It might be pointed out here that the Supreme Court itself was affected by the ideological limitations of the time. The position maintained by Sumner had been adopted by the Supreme Court and Senator Sparkman, when in one of the earliest civil rights cases, *Plessy vs. Ferguson (1896)*, a black man's challenge of Jim Crow legislation was rejected on the grounds that civil rights could not be legislated but required a long process of education. The inconsistency in the positions of Sumner and the Supreme Court is quite obvious: if the laws are ineffectual against segregation and discrimination, why are laws needed to maintain and enforce them? The indifference of the Supreme Court to the plight of the black man drew this comment from James Weldon Johnson:

> More than once, he took his case to the Supreme Court of the United States, but the court pointed out that he had failed to show that the State had abridged or denied his right to vote, or that persons who prevented him from voting had done so because of his race, color or previous condition of servitude. So unable to prove that the committee which had met him at the polls, with a shotgun, was actuated by any such base and unconstitutional motives, he found his case thrown out. In the last analysis he lost his vote because of the attitude of the Supreme Court.[38]

To proceed with our analysis of the sociologists' thinking, we find that Franklin H. Gidding maintained a similar position with regard to the poor. He stated that "The poor were unfree task-workers, not because society chooses to oppress them, but because society has not yet devised or stumbled upon other disposition to make of them."[39] Lester Ward, who regarded social factors as important in contributing to social ills, was very ambivalent when it came to racial questions. He drew a distinction between the "historic" or "favored" races which had originated in Europe, and other great groupings of black, red and yellow races. While arguing that these races had more ability than they had been given credit for, Ward approved Auguste Comte's statement that the black races are as much superior to whites in feeling or sentiment as they are below them in intelligence, and that the yellow races are superior to both whites and blacks, in "activity" though they are inferior in "intelligence and feeling."[40] Ward's position was so ambivalent that Gossett observed: "One can easily visualize an imperialist agreeing with Ward that primitive peoples might at some future time develop a civilization as high as that of the white races, but that it would take hundreds, if not thousands, of years for the germ plasma of the inferior races to improve to this extent.[41] We may point out that the hangover of Wardism still finds itself in present day jargon as it is applied to what are called underdeveloped countries: "They are not yet ready" for independence; or "They are becoming Westernized"; or "They are modernizing," all of which assumes that the West is the ultimate of development.

The other Founding Fathers of American sociology, Cooley and Ross, though opposed to the individualism of social Darwinist theory, were also racists in their attitudes toward the black. Cooley, for instance, declared that the Anglo-Saxon had courage, and that it was no accident that Beowulf had claimed: "Death is better for every clansman than coward life."[42] And Ross argued at one time that "the energy and character of America was lowered by the presence in the South of millions of an inferior race."[43]

Nineteenth and early twentieth century sociological and anthropological theory as it relates to the black and other non-white races has a particular significance. It illustrates why an analysis of the social thought of a given historical period, and a given stratum in society, must concern itself, not merely with ideas and modes of thought that appear most flourishing, but with the whole social setting in which this occurs.

> To look at a thing from a "structural" point of view means to explain it, not as an isolated, self-contained unit, but as part of a wider structure; the explanation itself is based not so much on the properties of the thing itself as on the place it occupies within the structure. Adopting this "structural" approach, one sees that the "meaning" of some individual phenomena, e.g., an utterance can be determined only in reference to the conceptual system to which it belongs.[44]

This approach means that we must of necessity take into account hidden factors that are responsible for the acceptance or rejection of certain ideas by certain groups in society, and the motives and interests that prompt certain studies on race to accept and promote these ideas. Calverton wrote of the early anthropologists:

> All the scientific studies on race, "whether they involve anatomy, intelligence tests, brain size, the skull size, feet, legs, shape of the face, hair texture, and color of the skin, were an immense superstructure of immoral ideas with no basis in fact. It was wish fulfillment thought, superimposed on anthropological edifice, and was widely accepted for just that reason. The social sciences have always been prone to accept such protective logic. In the days when *laissez-faire* was orthodox theory, economists and sociologists were its uncritical advocates; only today, when *laissez-faire* has lost its influence, do economists and sociologists criticize and at times cease to defend it. Only the breakdown of a principle or an institution makes it possible for its former advocates to view it objectively.[45]

Burrows Dunham suggested that "nobody will ever know the full range of possible errors unless he looks at society to see those errors rising upon him."[46] We suggest that he will have to look carefully indeed, because the rise of error has all the subtlety of infection. Living in any society requires the sharing of many things, among them ideas and prejudices. The infection begins at an early age, long before an individual is capable of understanding such things as ideological illusions, or even outright deceit. This becomes quite obvious when we examine the works of sociologists who wrote at the turn of the century. Many of them were honest men with extremely critical eyes, but their critical faculty, sharp as it was, was not able to sift out some errors, let alone scan them all.

I have undertaken this survey of American thought and the place it assigned to the black because, as Parson says:

> There is a fundamental symmetry in the relations, on the one hand of science and ideology, on the other of philosophy and religious ideas. In both cases the transition to evaluative category means a change in the "stakes" the actor has in the belief system, it means a change from acceptance to commitment. The primary question is no longer that of interest in whether a proposition is "true," but in addition to that, in a commitment to its implications for the orientation of action as such.[47]

In the late 19th century, Darwinism was politicized and the "survival of the fittest" and the "natural law of selection" became part of a ruthless celebration of racism and imperialism: these axioms established a ceiling on black political, economic and social aspirations. They did so in the name of inherent destiny inscribed in the nature of things. Blacks knew just as all other oppressed strata in societies have known that this was not true,[48] that given a place and given the necessary education, the naturalness of their inferiority could be proved wrong. For instance, the Niagara Movement, which met on August 15-19, 1906, to commemorate the 100th birthday of John Brown and the jubilee of the Battle of Osawatomie, passed a resolution which declared that ". . . never before in the modern age has a great and civilized folk threatened to adopt so cowardly a creed in the treatment of its fellow citizens, born and bred on its own soils. Stripped of verbiage and subterfuge and in its naked nastiness, the American creed says: 'fear to let black men even try to rise lest they become the equals of the white.' "[49]

Faced with a choice between permanent second-class citizenship and a place where this circumscription would be absent, it was natural that the attraction of Africa became stronger for certain sections of the black population as their experience among racists who maltreated them with impunity convinced them that white people were in no mood to do justice to the black people. Perry Anderson observes quite rightly that a great gulf had developed between Social Darwinism, the inhumane rationale for imperialism, and the initial optimistic exuberance of enlightenment philosophy in which it had its beginnings.[50] This ideology fostered among blacks in America a state of psychological disarray which was only somewhat alleviated by such messianic movements as "Back to Africa" which began to rebuild the distorted image of Africa and restore its meaning to the black population.

Every sociological theory has an ideological force by reason of its influence upon thoughts and actions of men in their everyday life. The concepts of Social Darwinism and white supremacy were impregnated with doctrines which persuaded whites to conceive of their lives as those of rulers. This chapter serves to point out that the oppression of the black was not just physical; what made it more exasperating was what Karl Mannheim once called the will to "psychic annihilation." In the next chapter I will discuss the meaning of Africa to the American black and will try to show how its degraded image became detrimental to the black self-conception.

Notes

[1]Herbert Aptheker, *Afro-American History: The Modern Era*, The Citadel Press, New York, 1971, p. 31.

[2]Burrows Dunham has written that "if philosophy could not claim leadership by right of content, it would nevertheless acquire it by surrender. Sciences have for many years been explicit concerning what their content is not, as much as concerning what it is." the subject that we call "man and his place in nature" has been the preoccupation not only of politics, but of many other social sciences. But as Dunham points out, "Politics rule everything except economics and economics rule politics. Beneath these lordly hierarchies all other disciplines must find their place." Dunham, *op. cit.,* pp. 11-12.

[3]Banton, *op. cit.*, p. 56.

[4]Quoted in *Ibid.*, pp. 62-63.

[5]Alexis de Tocqueville, *Democracy in America*, Schocken Press, New York, 1964, pp. 454-55.

[6]Cf. Harold M. Baron, "The Demand for Black Labor: Historical Notes on the Political Economy of Racism," *Radical America*, Vol. 5, No. 2, 1971, p. 3.

[7]Darcy Ribeiro, "The Cultural-Historical Configurations of the American Peoples," *Current Anthropology*, Vol. 11, No. 4-5, Oct-Dec. 1970, p. 405.

[8]The following section owes a great deal to Perry Anderson's "Portugal and the End of Ultra-Colonialism, Part 2," *New Left Review* 16 (1962). The quotations are taken from pages 104-115 of the article.

[9]Karl Kautsky, *Foundations of Christianity*, Russell and Russell, New York, 1953, pp. 355-56.

[10]Similar to L.E. Khortus in "A Critique of the Theoretical Foundations of Bourgeois 'Sociology of Knowledge,'" *Soviet Sociology*, Vol. 3.

[11]Karl Marx, *The Eighteenth Brumaire of Louis Bonaparte*, Foreign Language Publishing House, Moscow, undated, Chapter I.

[12]Bernard Crick, *In Defense of Politics*, Pelican Books, London, 1962, p. 84.

[13]Quoted in Banton, *op. cit.*, p. 68.

[14]*The Nation*, 24 May 1965, p. 593.

[15]Dunham, *op. cit.*, p. 52.

[16]Woodward, *The Strange Career of Jim Crow*, Oxford University Press, New York, 1955, p. 13.

[17]*Ibid.*, pp. 6-7.

[18]Cf. C. Van Woodward, "Our Own Herrenvolk," *The New York Review of Books*, Vol. 17, No. 2, August 1971, p. 11.

[19]Caudwell, *op. cit.*, pp. 116-55.

[20]Robert Chambers, *Vestiges of the Natural History of Creation*, London, 1844, p. 226.

[21]DuBois in his autobiography, *Dusk of Dawn*, writes: "The mind clung desperately to the idea that the basic differences between human beings had suffered no change; and it clung to this idea not simply from inertia and unconscious action,

but from the fact that, because of the modern slave trade, a tremendous economic structure and eventually an industrial revolution had been based upon racial differences between men, and these now had been rationalized into a difference mainly of skin color . . . Color had become an abiding unbridgeable fact chiefly because self-conscious instincts and unconscious prejudice had arranged themselves rank on rank in its defense. Government, workers, religion, education, became based upon and determined by the color line. The future of mankind was implicit in the race and color of man."

[22]Gossett, *op. cit.*, p. 83. (See p. 37).

[23]Quoted *Ibid.*

[24]*Chambers Encyclopedia*, Vol. IV, George Newness, Ltd., Dover House, London, 1959, p. 439.

[25]The rehash of these pseudo-scientific theories is important (no matter how offensive they may be to read today) because they, together with the previously discussed African image, formed the reality in which the early manifestations of African consciousness among the Afro-Americans took place. The memory of these ideas is still present today like a ghost that haunts and orders memory and imagination when the black tries to define his relationship to Africa.

[26]Lord Selborne in February 1909, on the occasion of the Annual Degree Day of the University of Cape Town, presented a typical imperialist argument emphasizing the unbridgeable differences between Whites and Africans. He said among other things: "It is impossible for us, who are sprung from races which were in contact with the Roman Civilization before the Christian era to look at questions from the same point of view as these Bantu races who are totally different. So far as we can form an opinion, our forefathers, 2,000 years ago . . . were distinctly less barbarous than were the Bantu races when they came into contact with white men less than 100 years ago. Nor has the Bantu hitherto evinced a capacity for civilization equal to that which our forefathers evinced from their first contact with it . . . Speaking generally . . . so far as we can foresee, the Bantu can never catch up with the European, either in intellect or in strength of character. As a race, the white race has received a superior intellect and mental endowment . . . The White man is the racial adult; the Black man is the racial child." Quoted by S. Herbert Frankel, *Supplement to Optima*, December 1960.

[27]Anderson, "The Origin of the Present Crisis," pp. 40-41.

[28]James Hosmer, *Short History of the Anglo-Saxon Freedom*, G. Scribner and Sons, New York, 1890, p. 8.

[29]John W. Burgess, *Political Science and Constitutional Law*, Ginn and Company, Boston, 1890, pp. 3-4, 44-45. Marx could have argued with Burgess that he advocated "a school which legalized the baseness of today by the baseness of yesterday" and that "those who seek their freedom beyond their history, in the Teutonic forest" sought a freedom which was no different from the "history of the Boers, if it can be found in the forests. Besides it is common knowledge that the forest echoes what you shout into it. So peace with the ancient Teutonic forests!"

[30]Dunham, *op. cit.*, p. 24.

[31]Gossett, *op. cit.*, p. 174.

[32]Karl Marx and Frederick Engels, *Selected Works*, Vol. I, Foreign Language Publishing House, Moscow, 1962, p. 272.

[33]V.F. Calverton, *The Making of Man: An Outline of Anthropology*, Modern Library, New York, 1931, p. 5.

[34]Quoted in Woodward, *op. cit.*, p. 80. This argument was also presented in 1896 by Frederick L. Hoffman in his book, *Race Traits and Tendencies of the American Negro*; his conclusions were definite: "All facts brought together in this work prove that the colored population is gradually parting with the virtues and moderate degree of economic efficiency developed under the regime of slavery. All the facts prove that low standard of sexual morality is the main underlying cause of lawlessness and anti-social conditions of the race at the present time. All facts prove that education, philanthropy and religion have failed to develop a higher appreciation of the stern and uncompromising virtues of the Aryan race." The Moynihan Report's conclusions on the Negro family sound very much like those of Hoffman. Among its sweeping conclusions it states: "At the heart of the deterioration of the fabric of the Negro society is deterioration of the Negro family. It is the fundamental source of the weakness of the Negro community at the present time." Quoted in *The Nation*, Vol. 200, No. 20, 22 November 1985, pp. 381-82.

[35]Josiah Royce, *Race Question, Provincialism, and Other American Problems*, Macmillan, New York, 1980, p. 10.

[36]Frederick Engels, *The Origin of the Family, Private Property and the State*, International Publishers, New York, 1963, p. 235.

[37]Quoted in Gossett, *op. cit.*, pp. 153-154.

[38]James Weldon Johnson, *Negro Americans, What Now?* Viking Press, New York, 1983, pp. 56-57. A similar sentiment was expressed by Kelly Miler in a letter to President Wilson, dated 4 August 1917: "It is but hollow mockery of the Negro, when he is beaten and bruised and burned in all parts of the nation and flees to the national government for asylum, to be denied relief on the grounds of doubtful jurisdiction. The black man asks for justice and is given theory of government. He asks for protection and is confronted with a scheme of government checks and balances." *Anthology of American Negro Literature*, edited by V.F. Calverton, p. 368.

[39]"Applied Sociology," pp. 197)8; Auguste Comte, *Systems of Positive Polity*, II, p. 378.

[40]Quoted Gossett, *op. cit.*, p. 159.

[41]Gossett, *op. cit.*, p. 164.

[42]Charles S. Cooley, *Human Nature and the Social Order*, Free Press, Glencoe, Illinois, 1956, pp. 209-210 (First published 1902).

[43]*American Sociological Review*, Ward/Ross correspondence, June, 1939, p. 387.

[44]Karl Mannheim, *Essays on the Sociology of Knowledge*, Routledge and Kegan Paul, London, 1959, p. 9.

[45]Calverton, *op. cit.*, p. 23.

[46]Dunham, *op. cit.*, p. 23.

[47]Parsons, *op. cit.*, p. 332.

[48]The blacks confronted the heritage of slavery and reacted indignantly to the accusations and assumptions of Western educatiors that the black was a sub-human species incapable of development. They ransacked the whole black past all over the world, in search of evidence against the idea. Rogers' pamphlet, "100 Amazing Facts About the Negro," which has gone through several printings, indicates the thoroughness of this attempt.

[49]*A.B.C. of Colour*, Seven seas Books, Berlin, 1964, p. 32.

[50]Perry Anderson, "The Myths of Edward Thompson," *New Left Review*, 35, 1966, p. 25.

CHAPTER FOUR
The Genesis of the Afro-Americans' Perception of Africa

Behold a stranger at the door;
He gently knocks, has knocked before
Has waited long, is waiting still
You treat no other friend so ill.

—A popular hymn

Wﻻilliam Roscoe Thayer wrote in his *Dawn of Italian Independence*: "We must look for signs of progress in the aspirations rather than in achievement of anything conspicuous. For this movement was inward and subtle, and its outward expression in deeds was stubbornly repressed. For no man can speak the truth that is in him, when the hand of the oppressor is on his throat."[1] The American blacks' consciousness of Africa was for a long time a purely emotional phenomenon. Its resurgence in the dawn of African independence movements was a crystallization and sharpening of these emotions into a more concrete awareness, but its roots are deeply grounded in the past. Now and again this awareness was distorted, ambivalent, and at times even reactionary. At certain periods it was no more than verbal expressions, and these can be traced back to pre-revolutionary America when African memories were still strong among the captive Africans. Some enslaved blacks are known to have committed suicide in the hope that their spirits would return to Africa.

The sociologist who wants to understand the ideology of Africanism today must be prepared to trace it far beyond its present manifestations. The matrix out of which it has evolved is, of course, the slave trade to the New World with its concomitant development and the various movements and organizations which grew out of these—as, for instance, black churches, lodges, fraternities, and, more important, the underground railroad. Of greater significance for my purpose were the territorial consequences of slavery, such as the founding of the states of Sierra Leone and Liberia, and the European settlement in Africa both before and after the imperialist scramble.

During the first half of the 19th century free blacks in the United States had become increasingly unwanted. This produced in them extreme discontent with their lot in the South. Through many channels they endeavored not only to provide for the individual self-expression which they lacked in the South, but also to achieve full citizenship rights within the American nation. It should be made clear from the very beginning that the American black, oppressed and abused, could not remain immune from the influences of the larger country in which he lived. Sometimes he had faith in the so-called American creed and democracy.[2] It is important to understand this because it puts into a clear perspective the nature of African consciousness and the whole question of nationalism among the American blacks. Since they had been brought here against their will, and since they worked and died in serving this country, it was only natural that their goal should be that of integration into the American society. it was only when this goal continued to be unattainable that black leaders began to think more and more in terms of emigration and self-government.

During the first half of the 19th century, as a result of the discovery of the spinning jenny, the demand for cotton increased; as a consequence, there was in the South a corresponding increase in the proscriptive laws and a corresponding change in the nature of the black-white relationship. Slavery, which had had some paternalistic attributes, qualitatively changed into an exploitative system. The North, which in the minds of most blacks was a refuge, was becoming increasingly less and less hospitable. Where then might the blacks turn? Some saw the answer in a kind of a racial government within the United States; others, weary of the struggle for equality in America, saw the answer in emigration. This emphasis on emigration and black sovereignty, which can be described as a kind of black nationalism, was a dominant factor affecting free Negroes in the decade before the Civil War.[3]

An earlier interest by the Afro-American in Africa was based in part on the false assumption that since slave trading had its roots among Africans themselves, it could only be exterminated thoroughly by Christianizing the Africans. This argument attributed to Christianity a moral force that could prevent Africans from selling one another; but because of its naiveté, it could not account for the fact that the people who did the buying were Christians, or that one of the ships used for this traffic in men was even called the *Jesus*. It was on the basis of such assumptions that Reverend Samuel Hopkins of Newport, Rhode Island, proposed to Ezra Stiles, later president of Yale, the sending of well-educated blacks to Africa. Stiles seemed to think that an actual colony could be founded, and later two blacks were said to have sailed to Africa as missionaries.[4]

There was not at that time any clear-cut distinction between the colonizationist and the emancipationist efforts. From the very beginning of the anti-slavery movement, there was an effort to provide for the restoration of Africans to their natural homeland. (Probably very much like the present-day migratory labor system in Africa, whereby Africans go to labor in what are called "European" towns and mines, and when they have ceased to be functional, are sent back to reservations to spend their last miserable years.) George Keith, a Quaker, inspired this movement as early as 1713. It is not surprising that in 1788 the Negro union of Newport, Rhode Island, proposed to the Free African Society of Philadelphia a general exodus to Africa on the part of at least free blacks. This "Back to Africa" movement was to recur time and time again in the ideology and philosophy of American blacks. At times it commended itself not simply to the inexperienced and reactionary demagogue, but to the prouder and more independent blacks, as well as to that black man who had simply tired of begging for justice and recognition (which should have been his by virtue of his humanity) from whites who seemed to have no intention of being just or no intention of recognizing the blacks as men. This current of thought was strong during the active days of the Colonization Society and succeeded in convincing some leading blacks, like John Russwurm, an early black college graduate, and Lott Carey, the powerful Virginia preacher, that manhood for the black was impossible in white America.

THE AMERICAN COLONIZATION SOCIETY

In December 1816, the American Colonization Society was formed by prominent white people, among whom were included some slaveholders. Its object was to transport free blacks to Africa on the grounds that they were incapable of serving useful lives in the United States. The society appealed to slaveholders by informing them that the removal of free blacks would make more secure the institution of slavery. Because of its rather dubious position, the society and the ideas it represented met opposition from blacks themselves. While it offered the possibility of a practical alternative to a life of continual limitations, the price of a stronger slave system was too much to pay. Moreover, abolitionists and some free blacks opposed the schemes of the Colonization Society because of the acquiescent attitudes of the colonizationists toward the persecution of the free blacks both in the North and South. David Walker expressed sharp disagreement with the Colonization Society in his famous Appeal:

> Here is a demonstrative proof of a plan got up by a gang of slaveholders to select the free people of colour from among the slaves, that our more miserable brethren may be the better secured in ignorance and wretchedness, to work their farms and dig their mines, and thus go on enriching Christians with their blood and groans. What our brethren could have been thinking about, who have left their native land and have gone away to Africa, I am unable to say. This country is as much ours as it is the whites, whether they will admit it now or not, they will see and believe it by and by.[5]

The abolitionists' position on the inconsistencies of the Colonization Society was logically developed by William Lloyd Garrison in his book, *Thoughts on African Colonization*, which demonstrated, among other things, the practical impossibility of deporting such large numbers of persons. Garrison, like Walker, pointed out that there was no more reason for thinking of the black as a native of Africa, and therefore deserving of deportation to that country, than of thinking of whites as natives of Great Britain. He could see no reason for persecuting these free blacks to the extent of making it so intolerable for them that they would prefer to emigrate. He concluded that the Colonization Society was founded upon selfishness, and that it was antagonistic to instant emancipation:

> It apologized to the slaveholders, it recognized slaves, it ultimately aimed to drive out the blacks from this country, it slandered the character of the free Negroes, it declared the elevation of the black people impossible in America, while claiming that it was possible in Africa, and it tended finally to misinform and dupe the whole nation into a scheme worked out in the interest of slaveholders.[6]

Though the free blacks were generally opposed to the scheme of colonizing them in Africa, they sometimes manifested ambivalence. This was particularly true around 1845 when their fortunes in the United States were rapidly deteriorating. Exploitation of slaves was intensifying during this period in response to the improved technology of the industrial revolution. More and more cotton was needed to supply the mills and more and more labor was being demanded of the slaves.

The free blacks became unwelcome in the eyes of the slaveholders, and antipathy toward them deepened. They came to be regarded as threatening, potential disrupters who would influence their enslaved brothers to desire freedom and to try to escape. From that time on the sons of prominent blacks who were active in anti-colonization movements were often found temporarily seeking their fortunes in Liberia or Haiti, the British West Indies, or California. Visiting Liberia in 1846, William C. Cornish, the son of Samuel Cornish, minimized the disadvantages of climate and spoke highly of the government there.[7] Two years later Robert Douglas, the son of a prominent Philadelphia minister, was in Jamaica but found it economically inexpedient to stay long.

In 1847 the National Negro Convention of Troy, New York, was ready to listen respectfully to a plan for commercial ventures involving blacks of Jamaica, the United States, and Africa. The proposition called for the development of a company owned and operated by people of African descent. As Howard Bell points out, this formal interest was particularly significant since it was the first time that serious national recognition by black leaders was given to an African project, and since it initiated a growing interest in emigration.[8] By 1848 A.M. Summer of Ohio was seeking a passage to Africa. He believed that a sizable minority of the blacks were seriously considering emigrating, but he was not convinced that Africa was the place. He intended to publish the truth about what he had found, "should I live to return."[9]

In 1847 Liberia obtained its independence, and this became a further stimulant of interest in Africa. A black nation had replaced the suspect American Colonization Society as chief authority in the Anglo-American settlement. By 1848 the population of Liberia included some 3,000 persons of African descent who had emigrated from the United States and the Caribbean. It should not be assumed that Liberian independence was responsible for the new ideas concerning emigration. The birth of the Republic fitted and encouraged a trend that was already underway due to the impossibility experienced by the freed men to lead unencumbered lives. Whenever the blacks enjoyed freedom in the North, they did not easily embrace the idea of expatriating themselves. Northern blacks, like David Walker quoted above, usually took the position that their fathers fought, bled, and died for this country; here they were born, and here they would die. Frederick Douglass expressed it cogently:

It is idle—worse than idle, ever to think of our expatriation or removal. We are here, and here we are likely to be. To imagine that we are ever to be eradicated is absurd and ridiculous. We can be remodified, changed, and assimilated, but never extinguished. We repeat, therefore, that we are here, and that this is our country; and the question for the philosophers and statesmen ought to be, "what principles should dictate the policies of action toward us?" We shall neither die out nor be driven out, but shall go with these people *either as testimony against them, or as evidence in their favour throughout their generations* . . . The white man's happiness cannot be purchased by the black man's misery . . . It is evident that the white and black must fall or flourish together.[10] (My emphasis)

The "Douglass Dictum," published in the *North Star*, in 1849, under the heading, "The Destiny of Colored Americans," pointed at and squarely faced an objective, historical situation. It provided an answer to the wishful schemes expressed by the various colonization movements sponsored by both whites and blacks. But it underestimated the subjective feelings of the blacks whose frustrations pointed to one option—escape. From time to time the American Colonization Society received from prominent blacks letters which were an expression of this subjective sentiment. The following two letters, selected from among others, show this motive for emigration:

I am a free man of colour, have a family and a large connection of free people of colour residing on the Wabash, who are all willing to leave America whenever they shall be opened [sic]. We love this country and its liberties, if we could share an equal right in them, but our freedom is partial and we have no hope that it will ever be otherwise here therefore, we had rather be gone, though we should suffer hunger, and nakedness for years. Your honor may be assured that nothing shall be lacking on our part in complying with whatever provisions shall be made by the United States, whether it be to go to Africa or some other place, we shall hold ourselves in readiness, praying that God (who made man free in the beginning, and who by kind providence, has broken the yoke from every white American) would inspire the heart of every true son of liberty with the zeal and pity to open the door of freedom for us also.[11]

Another letter expressed the same sentiment:

This is an era, however, in our affair, that we cannot shut our eyes to and it must appear to the philosopher, the Christian, and sagacious politician, a period of deep and conscious solitude, as regards the future prospects, hopes and interests of a people little known, but as nuisance and mere labourers in the most menial capacity, at best a people who seldom deserve notice or the exercise of charitable acts bestowed on them.[12]

Among the American blacks both African consciousness and a desire to emigrate were inspired in part by the oppressive conditions obtaining in the United States in the period 1840-58, and in part, by the philosophical proposition advanced by Martin R. Delany in a lengthy report, "Political Destiny of the Colored Race." This report was presented and accepted by the Cleveland (Ohio) National Emigration Convention, August 24-26, 1854. Among other things, the report denied the citizenship of the black man in America, and contended that freedom existed only where a racial group constituted a majority. It approved of emigration to the Caribbean area via Canada and warned that the rights withheld by a majority were never freely given but must be seized. On the other hand, the emigrationists were far from convinced that they would have to deal forever with white supremacy. "The white race are but one-third of the population of the globe—or one of them to two of us—and it cannot much longer continue that two-thirds will passively submit to the universal domination of this one-third."[13]

The editor of the *Culombian*, January 4, 1854, wrote of this National Emigration Convention of 1854:

> It is a gallant faith (and not without data to rest upon) which prompts the manly declaration! I believe it to be the destiny of the Negro to develop a higher order of civilization and Christianity than the world has yet seen. When any considerable number of black men come to a true and sublime faith, in such a destiny their lives will soon begin to compel the world to award them some praise.[14]

The writings of Martin R. Delany, who has been described as the father of black nationalism, expressed the idea of nationality linked with settlement in Africa quite vigorously. The movement failed for several reasons, among which we can mention a few: in a few years the Civil War was fought, the blacks were emancipated and, between 1868 and 1877, there were definite attempts at integrating the blacks into the "mainstream" of American society by various amendments to the Constitution—the most important of which were the 13th and 14th. The emigration issue was peripheral to the objective question: that the black was in America for good or worse. Emigration only became an issue when this objective fact became impossible to realize.

However, it was not long before the Tilden-Hayes Compromise was struck and gradually thereafter the rights of the blacks began to be whittled away one by one. Again the blacks were shocked into the realization that only within their own sovereign nation or within a state where being black did not matter could they enjoy citizenship with dignity and respect, because the one authority that seemed to be universal, embracing with its prescriptions and demands the lives of individuals, was that of nationalism. After the Civil War and the failure of Reconstruction, the blacks once again revived the issue of national independence. This new movement was to culminate in the prominence of Marcus Garvey between the years 1915-25.

EMIGRATION MOVEMENT AFTER EMANCIPATION

In 1857 the Dred Scott decision was made (later nullified by the 13th Amendment) declaring that a man of African descent, slave or not, was not and could not be a citizen of the United States. At the time when this decision was made blacks were experiencing ever-increasing repression both in the North and in the South. Moreover, it must be emphasized that only persons of African descent, not Chinese, Japanese, Arabs or Indians were singled out for exclusion from citizenship. In the minds of many blacks this stigmatization stemmed from their African background, and it had diverse implications for those who suffered from it. It is not surprising that many blacks at the time of the ascendancy of white hegemony made themselves caricatures in the effort to shed their burden-some African heritage. The negative portrayal of Africa in white institutions was bound to create a negative image among the black folk. The process of brainwashing is not new, and the victims usually recoil consciously or unconsciously from their former beliefs. Incidents like the Dred Scott decision and sentiments like these expressed by Abraham Lincoln only helped to alienate the black from himself. Lincoln said on one occasion:

> I will say then, that I am not, nor ever have been, in favor of bringing about in any way the social and political equality of the white and black races—that I am not nor ever have been, in favor of making voters or jurors of Negroes, nor of qualifying them to hold office, nor to intermarry with white people; and I will say in addition to this that there is a physical difference between the white and black races which I believe will forever forbid the two races living together on terms of social and political equality. And inasmuch as they cannot so live, while they do remain together, there must be the position of superior to inferior, and I, as much as any other man, am in favour of having the superior position assigned to the white race.[15]

From the earliest days of his political career, Lincoln had believed that colonization offered the only constructive solution to the black problem and he therefore supported the efforts of the American Colonization Society.

On June 26, 1857, in a debate with Senator Douglas, he said in favor of emigration:

> Such separation, if ever effected at all, must be effected by colonization, and no political party as such is now doing anything directly for colonization. Party operations at present only favour or retard coloniz-ation incidentally. The enterprise is a difficult one, but "Where there is will there is a way," and what colonization needs most is a hearty will. Will springs from two elements of moral sense and self interest. Let us be brought to believe it is morally right, and at the same time favorable to, or at least not against our interest, to transfer the African to his native clime, and we shall find a way to do it, however great the task may be. The children of Israel, to such number as to include 400,000 fighting men, went out of Egyptian bondage in a body.[16]

During the first two years of the Civil War, Lincoln continued to cling tenaciously to the idea of linking emancipation of the blacks with a proposal to repatriate and colonize them outside the United States. In appropriating $1 million to pay the slaveholders in the nation's capital to free their bondsmen, Congress, to Lincoln's delight, voted an additional $100,000

> to be expended under the direction of the President of the United States to aid in the colonization and settlement of such free persons of African descent now residing in said district . . . as may desire to emigrate to the Republic of Hayti or Liberia, or such other country beyond the limits of the United States as the President may determine.[17]

This was followed two months later by an actual appropriation of $800,000. Faced with the task of executing this legislative mandate, Lincoln cast about to find a place where the blacks could be sent. He was opposed to Liberia because he believed the climate to be unhealthy and because the cost of transportation there would have been prohibitive. A province in Panama, then a part of the Republic of Colombia, was seriously considered, but when this interest became known several governments of Central America protested the scheme.

Still undaunted Lincoln turned to Haiti. There one agent offered to resettle 5,000 Negroes immediately, providing houses, employment, schools and hospitals. The amount of $600,000 was appropriated for this venture and the government signed a contract with a certain Mr. Bernard Kock, a promoter who procured a lease on the Island of Vache off the coast of Haiti. He turned out to be "an irresponsible and untrustworthy adventurer" according to Lincoln, and his contract was cancelled. Meanwhile, the first boat had sailed with a contingent of 500 men, women, and children. Despite his reputation, Kock was sent along to govern the colony. The venture proved a miserable failure. Two hundred of the emigrants died, Kock was driven from the island, and Lincoln brought back the survivors under strong criticism from the abolitionists. The Bill for Negro Colonization was repealed, not to be heard of again until President Grant's administration. As late as 1939, Mississippi Senator Bilbo, with typical obtuseness, introduced a bill to colonize blacks in Africa.[18]

If an historical warrant were necessary to justify and explain black national consciousness and African awareness, whether positive or negative, these incidents would be enough. The American black has always been surrounded and conditioned by his concept of white people, and he has also been treated in accordance with the concept that white people have of him.

DuBois wrote in 1940 that:

> American Negroes have always feared with perfect fear their inevitable expulsion from America. They have been willing to submit to caste rather than face this. The reasons have varied but today they are clear. Negroes have no Zion. There is no place where they can go today, and not face or be subject to worse caste and greater disabilities from the dominant white imperialistic world than they suffer here today.[19]

However, we have reached the end of the era of white hegemony, which but a few years ago seemed omnipotent and eternal. This has introduced a new era of consciousness about Africa among the blacks.

When looking at black ambivalence towards Africa in the era of total white dominance, in particular their uncertainty as to what name would best describe them, one realizes more than ever before the primacy of the hegemonic class as a determinant of consciousness. That the word "Africa" had come to be associated with degradation by some American blacks is perfectly understandable. J.C. Smyth expressed the dilemma of the black about Africa in 1896 as follows:

> Negroes are averse to the discussion of Africa, whenever their relationship with that ancient and mysterious land is made the subject of discourse or reflection. The remoteness of Africa from America may be a reason for such feelings; the current opinion in the minds of the Caucasians, whence the American Negores' opinions are derived, that the African is by nature an inferior man, may be a reason. . . The illiteracy, poverty, and degradation of the Negro, pure and simple, as

known in Christian lands, may be a reason in connection with the partially true and partially false impressions that the Negroes or the Africans are pagan and heathen as a whole and as a consequence hopelessly degraded beings. These may be some of the reasons that make the subject of Africa discordant and unmusical to our ears. It is amid such embarrassment that the lecturer, the orator, the missionary must present Africa to the Negro in Christian America.[20]

The slave heritage in mind and body was to be perpetuated by a compulsory ignorance.[21] As Carter Woodson pointed out, most Western nations deliberately kept the people they exploited in a condition of ignorance and disorganization, since awareness and unity might have led to self-assertion.[22] Ignorance about Africa could not be mitigated by a few insightful individuals who, aware of the falseness of white assumptions, tried to penetrate this curtain of misinformation by brilliant assaults. The pervasive negative image of the dark continent was not simply the result of ethnocentrism or ill-will, but included a more powerful motivation in the urge to build wealth and comfort for the white races on the backs of the black slaves. This was the first experiment in history where the color of the skin became the qualification for aristocratic pretensions. The American black lived in a physical and social environment where the ideas and customs, laws and notions of white supremacy molded his outlook of himself and his putative African kinfolk; where these ideas were accepted for the most part without questioning: DuBois expressed it thusly:

I was not an American, I was by long education and continual compulsion and daily reminder, a colored man in a white world, and that world often existed primarily, so far as I was concerned, to see with sleepless vigilance that I was kept within bounds. All this made me limited in physical movement and provincial in thought and dream.[23]

Political philosophy is a social reality; it is an ideology in terms of which certain institutions and practices are justified and others rejected; it provides the phrases through which demands are raised, criticisms made, and exhortations delivered, that even the word "African" had come to be associated with degradation by some blacks is born out by the controversy it provoked among certain educated classes during the 19th century. The Reverend Benjamin Tucker Tanner, according to Essien-Udom, was forced in 1860 to defend the use of the word African in the denominational title, African Methodist Episcopal Church. His argument illustrates the criticism he faced:

What then is the intended force of the title Africa? Is it doctrinal or national? It is first "doctrinal" and secondarily "national." It is doctrinal, because a whole race was systematically ostracized and the goal to which Richard Allen, founder of the A.M.E. aspired, was the humanity of the Negro . . . a church wherein the claims to humanity of this despised class would be practically recognized. The title African is but the finger-board, the index of this sublime truth; a means only, that men of African descent are to be found there and found as men, not slaves; as equals, not inferiors. The doctrine of the Negro's humanity is its primary signification.[24]

When he was accused of parochialism and discrimination against the whites because of his use of "African" in the title of his denomination, a cynical and highly hypocritical charge at best, Rev. Tanner retorted:

It doesn't mean, neither does it say, that none others are admitted or found there, but it does say and mean that whoever else you may find, you will be sure to find this notable individual. But why this prominence? Save for the simple reason that other churches would not receive him as a man, this one would, and God having given it a tongue to speak, it said so.

To those who were anxious to omit the word "African," Tanner argued:

And here we say, in view of the fact that many are making haste to blot out the hated adjective, that it is generally thought to be ample time to remove an effect when the cause ceases. When the American people and churches . . . shall have learned . . . to speak the tongue peculiar to Paul and the Negro—the language of man's humanity; then let the doctrinal (not national as some have asserted, and others argued) insignia so long floated at our masthead be removed, let it be hauled down, when the malice of war has ceased.[25]

Tanner's assumptions and stand are quite clear. The Americans of African descent had a humanity which was being trampled underfoot and degraded, and they had a duty to reassert it. They could be integrated as full-fledged and respected American citizens, or they could achieve this by developing themselves to a point where they could compel respect.

The latter point of view was explicitly formulated in another of the resolutions of the 1854 Cleveland, Ohio, National Emigration Convention of Colored People. The resolution affirmed:

That no people, as such can ever attain to greatness who lose their identity, as they must rise entirely upon their own native merits. That we shall ever cherish our identity or origin and race, as preferable in our estimate to any other people; that the relative terms Negro, African, black, Colored, and mulato, when applied to us, shall be held, with the same respect and pride and synonomous with the terms Caucasian, White, Anglo-Saxon and European, when applied to that class of people.[26]

CONSCIOUSNESS OF AFRICA FROM 1877-1900

We have pointed out that ideas of emigration among the blacks always surfaced and became an issue when the heel of oppression descended heavily upon them. Therefore, it is not surprising that from the end of the Civil War to 1877 there was no agitation for emigration. This was the period which saw significant efforts by the federal government to integrate blacks into American society. But with the Tilden-Hayes Compromise of 1877 the trend was reversed. It became clear as the decades went by that once again the nation was trying to revert to the period before the Civil War when it existed "half-free and half-slave." Despite the several amendments to the Constitution that had been passed since the end of the Civil War, the federal government seemed unable to enforce its own statutes. In the North and in the South there was acceptance by silence of the possibility that there was a middle state between slavery and freedom; and that a black, permanently disenfranchised peasantry could exist under American institutions without contradicting the specific provisions of the Declaration of the Rights of Man in the Preamble to their Constitution.

When the "Black Codes of South Carolina" were published in 1866, H. Melville Myers, the editor, explained in the preface why such laws were necessary. "The Negro race," he declared, had at all times "been excluded, as a separate class, from all civilized governments and the family of nations," since it was "doomed by a mysterious and Divine ordination . . . The war had settled the matter of the abolition of slavery, but this did not mean that the Negroes were considered as citizens." They were to be "equal before the law, in the possession and enjoyment of their rights of person—of liberty and property," but they were not to be voters and jurymen. "To institute . . . between the Anglo-Saxon, the high-minded, virtuous, intelligent, patriotic Southerner and the Freedmen a social or political approximation more intimate—to mingle the social or political existence of the two classes more closely," said Myers, "would surely be one of the highest exhibitions of treason to the race."[27]

What Myers said was to become the guiding philosophy of the South.
Having lost the war, the South after 1876 was to make a determined effort to
ensure that the blacks never became socially and economically equal to the
whites. Thus Ben Tillman, a Senator from the South, could boldly declare
that South Carolina had disenfranchised all the "Colored" people it could.
"We have done our level best," he added: "We have scratched our heads to
find out how we could eliminate the last of them. We stuffed ballot boxes.
We shot them. *WE ARE NOT ASHAMED OF IT.*"[28] What Myers said
and Tillman corroborated was to make the situation very inhospitable for
the black, and once again, agitation began for escaping the South. There
was a revival of the colonization movements under Bishop H.M. Turner,
who wrote in January 1883:

> There never was a time when the Coloured people were more
> concerned about Africa in every aspect, than at present. In some
> portions of the country it is the topic of conversation; and if a line of
> steamers were started from New Orleans, Mobile, Savannah or
> Charleston, they would be crowded to density in every trip made to
> Africa. There is general unrest and a whole dissatisfaction among our
> people in a number of sections of the country to my certain knowledge,
> and they sigh for conveniences to and from the continent of Africa.
> Something has to be done, matters cannot go on as present, and the
> remedy is thought by tens of thousands to be a Negro nationality. This
> much the history of the world establishes, that races either fossilised,
> oppressed, or degraded must emigrate before any material change takes
> place in their civil, intellectual or moral status, otherwise extinction is
> the consequence.[29]

Bishop Turner's efforts, with the encouragement of Senator Morgan of
Alabama, seemed to have a chance of success. The reactionaries were
succeeding and had advanced very far in their task of depriving the black
man of his rights. Their former friends were weakening and the blacks
turned to their enemies in the ancient strategy of "riding the devil across the
Red Sea."[30] This accounts for the close collaboration between black leaders
and Senator Morgan of Alabama, who believed that the black should go to a
foreign land to develop independently a nation of his own. Some blacks
thought again of Africa, but the memory of the antebellum struggle to defeat
white colonization schemes made that continent too "frightening" to attract
many. In the early 1890s a few blacks emigrated to Mapini, Mexico, but
after many hardships they returned to their homes in Georgia and Alabama.
Resorting to Africa, 197 blacks sailed from Savannah, Georgia, for Liberia
in 1895.

In the meantime the reign of terror, initiated to overthrow the carpetbagger governments by means of the Ku Klux Klan, continued to the turn of the century, and it became a special delight of the poor whites to humilitate and persecute blacks who had acquired some education and some wealth. These actions were to make the black realize that he lived in a white man's country in which law for the black is the will of the white man. Blacks were in effect being punished for having presumed to undertake the task of government during Reconstruction and they were being shown that such an eventuality would never again be permitted to occur.[31] America became from the demise of Reconstruction to 1920 a "kith and kin" democracy. The Jim Crow laws were an affirmation of this.

What were the blacks to do in this hostile environment? Segregation was extended abroad wherever the United States government in particular, and the white settlers in general, were in control or had influence. Though the United States Supreme Court had ruled that the Constitution did not follow the flag, color caste did. The intervention of the United States in the war between Cuba and Spain and the acquisition of Cuba and Puerto Rico, construction of the Panama Canal, the conquest of Haiti and the Virgin Islands, all opened promising fields for the extention of the caucasian autocracy in the West Indies. Where persons of color had formerly been treated as members of the human family, United States citizens now instituted a rule of white supremacy. Cuba and the Canal Zone were subjected to strict segregation, Haitians were placed under the domination of the descendants of slave drivers, and Virgin Islanders were deprived of the opportunities for development which Danish control had made possible.[32]

The increasing encroachment on their rights accompanied by severe brutality convinced many southern blacks that they should no longer endure such treatment. They could not educate their children at public expense, although they were taxed to support public schools; they enjoyed little security in the possession of property and dared not defend their families from insults. Emigration to the North increased, creating there the so-called race problem. The events of the last two decades of the 19th century left the black in a morbid state of mind, with a feeling of despair mingled with hate. An Englishman who visited the United States in the autumn of 1884, wrote of the American blacks in *MacMillan's Magazine*, July 1885:

> The Negro is eager to learn, and is steadily improving his position. But the old antagonism of the races is as strong as ever, if indeed not stronger than ever . . . The black man is despised as of old, and no one hails him as a brother. His children must go to separate schools—he must travel by separate cars on the railway. *Will it be so always with*

these six millions of free citizens of the American Republic? It is a
grave and difficult question . . . In an alien land, he has not the
independence, vitality which gains respect for its originality and
strength, at best he is but the meek imitator of his old enslaver. What
may be the future of the dark continent and its inhabitants is one of the
great problems of the World. *But it is my conviction that the tribes and
peoples which have been sold from it into slavery will never reach the
heights of perfect manhood in the countries of their exile* until the race
from which they sprang develops a new endemic civilization in Africa.
The experiment with the African must be made in his own magnificent
home. (My emphasis)

It must be quite obvious by now that more than anything else, it is
precisely the recoil from a system of deliberate and systematic prejudice,
accompanied at times by extremely bestial brutality, that forcibly reminds
American blacks that they are not of European and Anglo-Saxon origin, but
that they have a kinship with those races of humanity who are victims of the
white man's oppression and exploitation. It is this background that impels
the black in America in his quest for an ancestral culture and history.
DuBois, the most eloquent spokesman of the black people, understood this
very well:

My African racial feeling was then purely a matter of my own later
learning, my recoil from the assumptions of the whites, my experience
at Fisk. But it was nonetheless real and a large determinant of my life
and character. I felt myself African by "race," and by that token was
African, and an integral member of the group of dark Americans who
were called Negroes.[33]

Between 1890 and 1892 the Afro-American Council and the Afro-
American League were resurrected. In 1892 Bishop Alexander Walters
expressed the need for the Afro-American Council so long as the black
citizens "were being deprived of the ballot by the unjust enactments. The
ballot is the badge of political equality . . . and obtaining it should be
the ambition of every man, whether white or black."[34] Earlier, in 1881,
there had been established the African Emigration Association which
was an indication of the persistent idea among some Afro-Americans
that they were not accepted in the mainstream of American society, and
that only their own nationality could confer on them those rights they
were deprived of in a white man's democracy. Their desire to form a
black state in the Midwest was expressive of the same sense of grievance.

In 1886 the African Emigration Association sent the following resolution to the Senate and the House of Representatives of Congress:

> Whereas we the Negroes of the United States were brought from Africa and sold as slaves in this country and served as such from 1620 to 1865, and whereas we were set free without a penny, and left to the mercy of our late masters, and their brothers, who owned all this country, from the Atlantic to the Pacific; and who, for over 200 years had regarded us as inferior, and slaves, and whereas there are sixteen thousand of us who have already returned to Africa; and whereas there are thousands of us in humble circumstances, who yet wish to return to Africa, modelled after this government and under the protecting care of the same for the elevation of the African and other troubles, etc.

> Therefore:
> We the members of the African Emigration Association, and such citizens as are willing to aid and encourage us, ask for an appropriation to be disbursed through such channels as in your judgement may direct. It is the purpose of this petition to ask only those who wish to go to Africa, in whatever part of the United States they may be.[35]

The concept of Negro nationality, particularly in Africa, had been projected in the 1850s by such eminent blacks as Martin Delany and Sojourner Truth. In nearly all black emigration efforts we recognize the same ideology incorporating explicit political goals. In the 1890s when the question of establishing a black state in the West or in Africa arose, we find editorials in the black press like the following from the *Christian Recorder* of March 13, 1890:

> What do you think of making a great Negro state under this government as a way out of their race trouble? We think nothing of it; if the two classes cannot live in this country as they are, they certainly cannot live in such relations as must necessarily result from any such plan.

A few months later, on June 26, 1890, the same paper carried an article entitled "Is the Negro Capable of Self-Government" by the Reverend A.B. Gibson, who had this to say:

> The people were ordered to stop going to the territory, it was not made a Negro state; McCabe was not appointed governor. Oh! we were sorry. He must still remain where he does not desire to stay . . . [*sic*]. Could he live in a country ruled and governed entirely by Negro judges, lawyers,

doctors, sheriffs, deputies, mayors, councilmen, legislators? Could he live: having asked those questions, I will now ask another. Would he be successful under Negro rule and government as he is under the white man's! This is a white man's country and government and he has proven it North and South, East and West, democrats and republicans. For my part, I am tired of both parties, the Negroes' back is sleek where they have rode him so much.

Another editorial under the title "A Negro State" in the *Indianapolis Freeman*, July 29, 1905, had this to say:

> The more we think about this subject, the more we are convinced that it is not only possible, but it would be easy for the Colored people to make Oklahoma, an Indian territory, a State under their own control and management, where all opportunities of any other American would be theirs.

All that we have said on this subject and all the evidence we have produced to explain the nature of what we have called the blacks' spiritual yearnings could be dismissed as expressions of only a small section of the black community, a minority suffering from an utopian mentality. This we cannot dispute. It can also be asserted that this movement is and was insignificant in terms of the aspirations of the majority of the blacks, but this we find arguable. The latter point of view takes the position that a focus on Africa is in fact detrimental to the black cause and incongruent with black reality in the United States. According to this perspective American blacks are unassailably American in culture and psychology and their problem is one of assimilation. The solution to their dilemma therefore is seen, not in an emphasis on their African roots, but in a repudiation of them, and in an unremitting effort to incorporate every aspect of American socio-cultural standards and values, becoming, if possible, more American than the whites.

This sort of argument represents the sublime nonsense current among certain intellectuals who eschew race consciousness, and would *really* like to see the black as an integral part of the great American society. But wishing and understanding the fundamental nature of the problem are two different things. When one discusses African consciousness in the United States one must deal with this ideology as it appears, and trace it to its roots in the white social structure. In this society, as long as the black is not amalgamated socially, politically, and economically, black nationalism will develop. This reality must be dealt with despite liberal objections.

> Had it not been for the race problem early thrust upon me and enveloping me I should have probably been an unquestioning worshipper at the shrine of social order and economic development into which I was born. But just that part of that order which seemed to most of my fellows nearest to perfection, seemed to me most inequitable and wrong, and starting from that critique, I gradually as years went by found other things to question in my environment.[36]

DuBois was here pointing out how the black came to find it imperative to develop African consciousness or black nationalism. Those who have articulated this African consciousness among the blacks were expressing what their group thought and felt. In our analysis we have tried to show how in their experience the American blacks could not shed their "burdensome" African origin.

We have shown that the blacks doubted that they were inferior or that Africa was without a history, let alone a pre-history. They went back to exhume their past partly to find out who they were and partly to find material to refute white assumptions and assertions about them.

Progressive scholars on both sides have done yeoman service in unearthing the black's pre-American past; in piecing together that broken line of black history and the contribution the black man has made throughout the world. They have refuted the spurious race sterotype depicting the black as an inferior, a man without a past and therefore unworthy of an equal place at the "table of civilization," to use Martin Luther King's biblical rhetoric. Scholars have shown and are showing that the black is an inheritor of a rich historical tradition with antecedents reaching far back into the dawn of civilization itself.

Black scholars like W.E.B. DuBois, Carter Woodson, George Washington Williams, and many more were pioneers in this field. Their writings brought to the consciousness of the American blacks the missing pages of their civilization. Describing the importance of the formation of the Niagara Movement, William H. Ferris states that "it is a protest against this low estimate of thought and feeling, manifesting themselves in the Negro consciences. It is but the *zeitgeist* affecting the Negro minds, it is but the stirring within the Negro's soul of the immanent World spirit. It shows that the Negro is human and sensitive to slights and insults."[37]

In the United States—or in the general historical relations between blacks and whites—one can appreciate the importance of such phenomena as African consciousness. It aimed at dissipating the popular illusions imposed by a white hegemonic system of rule, oppression and exploitation. Under this system the black man was manipulated by a heartless system which he usually did not understand. The economic part of this oppressive system created the alienated individual who was tied to it by nothing more than the *law of value*. This law of value permeated his whole life and guided his destiny. This, coupled with color prejudice, caused the black soul to see a horizon which often appeared to be at an infinite distance. In any case, that is the way the racist propagandists presented reality. They tried to make the blacks believe the story of their innate racial inferiority. They never suggested that African resources and African labor built or aided in building Western industrial civilization. What the black man got in return for forced services was abuse and castigation.

The scholars and historians who labored to rediscover the black's African past assumed naively that it was possible to expose the myth of black inferiority as mendacious, and they hoped that by eradicating error they could establish accepted criteria of objectivity in the relations between blacks and whites. To suspect that one's opponent is the victim of an ideological delusion does not necessarily mean that one excludes him from discussion, which can be based on a common theoretical frame of reference. This has been both the strength and weakness of liberalism and the Civil Rights Movement: they did not see that the American social structure, which gave prejudice its income-bearing value, was the *cause* and merely not the result of race theories. They did not take into account that the income of the cotton kingdom, based on black slave labor caused the passionate belief in black inferiority and a determination to enforce it even with arms. In accordance with the demands of this system the American social structure justified not only black slavery but exploitation of the Asiatic coolie and the South American peon; all were profitably used, and the color bar was the historical product of this system.

A state of mind is utopian when it is incongruous with the reality within which it occurs.[38] But the blacks' search for their African history or even their desire to repatriate themselves is not utopian, it is congruous with their existential reality. Gibbon, for example, thought that the Irish and Scottish historians wanted to idealize their ancestors, and he observed: "A people dissatisfied with their present condition grasp at any vision of their past or future glory." Hume, too, complained of the "rather fabulous annals which are obtruded on us by the Scottish historians."[39] This tendency has been very true for the Anglo-Saxons, who always carried the explanation of everything good in their English civilization back to the Teutonic forests whence they emerged. Why not allow the black the liberty at least to go back to the African jungle to cry out so that he may receive those echoes which seem to be so essential to the integration of one's personality?

Augustus Cornu has written that "Ideologues divorce ideas from the individuals who conceive them and the empirical circumstances out of which they arise, and attribute an absolute creativeness to the spirit, independent of real life and practical activity."[40] Thus a critic of African consciousness such as Albert Murray could write that:

> Nobody has yet explained how messing with African history and culture is going to give the young United States Negroes a greater sense of identification with the United States. What really counts for identification in this country is not one's old world ancestry. If it did, then the overwhelming majority of the U.S. [sic] white people would be as embarrassed as hell all the time. Their ancestors couldn't make it in the old country![41]

One wishes that things were as stated by Murray, but unfortunately they are not. One can only remind Murray that not *one* black came to the United States because his parents could not make it in the Old World; so thank God they have been saved at least one embarrassment. Among the nationalists who seek a sense of identification with Africa are some reactionaries and self-seeking demagogues; but there are also genuine neonationalists who are repelled by the assumptions of the white world that it alone has an historical tradition and a glorious past, and that, therefore, this entitles it to dominance over other groups. Those blacks who have looked back in search of their history did so because they felt that their ancestors were worth more than anthropological research. White hegemony never ceased to maintain that the black is a savage, that Africa was a haunt for savages, that it was a country overlaid with all of God's infirmities and therefore destined for contempt forever. The American black whether or not he "messed with" African history was African in background, and he could never escape from the burdensome infirmities of that continent. Fanon pointed out that white assumptions produce as a counter-reaction, "a passionate research," and "anger kept up at least by the secret hope of discovering beyond the misery of today, beyond self-contempt, resignation and abjuration, some very beautiful and splendid era, whose existence rehabilitates us both in regard to ourselves and in regard to others." This despite the fact that "by a perverted logic," the oppressor "turns to the past of the oppressed people, and distorts, disfigures and destroys it."[42]

The distortion and the devaluation of pre-colonial black history has taken on a dialectical significance today, because it reacts and is reacted upon by the independence movements in Africa. It is therefore not the existence of black nationalist movements in America that is fantastic. Their programs might be a utopian dream, but the fact of their existence challenges most of the analyses which have been proffered to explain the black situation in America. The central theme of most studies on the black regrets the fact that the American creed of democracy and freedom is negated in the treatment of the black. The Negro problem for most social scientists is basically a moral dilemma which should not exist at all in American society. They claim that if only the whites could be convinced that blacks are as good as the whites, the problem would be solved. The fundamental economic and cultural issues at stake in the conflict between black and white cannot be dealt with within the assumptions of most schools of race relations in America. They talk of Americanizing all the varied racial elements in the United States. However, it is clear that certain racial elements are not being melted socially, economically, or culturally; so the sociologists proffer more studies on the nature of prejudice. Huge sums of money are spent in interracial schemes to minimize prejudice. Going hand-in-hand with this idealistic approach is an abiding faith, an eternally optimistic though sometimes desperate faith in democracy despite all negative evidence. These studies are superficial, ahistorical, and often limited to describing events after the fact. Thus if members of a minority group are assimilated, the explanation for that is the melting pot approach; if the minority groups do not melt but remain segregated and apart, then that is euphemistically called cultural pluralism. American sociology stubbornly or blindly—and therefore stupidly—refuses to examine its material from a nomothetic or generalizing perspective. It continues to move in a closed circle, unaware of the truly explanatory power of its own data, and therefore, unable to formulate those basic laws or principles which would lead to a sorely-needed understanding.

It is in the context of the events, ideas and prejudices that we must understand the phenomenon of Garvey, which is the subject of the next chapter.

Notes

[1] Quoted in Georg Lukacs, *The Historical Novel*, Beacon Press, Boston, 1963, p. 67.

[2] According to Perry Anderson, "If a hegemonic class can be defined as one which imposes its own ends and its own visions on society as a whole, a corporate class is conversely one which pursues its own ends within a social totality whose global determination lies outside it. A hegemonic class seeks to transform society in

its own image, inventing afresh its economic system, its political institutions, its cultural values, its whole mode of insertion into the world. A corporate class seeks to defend and improve its own position with the social order accepted as given." "Origins of the Present Crisis," *op. cit.*, p. 41.

[3]For an extended discussion see Howard H. Bell, "The Negro Emigration Movements, 1849-1854: A Phase of Negro Nationalism." *Phylon*, Vol. 20, No. 2, 1959, pp. 132-142.

[4]Woodson, *The Negro in Our History*, p. 279.

[5]Walker, *One Continual Cry*, p. 121.

[6]William Lloyd Garrison, *Thoughts on African Colonization*, Knopf, Boston, 1832, p. 14.

[7]*The African Repository and Colonial Journal*, October 1846, pp. 303-4.

[8]Bell, *op. cit.*, pp. 132-42.   [9]*African Repository*, August 1848, pp. 243-44.

[10]Frederick Douglass, "The Destiny of Colored Americans," *North Star*, 16 November, 1849.

[11]American Colonization Society, *Colonization Reports*, Vol. 1, p. 116.

[12]*African Repository*, Vol. II, pp. 239-43.

[13]Quoted in Bell, *op. cit.*, pp. 132-144.

[14]*The Culombian*, 4 January, 1854.

[15]Quoted in William Pickett, *Abraham Lincoln's Solution*, Pittman, New York, 1909, p. 306.

[16]*Ibid.*, pp. 301-2.

[17]Charles Benjamin, *Lincoln and the Negro*, Oxford, New York, 1962, p. 109.

[18]Senator Bilbo stated his case in the following words: "It never occurred to Jefferson when writing the Declaration of Independence, or at any time thereafter, to assume the false pretense of recognizing the Negro upon terms of perfect equality with the white man. The Declaration of Independence was written by a white man, the Constitution of the United States was formed by a white man, and both are conceived exclusively in the interest of the white man." *Congressional Record*, 24 May 1938. Senator Bilbo went on to claim that he already had two million signatures of blacks who were willing to go back to Africa.

[19]DuBois, *Dusk of Dawn*, p. 305.

[20]"The African in Africa and the African in America," *Addresses and Proceedings of the Congress on Africa, December 13-15, 1895*, Gouman Theological Seminary, Atlanta, 1896.

[21]Montesquieu observed: "Nothing more assimilates a man to a beast than living among freemen, himself a slave." Quoted in W. Sypher, *Guinea's Captive Kings*, Chapel Hill, 1942.

[22]Woodson, *The Negro in Our History*, p. 433.

[23]DuBois, *Dusk of Dawn*, p. 136.

[24]Benjamin Tucker Tanner, *An Apology for African Methodism*, Baltimore, 1867. Quoted in Essien-Udom, "Relationship of Afro-Americans to african Nationalism," *Freedomways*, Vol. 2, No. 4, 1962, pp. 393-4.

[25]*Ibid.*, p. 394.

[26]*Ibid.*, p. 395.

[27]Quoted in Gossett, *op. cit.*, p. 256.

[28]Quoted in Logan, *op. cit.*, p. 99.

[29]Quoted in Blyden, *op. cit.*, p. 123.

[30]C. Van Woodward says of those who befriended the blacks in this period, "Public spirited professional people of a humanitarian bent gathered at periodic conferences to discuss the race problem and they took a pessimistic or despairing view of the Negro. They emphasized increased Negro crime and became convinced that the race was rapidly deteriorating in morals and manners, in health and efficiency, and losing out in the struggle for survival. They resolved that the Negro was incapable of self-government, unworthy of the franchise, and impossible to educate beyond the rudiments. They devoted much of their time and efforts to the promotion of Negro eduction, but the limitation of their aims are indicated by Booker T. Washington when he said in welcoming a conference of white Southern university presidents to Tuskegee in 1912, "We are trying to instill into the Negro mind that if education does not make the Negro humble, simple and of service to the community, then it will not be encouraged." *The Strange Career of Jim Crow*, pp. 95-95.

[31]Woodson, *The Negro in Our History*, p. 435.

[32]*Ibid.*. p. 491.

[33]DuBois, *Dusk of Dawn*, p. 115.

[34]Alexander Walters, *My Life and Work*, Fleming and H. Revell Company, 1917, p.

[35]Herbert Aptheker, *The Documentary History of the Negro*, Citadel Press, New York, 1965, Vol. 2, pp. 647-48.

[36]DuBois, *Dusk of Dawn*, p. 27.

[37]Ferris, *op. cit.*, p. 199.

[38]Mannheim, *Ideology and Utopia*, p. 192.

[39]Quoted in Gossett, *op. cit.*, p. 85.

[40]Augustus Cornu, *The Origin of Marxian Thought*, Springfield, Illinois, 1957, p. 107.

[41]Albert Murray, "Social Science Fiction in Harlem," *New Leader*, Vol. 49, No. 2, 17 January, 1966, pp. 22-23.

[42]Franz Fanon, *The Wretched of the Earth*, Grove Press, New York, 1961, p. 170.

CHAPTER FIVE
Garveyism and the Afro-American Image

I believe in pride of race and lineage and self: in pride of self so deep as to scorn injustice to other selves, in pride of lineage so great as to despise no man's father, in pride or race so elevating as neither to offer bastardy to the weak nor bed wedlock to the strong, knowing that men may be brothers in Christ, even though they be not brothers in law.

—(from *Dark Water* by W.E.B. DuBois)

Marcus Garvey remains an enigmatic figure in the history of black people and their struggle for liberation from the tribulations of white rule and exploitation. Born in Jamaica in 1887, Garvey has been the subject of many biographies and his papers are being edited by Professor Robert A. Hill and published by the University of California Press, in Los Angeles. From 1919 to the time of his death in 1940 millions of black folks heard his message and responded to the call of Garvey's United Negro Improvement Association; they read its newspaper, *The Negro World*, bought shares in the business ventures he created, and attended meetings and rallies in large numbers. In 1920, the *Crusader* of November reported that some 50,000 blacks marched in a mass UNIA rally in Harlem.

The UNIA's impact was felt internationally as much as in the United States. Claude McKay wrote: "In the interior of West Africa, new legends arose of an African who had been lost in America, but would return to save his people."[1] On the Nigerian coast Africans lit bonfires and slept on beaches waiting to guide in the ships of "Moses Garvey." Dr. Kwame Nkrumah, the first Prime Minister of Ghana, acknowledged that Garvey was an important influence on his political awakening. In South Africa, Clements Kadalie, whose 250,000-member Industrial and Commercial Workers Union was the largest working-class political formation in South

Africa, said he had been much influenced by Garvey's UNIA. The Garvey Movement, in Nkrumah's words, "raised the banner of African liberation" on three continents.[2]

Many other leaders of the struggles for independence in Africa have told how their thinking changed radically when they were exposed to Garvey's ideas.

> The King of Swaziland told Mrs. Marcus Garvey that he knew the names of only two black men in the Western world: Jack Johnson, the boxer who defeated the white man Jim Jeffries, and Marcus Garvey. Jomo Kenyatta has related . . . how in 1921 Kenya nationalists, unable to read, would gather round a reader of Garvey's newspaper, *The Negro World*, and listen to an article two or three times. Then they would run in various ways through the forest, carefully to repeat the whole, which they had memorized, to Africans hungry for some doctrine which lifted them from the servile consciousness in which Africans lived. Dr. Nkrumah . . . has placed on record that of all the writers who educated and influenced him Marcus Garvey stands first.[3]

Within the United States itself some of the more radical leaders like the assassinated Malcolm X traced their ideological inspiration to him. In his own time Garvey could not be ignored. The accommodationist leaders feared him as he despised them. When he died in London in 1940, the *Journal of Negro History* in its obituary pages wrote:

> Marcus Garvey died in London on the 10th of June . . . There he was educated and learned to think seriously of the social repression which his people suffered there and their untoward status throughout the world. . . The white man's hostility toward the Negro and the fixed policy of treating the race as an inferior had so rankled in the bosom of Marcus Garvey as to make him hate white people. He had learned also to despise the mulatto class of Negroes who were used by the whites as a buffer between themselves and the blacks. To get rid of the evils confronting the black people in the Western Hemisphere he organized the Universal Negro Improvement Association by which he endeavored to obtain money to purchase land, ships, and facilities for the transplantation of the Negro to that foreign shore and the development of trade with them and other parts of the world. . . To the highly educated Negroes in the United States, with the exception of a few who followed Marcus Garvey for whatever they could strip him of, his idea was considered as most nonsensical and absurd. The effort to

transplant the Negro from the New World to Africa was nothing new. . . It was bolder, however, in that Garvey attacked the economic imperialist and proclaimed his program of dislodging them from the shores of Africa where they had preempted all African territory at the time with the exception of Liberia and Ethiopia. The Negroes of Africa even felt the impact of his movement, and here and there on the continent were found evidences of their belief that Marcus Garvey would some day come as a deliverer of the blacks from the stranglehold of the European imperialist. The European nations, therefore, feared Garvey as an evil influence; and complaints were sent to the United States to the effect that his operations were hostile efforts against the economic imperialists with whom the United States Government was supposed to be on friendly terms.

And as though these commonplace prejudices were not enough, the obituary ends by stating:

Whatever may be said about Garvey's mistakes, he cannot be recorded in history as a fanatic or a fool. His plans showed just as much sanity as those of Hitler who happened to be able to get control of a nation of his blood with sufficient military equipment to dominate the Western World with the idea of the supremacy of the German people. Garvey might have succeeded in his enterprise if he had such possibilities. His claim to be recorded in history lies in the fact that he attracted a larger following than any Negro who has been developed in modern times. Negroes here and there in America have been hailed as leaders, the press has given them great praise, and their friends have sung of their virtues in high tones; but a thorough analysis of these famous Negro leaders will disclose the fact that they owed their prominence mainly to white men who considered such spokesmen as those persons through whom they could work to keep the Negro in his place.[4]

I have quoted this article at such length because it shows what a complicated personality Garvey was. He was at once according to this article a white man hater, a despiser of mulatto Negroes and a creator of uneasiness among imperialists. He could have been a Hitler and unlike the "promoted" black leaders he had a real following. This article in its attempt to be objective and fair leads to confusion and even to the erection of a strawman. It obscures while enthroning ignorance. Indeed, a strange and shoddy piece of cloth is woven and Garvey is clothed in it. To compare

Garvey to Hitler is not just far-fetched, it is the height of absurdity. The economic imperialism which Garvey threatened was a system which, with grandiloquent and sweet phrases, had violated the world . . . "as a senile old man violates a young, healthy woman, whom he is impotent to impregnate with anything besides the diseases of senility."[5] It may be convenient but certainly not realistic or enlightening to compare Garvey to Hitler. The latter's racism was based on the obnoxious assumption that psychocultural traits and capacities are determined by biological race and that races differ decisively from one another. Modern racism is a European product where it became institutionalized to determine black/white relations; and the non-white people merely react to prove that they are not inferior, but never themselves attribute inferiority to others. Even the US Black Muslims do not believe in white inferiority but do say that the behavior of whites towards non-whites is primitive and of the lower order in the animal kingdom. How realistic can a scholar be if he chooses example and comparisons for convenience and character assassination rather than for a heightened understanding?

The reality of the black position is unique in American society, and its uniqueness lies in the fact that, even though America has gone through two revolutions the black has not been integrated into the American social structure. The black people were not freed by the War of Independence of 1776, nor fully emancipated by the Civil War and Reconstruction.

The Garvey movement in its aims, programs and assumptions must be understood as pointing to these failures to accept the blacks as Americans. The American blacks are not just another minority which experienced stereotyped behavior and which is likely with the passage of time to be integrated and to disappear. Of all the minority groups which came to America, the blacks are the only ones who in the early 1960s were still fighting for the vote and other elementary civil rights.

This is the historical reality which has informed the experience of the black folk, in its continuity in American society. It is important to understand the structural position of the black people, in particular to see how it induces and fosters a kind of black consciousness. Garvey is truly the product of white hegemonic dominance of the black masses. He dreamed dreams of black independence. This dream of course was an embarrassing nuisance to many. The black middle class who also happened to be mulatto were made very uncomfortable by Garvey and feuds developed with them which earned Garvey the epithet of a "hater." To be a mulatto in the time of Garvey was to be better than being pure black; and because Garvey rightly or wrongly rejected these assumptions and preached a black God as opposed to a white God, and a black Empire as opposed to a white Empire, he became in liberal circles an exponent of race hatred. Garvey's anti-imperialism and his emphasis on racial pride was, of course, a much-needed antidote to white racism and the cruelties of imperialism, which were carried out under a cloak of righteousness and labelled as acts of goodness and love, while they were most oppressive and exploitative. More than that, the racism of Garvey was the epiphenomenon of a racist society. The meaning and importance of Garvey's philosophies lie in their effects on the sorely-tried masses of black people. Garveyism was in its initial stages a movement of diverse sorts of poor people who can be lumped together as the proletariat, if we do not mean thereby only wage-workers. The very nature of movements like that of Garvey is to bring out from the hearts of the oppressed strata the essence of human hope, fear, suffering and triumph. But to do this they must invert reality, because dominance and oppression distort the human essence. Marx observed that:

> Consciousness can never be anything else than conscious existence and the existence of men in their actual life process. If in all ideology men and their circumstances appear upside down as in *Camera obscura*, this phenomenon arises just as much from their historical life process as the inversion of objects on the retina does from their physical life process.[6]

The advent of Garvey into the American scene and his attitude and designs about Africa, in my scheme of analysis, mark the reawakening of those sentiments and emotions which men and women have felt for their history, nationality and origins, particularly in times of stress and strain. They cannot be explained by the personality of the leader, and the significance of their meanings is not the verbal expressions, but the type of actions they produce.

Garveyism in its various forms becomes a powerful political and ideological protest against the despoliation of Africans and Afro-Americans. Blacks in America, because they shared the same soil with their oppressors, became the forerunners of this movement. Their presence in one of the centers of this world drama sharpened their awareness of the contradictions between ideal and practice, between the carryng of the white man's burden in Africa and their exploitation in white America.

The position of the black in the foremost Western democracy, in particular his treatment there, not only negated but made even more obvious the falsity of the whole notion of the Western mission to uplife the poor African savages. The significance of black nationalist movements, whether or not they advocate the Back to Africa ideology, is not a matter of their numbers:

> ... as a matter of fact, it derives in part from the very obscurity which surrounds the estimate of size.... Black nationalism is an extremist manifestation which arises out of deep and ancient fear and suspicion and which is nourished by contemporary frustration at the persistence of racial discrimination. If even a relative handful is sufficiently impelled to active and personally satisfying participation, and particularly if partial echoes of their arguments can be heard at nearly all levels of the Negro community; then there is more justification for thinking that the potential for espousal of black nationalist doctrines may be a good deal greater than the ascribed organizational base suggests.[7]

The transition of American capitalism to imperialism confronted black Americans, and indeed the entire black world, with fresh problems. Afro-Americans were subjected to the worst excesses of racism. In the southern states Jim Crow laws squeezed them out of electoral politics in order to force them back into peonage on the plantations. In the North they were forced to live in atrocious slums. The ruling class, through the Klu Klux Klan, was intent on driving out all vigor from the black movement for equality through the wide-scale use of repression, including the lynch mob. As if to drive the point home the United States got into World War I to "save democracy," and Afro-Americans were enrolled into the US Armed Forces and sent to Europe in large numbers as cannon fodder. Black folks made up 10 percent of the country's population, but 13 percent of the armed forces. All in all, 367,000 blacks were drafted into the US Armed Forces during World War I, 200,000 of whom crossed the ocean to take direct part in the War.

At the conclusion of hostilities black soldiers returned to the United States and found themselves facing abuse and lynch mobs. In Houston, Texas, in August 1919, clashes took place between local racists and a regiment of blacks, leading to the deaths of 16 whites including 4 policemen, and 4 blacks. At a trial 19 black soldiers were sentenced to death and hung; many others were given life sentences. In the same year, another tragic incident took place in East St. Louis where striking white workers lynched black workers. The reaction of the American authorities to these atrocities was characteristic. W.E.B. DuBois illustrated it graphically in a table which appeared as an editorial in the *Crisis:*

HOUSTON AND EAST ST. LOUIS

Houston	East St. Louis
17 WHITE persons killed.	125 NEGROES killed.
13 COLORED soldiers hanged.	10 COLORED men imprisoned for fourteen years
41 COLORED soldiers imprisoned for life.	4 WHITE men imprisoned 14-15 years.
4 COLORED soldiers imprisoned.	
5 COLORED soldiers under sentence of death; temporarily reprived by the President.	5 WHITE men imprisoned five years.
40 COLORED soldiers on trial for life.	11 WHITE men imprisoned under one year.
	18 WHITE men fined.
White policeman who caused the riot not even indicted.	1 COLORED man still on trial for life.
No white army officers tried. (Military law)	17 WHITE men acquitted (Civil law)[8]

The world events that led up to World War I and after had a great impact on black Americans and contributed significantly to their social and political alienation. The *Messenger*, a newspaper that had opposed black participation in the war, noted the bitter irony in blacks' being called upon to risk their lives in defense of freedoms that were denied them at home. In rejecting the contention that by their service in war, blacks would prove their patriotism and thus bring an end to discrimination, disfranchisement and lynching, an article by Chandler Owens noted:

> Since when has the subject race come out of a war with its rights and privileges accorded for such participation? . . . Did not the Negro fight in the Revolutionary War, with Crispus Attucks dying first . . . and come out to be a miserable chattel slave in this country for nearly one hundred years after? . . . Did not the Negro take part in the Spanish-American War? . . . And have not prejudice and race hate grown in this country since 1898?[9]

The intensification of racial discrimination and unemployment, and the increase in the number of lynchings during and after World War I, dashed any hopes among the masses of black people that their loyalty and patriotism offered any hope to improve their third-class citizenship.

This abbreviated discussion of the Afro-American experience during and after the war should provide the context for understanding the rise of the Garvey Movement. The failure by the US ruling class to live up to its promises made during the war solidified black resistance as never before. The fact that the United States had been a participant at the Berlin Conference at which Africa was partitioned, and the deals that were made after the war regarding the German colonies, drove the point home to most black Americans. Black workers and the black middle classes united against the colonial structures of oppression and dehumanization.

The Garvey movement arose and flourished in the conditions created by imperialism. It spread and became an anti-imperialist movement with incredible vigor and elan. At its peak in the early 1920s the Garvey movement was the greatest outbreak of black political activity since the Civil War. The new motion of black agitation in the United States caused disturbances that went far beyond the redress of grievances the British Directorate of Intelligence warned at the time. He pointed out further that the new motion of black politics assumed the form of "Pan Negroism" and combination with other colored races. In Berne, Switzerland, a military attache reported black agitation to be "international in its proportions. Great quantities of propaganda literature, such as *The Negro World*, had been shipped from the United States to the West Indies and Africa."[10]

The Garvey movement was a financial disaster; Garvey was to end up associating with the Ku Klux Klan and alienating the "colored" Negroes and intellectuals. However, the message which Garvey had for the black masses touched them as nothing before or since. When in the 1920s Garvey told tales of great African civilizations, and asserted the claim to full African independence, a few realized the far-reaching effects it would have upon black people; on their minds, on their emotions, and on their future struggles. Although now it may seem a simple thing to recognize that self-determination is the right of all peoples, in the 1920s black people felt the sheer weight on the mind and body of a system of slavery armed with the machinery of the states, all the legal and ideological weapons designed to obliterate from their minds the very capacity to think and do for themselves as human beings; if we visualize the steady insidious effect of the image of Africa as a dark continent, the brutalizing effect of white supremacist ideology—if we take all these things into account, we begin to form some idea of the magnitude of Garvey's conception of an independent Africa as the arm and shield of every black man.

"Africa for the Africans," "Renaissance of the Black race," "Ethiopia Awake." These were magic slogans to the downtrodden and abused. "Up you mighty race!" Garvey cried. "You can accomplish what you will. It is only a question of a few more years when Africa will be completely colonized by Negroes as Europe is by the white race. No one knows when the hour of Africa's redemption cometh. It is in the wind. It is coming. One day, like a storm, it will be here."

Garveyism as a body of ideas and hopes raised high the vision of an independent Africa in which her sons and daughters scattered all over the world could live in peace, free of torment and insult from their erstwhile rulers and exploiters. The Africa Garvey dreamt of would be completely independent, self-reliant, built around her own institutions and culture. It was to be an Africa that would not plead for acceptance from anyone. In other words, Garveyism expressed the deep-seated sentiments of the masses who had known white torment and abuses. Richard Wright was profoundly moved by Garvey's message and what it meant for his followers:

The one group I met during those exploring days whose lives enthralled me was the Garveyites, an organization of black men and women who were forlornly seeking to return to Africa. Theirs was a passionate rejection of America, for they sensed with the directness of which only the simple are capable that they had no chance to live a full human life in America. Their lives were not cluttered with ideas in which they could only half believe; they could not create illusions which made them think they were living when they were not; their daily lives were too nakedly harsh to permit of camouflage. I understood their emotions, for I partly shared them.

The Garveyites had embraced a totally racialist outlook which endowed them with a dignity that I had never seen before in Negroes. On the walls of their dingy flats were maps of Africa and India and Japan, pictures of Japanese generals and admirals, portraits of Marcus Garvey in gaudy regalia, the faces of colored men and women from all parts of the world. I gave no credance to the ideology of Garveyism; it was, rather, the emotional dynamics of its adherents that evoked my admiration. Those Garveyites I knew could never understand why I liked them but would never follow them, and I pitied them too much to tell them that they could never achieve their goal . . .

It was when the Garveyites spoke fervently of building their own country, of someday living within the boundaries of a culture of their own making, and I sensed the passionate hunger of their lives, that I caught a glimpse of the potential strength of the American Negro.[11]

George Padmore, like Wright, underlined the psychological therapy that Garveyism offered to the poor toiling masses:

> With his emphasis on the proud tradition of the African past, upon "race pride" and particularly upon the virtue of "blackness," Garvey put steel into the spine of many Negroes who had previously been ashamed of their colour and of their identification with the Negro group. Before his time, such things as coloured dolls or calendars with coloured families and heroes were a rarity; today they are commonplace. Garvey didn't get many Negroes back to Africa, but he helped to destroy their inferiority complex, and made them conscious of their power.[12]

Garvey's name still arouses fond memories in many present-day nationalists. The real significance of Garvey for our analysis is provided by the subsequent destiny of his social thought both among the blacks in America and among Africans. For the momentous, overwhelming fact of Afro-American and African history in the last 40 years has been the gradual acknowledgement of Garvey as a significant catalyst in the destinies of these peoples. Garvey's ideas and philosophy fundamentally define American black and African nationalist and cultural aspirations.

At the turn and the early part of this century American blacks stood alone as advocates of African nationalism, independence and Pan-Africanism. In the panorama of Afro-American advocates of African independence, stand Garvey, W.E.B. DuBois, George Padmore, Aime Cesaire, Bishop Turner, and others. Nothing is more striking than the fact that in field after field American blacks were among the decisive formative influences: Carter G. Woodson in African history, DuBois in Pan-Africanism, Bishop Turner and Smyth for the Christianization of Africa.

Ever since Africans were enslaved, the Western world stood for the total negation of Africa and its history. This situation could only be countered by the modes of thought that were articulated in Pan-Africanism and Garveyism. That is:

> Ideologies are situationally transcendent ideas which never succeed *de facto* in the realization of their projected content. Though they often become the good intentioned motives for the subjective conduct of the individual when they are actually embodied in practice, their meanings are most frequently distorted.[13]

On more than one occasion, some blacks in their moments of tribulation and persecution longed not only to return to Africa, but to move anywhere, if only to remove themselves physically and emotionally from their tormentors. Now and then a few hundred desperate individuals had actually set sail to settle on the African continent. The increasing manifestation of anti-black expressions and incidents during the Spanish-American War, according to Satewood, "quickened the black man's interest in emigration schemes. At this juncture emigration to Cuba, Puerto Rico or the Philippines appeared to provide the black American with an escape from the barriers to 'full manhood.' Cuba in particular was depicted as a 'paradise for colored men,' a place where racial distinctions were virtually non-existent and where vast wealth could be acquired by anyone with a little capital and a willingness to work. Only a little less unrealistic were descriptions of opportunities awaiting Negroes in Puerto Rico and the Philippines. Although several enterprises were actually launched by Negroes to establish colonies of black Americans in these islands, most such schemes never materialized."[14] These movements are important as historical antecedents to Garvey; but Garveyism introduced qualitative changes.

It is important sociologically to establish a point at which the structure of a particular society makes it imperative that a people have a messiah, who transforms situationally transcendent ideas into a force leading to the transformation of the existing order. There are many such factors; and Garvey perceived and took advantage of them. Garvey understood and articulated the deeply felt aspirations of both Africans and Afro-Americans. He made the masses of both groups consciously aware that the color-bar "was the cardinal principle of modern civilization."[15] DuBois had intellectually phrased it: "The problem of the twentieth century is the problem of the color line." But it was left to Garvey to bring this truth forcefully to the American blacks and the Africans everywhere. In the era of imperialism, Robert E. Park has written:

> The nation state, far from eliminating race relations, intensifies them, its ideology of correspondence of cultural and racial with political boundaries makes internal problems of what were external or international problems in the days of empire or in the more primitive times of tribal rule. It . . . made great numbers of human individuals aware of race as a fateful personal characteristic, determining the terms of struggle for a place. It . . . made whole groups of people conscious of themselves as having a status, not merely in their own regions but in the World.[16]

The deeply-rooted racial division in the United States confronted black leaders with many problems. Gunnar Myrdal observed that blacks and whites dealt with each other like two foreign countries, "through the medium of plenipotentiaries."[17] This always creates a problem of the inequality of power at the disposal of each of the two power blocs: the white leaders are not "accommodating." They are not acting as "protest leaders, either."[18] The black leaders who participate in this type of relationship are always at a disadvantage because they have to see to it that they do not "rock the boat." As Lerone Bennett said, the white leaders who "function as liaison agents with the Negroes usually 'fix the measure of value' of the Negro organization,[19] deciding not merely the question of how much to ask for, but also how to ask, and indeed whether the Negro should ask at all."[20]

The dilemma that faced black leadership in the era of unchallenged white supremacy is exemplified by the careers of Booker T. Washington and W.E.B. DuBois. The former became the first southern-based black person to be nationally accepted and projected by a fraction of the white bourgeoisie. Washington, according to historian Vincent Harding, generally assumed that this was indeed a white man's country and that it would always be so. His stance of accommodation was based on the imposing reality of white power.[21]

Accepting unchallenged white power and building on his experience at Tuskegee, in the heart of Alabama, he urged black folks not to search for pie in the sky but to do whatever was necessary to survive. His famous Atlanta speech of September 18, 1895, established an *entente* between "moderate" blacks and the "better element of the whites." For the masses of blacks Booker T. Washington advised, "Cast down your buckets where you are." This symbol he drew from a story of a water-famished ship's crew off the shore of South America, who casting their buckets into the sea, came up with fresh water from the Amazon River, where they had thought all was salt water. This was a graphic depiction of the black situation, except that when they cast their buckets instead of bringing up fresh water they brought up muddy racism and the scorn of white supremacists. What Booker T. Washington was saying was that black people should make the best of the situation confronting them, and not pursue emigration and political equality. He called upon the rulers of the South also to "cast down their buckets" into the rich labor source afforded by black people instead of wasting their efforts trying to attract white immigrants from Europe.

In return, Washington pledged that if this was done, black people would prove loyal to the master class:

> While doing this you can be sure in the future as you have been in the past that you and your families will be surrounded by the most patient, faithful, law abiding and unresentful people the world has seen. As we

have proved our loyalty in the past, in nursing your children, watching by the sick bed of your mothers and fathers, often following them with tear dimmed eyes to their graves, so in the future in our humble way we shall stand by you with a devotion that no foreigner can approach, ready to lay down industrial, commercial will and religious life with yours in a way that shall make the interest of both races one.[22]

Washington deplored the mistakes of the past made in seeking seats in Congress and the State Legislature and declared that the wisest among my race understand that the agitation of questions of social equality is the extremist folly. He said nothing about the terrible outrages suffered by the blacks during 1895; when his speech was delivered 113 blacks had been lynched in the South that year. What this philosophy meant was that blacks could not assert themselves and were expected to accommodate to the white hegemony which condemned them to perpetual exploitation while offering the mirage of self-development and improvement.

For W.E.B. DuBois, Washington's proposals were tantamount to denigrating black capacities, if not relegating them to perpetual purgatory. DuBois for his part established an *entente* between militant blacks and liberal whites. At the core of DuBois' philosophy at the turn of the century, was the role he assigned to the Talented Tenth. Like all races the black race would be saved by its exceptional men, trained to the knowledge of the world and man's relation to it. As teachers, ministers, professional men, spokesmen, the exceptional few must come first:

> To attempt to establish any sort of system of common and industrial school training without first, and, I says first advisedly, without *first* providing for the higher training of the very best teachers, is simply throwing our money to the winds.

DuBois did not deprecate the importance of industrial training, but argued that

> it is industrialism drunk with its vision of success, to imaging that its own work can be accomplished without providing for the training of broadly cultured men and women to teach its own teachers, and the teachers of the public school.[23]

DuBois, unlike Booker T. Washington, was both militant (particularly at this time) and conservative. His pronouncements were militant and sometimes devastatingly honest in their criticism of the white betrayal of the

"American Creed," but his actions were cautious and conciliatory. What was common both to DuBois and Washington was not only the unwillingness to act, but the unwillingness to involve the masses in the act of their own liberation. The National Association for the Advancement of Colored People exemplifies this tendency. Bennett described the politics of the NAACP as protest politics rather than mass politics:

> The word, protest, is a mask for inaction. The deepest strain in Establishment protest is sterile and socially irrelevant. Endless debate, polite petitions, the sending of telegrams and letters, the whole ritual of mimeograph machines and typewriters: all this has been a substitute for hard analysis and risky action. The word *risk*: this separates the establishment and its perennial critics, the radicals.[24]

Indeed, the NAACP was formed and organized largely by white folks who were both intellectual and biological heirs of the antebellum white abolitionists. Beginning in 1910, DuBois gave more than 20 of the most productive years of his life to the NAACP as editor of its organ, *Crisis*.[25] The relationship of Washington and DuBois to different factions of the white bourgeoisie explains the social distance between their leadership and the masses for whom they spoke.

The compromising leadership has no need for mass action because its methods of respectability and self-improvement fall outside mass action. This creates what DuBois called "the inner problem of contact with their own lower classes." When Ralph Bunche stated that the black elite "know very little, if any, more about the Negro in the mass than does the average white man," he was talking about this lack of social connection.[16] That is, the NAACP, the Pan African Movement, and the Urban League were all led by intellectuals whose problem was how to make contact with the masses. Garvey had no such problem.

The NAACP and the Urban League (the two oldest black organizations), while they can show on their credit side some spectacular constitutional victories, have by and large worked to accommodate the black masses to the misery of the status quo, rather than to organize them for an attack on the forces responsible for the misery. "Behind all the words and all the slogans is a terrible reality: millions and millions of men and women with deep fears and resentment and needs—fears and resentments and needs, it should be noted, that cannot be met by the appointment of a Negro federal judge or the filing of a court suit."[27]

It was these masses whose needs could not be satisfied that Garvey attracted and for a while led. For the lower strata of the black working masses the Garvey movement had both messianic and utopian qualities.

Karl Mannheim has suggested that the substance and form of a utopia does not take place in a realm which is independent of social life:

> An effective utopia cannot, in the long run be the work of any individual, since the individual cannot, by himself tear asunder the historical situation. Only when the utopian concept of the individual seizes upon currents already present in society and gives expression to them, when in this form it flows back into the outlook of the whole group and is translated into action by it, only then can the existing order be challenged by striving for another order of existence.[28]

If we accept what Mannheim says, then the Garvey Movement becomes a natural part of human history and experience under specific historical conditions. The person of the prophet (Garvey) becomes the point at which the past and the future converge. In Gramsci's words: "He gives a creative impulse to a prospective moment of history, and into him, in turn, flows the tradition which is history's moment of retrospection."[29]

The Garvey Movement was an answer to the accommodating black leadership which, because of its fear of mass action, considered the black masses incapable of organization, apathetic and demoralized. Garvey was able to articulate the desire of the black masses for freedom and self-determination. The accommodating black leaders and their white friends did not wish to—and could not—recognize Garveyism as a phenomenon legitimate in the exploitative structure of the post-World War I era, as this would have been equivalent to recognizing the legitimacy of protest by the masses against the established order.

Garveyism is quite different from other forms of messianic movements. Garveyism was a specific socio-historical phenomenon possessed of significant distinctive features. *Africa for the Africans! Renaissance of the Black race. The Black Star steamship line!* These were the wishes which informed the Garvey movement. Messianic movements have tended to grow among peasants as a form of political protest of a people at a given stage of their development. Garvey may not have provided a correct solution to the problems of black people, but he posed it significantly. He generated a durable consciousness among blacks which he linked with the fortunes of Africa at a time of complete white domination of non-whites. In the historic conditions which formed America, her economy, her classes, her states, in the reality of the world situation after World War I, we find the premise of the Garvey movement.

Garvey's black star made its appearance in the firmament of the white world, exhorting black people everywhere to gaze upon and follow it. When it appeared it seemed unreal and impractical, but Africa today is independ-

ent and Garvey survives in memory like the spectacular myth of an
unforgettable moment. As Gramsci says, "If men acquire consciousness of
their social position and of their function on the plane of the superstructure,
there exists a necessary and vital nexus."[30]

Garvey was calling upon an oppressed, downtrodden and dehumanized
African people to look to their own resources to free themselves, and to
redeem their colonized motherland. Black folks heard the message, and
many sensed the call to struggle which was implied. The Garvey movement
had serious implications for the white world. Addressing a meeting at New
York City's Carnegie Hall in 1919, Garvey said:

> We say to the white man who now dominates Africa, that it is to his inter-
> est to clear out of Africa now, because we are coming . . . 400,000,000
> strong; and we mean to retake every square inch of the 12,000,000
> square miles of African territory belonging to us by right divine.

Continuing that challenging theme, he placed the struggle for Africa in
the context of world revolution:

> Every American Negro and every West Indian Negro must understand
> now that there is but one fatherland for the Negro, and that is
> Africa . . . as the Irishman is struggling and fighting for the fatherland of
> Ireland, so must the new Negro of the world fight for the fatherland of
> Africa.

And what did all of this have to do with the daily oppression and death
faced by black people in America? To that question Garvey offered a
strange answer, a bizarre set of connections between the struggle for Africa
and the struggle for freedom in America. He solemnly promised the
Carnegie Hall gathering that:

> In the next few months we will be so organized that when they lynch a
> negro below the Mason and Dixon line, if we cannot lynch a white man
> there, and since it is not safe to lynch a white man in any part of
> America, we shall press the button and lynch him in the great continent
> of Africa.[31]

Was Garvey an unredeemed racist? In the drama of human experience,
Garvey reminds one of Shakespeare's Caliban, who said:

You taught me language, and my profit on't
Is, I know how to curse. The red plague rid you
For learning me your language![32]

That is, what the oppressed learn from their oppressor is a distortion of
themselves. The world in which Garvey and the black masses he led lived
distorted human potentialities. Shakespeare in *The Tempest* had no
illusions about the real world; he had a grasp of the potential sweetness of
human life and brotherhood when it was not soured by a corrupt society.
The challenge that Garvey posed was (and still is) to create a society that
will not corrupt humanity.

The struggle for liberation is an important landmark in the history of any
people, and it was doubly so for the black masses. After the abolition of
slavery, the former slaveowners seized power in the Southern states and set
up the economic and political conditions to establish a regime based on
white supremacy. Such was, and today still is, the economic basis of racial
discrimination.

The freedom that Garvey sought was different from that sought by
organizations like the NAACP and the Urban League. Garvey's teachings
and philosophy were not without precedents. Afro-Americans like John
Bruce, Hubert Harrison, Bishop Turner, Martin Delany and David Walker
had preached the gospel of self-determination. But the world in which
Garvey lived and worked was different. As Harding put it:

> What was new was the twentieth century. New were the confusing,
> exhilarating forces that were abroad, the new movements that deeply
> affected black people and their oppressors. New was Marcus Garvey
> and his extraordinary power as a publicist and an exhorter, and the
> availability of a mass print medium, *The Negro World.* New were the
> many signs Garvey had given that he might indeed be able to organize
> the children of Africa as no one had ever done before. By 1919, there
> were reports of dozens of branches of the UNIA, not only in the United
> States but in many other parts of the black world as well—including
> Africa. In addition to *The Negro World*, other UNIA businesses and
> subsidiaries began to be established, but none so electrified the black
> world as the organization of the Black Star Line.[33]

For the first time a black man was speaking to black people, saying that
they must remove themselves from the system under which they were

suffering. Garvey got black people to do something in America. They built Liberty Hall and they acquired petty businesses. He encouraged black people to do things for themselves and not to rely on the good will of the oppressor.

I have already referred to the savage treatment blacks suffered at the hands of the white people. The physical aspect of this treatment is well-known and has been adequately described in the literature of the lynch mobs. The psychological effects of being ruled by persons over whom one has not the slightest control, has only been touched upon slightly in the studies of colonies. Here I can only point out that dependency damages group psychology and warps perspective, leaving a feeling of disparagement and social disillusion. It destroys the culture of a subordinate group without offering a substitute, while sheer physical fatigue stupefies the masses. The problematic nature of the black's perception of and relation to Africa is a symptom of this. The masses of people in such a society feel the oppressive and psychological torments, but they do not always understand or know the reasons or causes for this feeling. Such a situation frequently produces what Joseph Schechtman described as a "deep longing for a hero." The masses yearn for some strong figures to bring them relief from the dismal round of their daily lives, to provide the direction and confident leadership that will release them from their oppressive bondage. Too often, however, the desire is "for a hero to bow before and follow blindly. The danger of a hero worship is implicit in the human need for heroes."[34]

The intellectual elements claim to know the conditions which bring this about, but do not always understand, let alone feel it. The lack of understanding by the masses, and the absence of feeling in the leadership, ends by producing the type of black leadership such as that in the NAACP and the Urban League, whose role is to interpret to the white power bloc the mood of the black. These interpretations are expressed in the classic statement "the Negro feels" or "the Negro believes" or "the Negro wants"; and more often than not, what the Negro wants, according to these interpretations of the black mood, is assimilation to the status quo. This alienation between the intellectuals and the masses leads to what Gramsci called two extremes: "Pedantry and philistinism on the one hand and blind passion and factiousness on the other." Gramsci's discussion helps explain the attitude of Booker T. Washington and DuBois at the turn of the century, an attitude which has characterized most Negro civil rights organizations:

> The error of the intellectual consists in the belief that one can know without understanding, and in particular without feeling and being impassioned . . . the intellectual can be such a person (not a pedant)

detached and self-withdrawn from the nation and people, i.e., without feeling the elementary passion of the people, comprehending and so explaining and justifying them within the determined historical situation and integrating them dialectically with laws of history, with a superior concept of history of the world scientifically and coherently.[35]

When Garvey appeared, and became a principal figure on the stage of black self-consciousness, he was able to bridge that critical gap between the intellectuals and the masses, giving the people a handle to their own affairs and tapping for them the life-giving root of popular radicalism.

It is not merely generating a socially effective consciousness that is important for a leader; he must then be able to direct this mass consciousness to politically significant goals. From this point of view Garvey can be accused to having misdirected the popular radicalism which he was able to arouse, by directing it to the chimerical goal of Back to Africa. But if one looks at the influence his ideas exerted on later generations and at the importance of a free Africa for the black self-image, his teachings assume a different meaning. What Gramsci said about the worker in the following quotation applies equally to an oppressed group:

The salvation of the disinherited lies in their own hands. The worker daily wins his own spiritual autonomy and his creative freedom in the realm of ideas, battling against fatigue, against utter tedium, against the physical monotony which tends to mechanize and so kill the inner life.[36]

Hegemony for the oppressed group ultimately becomes an important instrument of cultural renovation. Garvey for the first time in the history of the black folks in the United States and black people everywhere, was able to point with unparalleled clarity to the subtle yet significant interplay of social and cultural values. Until the advent of Garvey the struggle for black humanity and liberation was expressed largely in religious and humanitarian terms, which dissociated black energies and focused them on meaningless targets instead of pointing out the connection between the economic plunder which went on in Africa and what the black experienced in America. The nature of humanitarian and religious rhetoric, as I have suggested before, is to accommodate the masses to the present state of social, economic and political distribution. This rhetoric flows freely because it costs nothing and is readily accepted by the rulers.

It was into this theological vacuum that Garvey introduced his Back to Africa movement. Until Garvey, no one was interested in organizing the black masses. They had no ideological focus except an appeal to abstract principles which acted chiefly as a mediating philosophy for the status quo. This type of political manipulation neither inspired the black masses nor won any victories, except token opportunities for the special individual who is always proclaimed the first. Garvey, however, organized in the 1920s the first truly international organization of Africans and people of African descent. On August 4, 1920, the *New York Tribune* estimated that 25,000 blacks "from all parts of the world" were assembled in the city for a 30-day convention of the Universal Negro Improvement Association. This meeting was so threatening to imperialist powers that Garvey's agents were not permitted to visit Africa.

Garveyism was the supreme effort involving the black masses and it lasted for less than a decade. Wrecked by its pitifully weak leadership and strategy, in the end it collapsed without a fight. Garvey himself was arrested and convicted of forgery and finally died without having set foot on Africa. With him the elan and combativity of the black masses disappeared, not to be experienced again for 30 years.

The tragedy of Garvey is not that he insulted the Negroes of light skin or that he eventually joined hands with the Ku Klux Klan or that he engaged in abortive business ventures. The real tragedy lies in his misunderstanding of the forces that kept Africa dismembered. He talked about a free Africa at a time when this was impossible, and consequently he paid the price of all visionaries. In the early part of this century, black nationalism and African independence had to remain a dream of a few intellectuals. Except for the African National Congress of South Africa, most African nationalist organizations, which is to say those in West Africa and Kenya, were formed in the 1920s. At that time nationalism in its modern sense came to Africa from outside. In other African countries such as Rhodesia, the Congo, the former French colonies and the Portuguese territories it took another 30 years of white domination and exploitation before the people were able to organize for national independence. Garvey's sober judgement of his role was significant: "Now we have started to speak and I am only the forerunner of an awakened Africa that shall never go back to sleep."[37]

It is no accident that in the flurry of African independence movements the contributions of the early Afro-American nationalists like DuBois, Garvey, and Padmore have been temporarily forgotten. In America, the shattering fiasco of Garvey's business ventures finally broke the morale of the early efforts at African Independence. The period after Garvey's death, when a few young black intellectuals were attracted to the activities of the Communist Party, was followed by the depression years and subsequently by the Italian attack on Ethiopia, which temporarily awakened black interest in Africa. But for the most part the blacks' interest in Africa went through what Perry Anderson, describing the English working class, called "prolonged catatonic withdrawal."[38] The once insurgent Black Nationalist became numbed and docile. Even the Pan-Africanism of DuBois which had been formulated in 1919 went into doldrums of non-activity until 1945.

While the drama of Marcus Garvey's rise and fall was unfolding in Harlem, another event, less colorful but equally important, had contributed towards resuscitating the black's African roots. This was the exciting, productive phenomenon called the Harlem Renaissance. While Garvey was attempting to emancipate the black spiritually, the Harlem Renaissance began his cultural emancipation. Alain Locke, the spirit behind this the "New Negro" movement, observed its two constructive channels: "One is the advance guard of the African peoples in their contact with twentieth century civilization; the other, the sense of a vision of rehabilitating the race in world esteem . . . "[39]

The Garvey movement and the Harlem Renaissance represent two different brands of black nationalism. The central theoretical assumption of black nationalism is that before the Negro can be truly free, he must effect a psychic separation from the idea of whiteness; that is, he must stop believing in it so much that he cannot believe in himself. The idea of separation, a part of the ideological armory of the nationalist movement, is a reiteration of this slightly more complex notion, which, by making it concrete puts it in terms the uneducated layman can understand.[40] If one can entertain the notion of a physical separation from whites, and can accept this idea with equanimity, then it becomes proportionately easier to come to grips with the idea of mere psychological separation. The nationalist realizes that identification of virtue, beauty or excellence with whiteness makes it impossible for the black to accept himself as something other than a stepchild of the human race. The values, the social structure and the propaganda of imperialism seemed always to whisper into the black ear: "The Good Lord took a hand in this color business and it is a sign of his displeasure if one is born anything but white." The historical class structure of the black community, where the colored occupied the intermediate position between the black masses and the white society, created the sociological notion of passing from what must have seemed the purgatory of blackness to the heavenly bliss of whiteness.

The distinctive facets of African consciousness and perception among American blacks, as it has developed over the past 100 years, can thus be summed up as follows: With the qualitative change in the nature of slavery at the end of the 18th century and the period preceding the Civil War, the free Negroes experienced many hardships, and with the encouragement of the American Colonization Society, a *few* blacks looked toward Africa as the solution to their persecution. After the Civil War, which formally emancipated the black without guaranteeing him the machinery to secure these newly-won freedoms, imperialism finally expelled black people from the citizenship of American society and from history. The eclipse of the black world physically and economically established the ceiling on black aspirations. Undisturbed by criticism from Europe and from American liberals, mesmerized by the successes of imperialism, the southern philosophy extricated the nation from its moral qualms. The masses of blacks, as a result of the untold brutalities of lynch mobs, lost nerve and ended up losing their sense of identity. The turn of the century saw various adjustive mechanisms at work among blacks as they tried to adapt to their fate in a white society. Booker T. Washington with his program of subordinate evolution within the apparently unshakeable structure seemed to provide one answer. W.E.B. DuBois insisted on equality as guaranteed in the Constitution, but this was merely a variation on the same theme of adjustment to the existing system. These two methods of approach merge in the formation of the NAACP and the Urban League. The elite of the black community working through the elite of the white community would manipulate the Constitution. In the meantime, the black masses would be restrained from rocking the boat. In 1943, Eleanor Roosevelt in an article called "If I Were a Negro" explicitly stated this philosophy. She advocated waiting on behalf of the Negro "until certain people were given time to think"; not being "too demanding"; accepting every advance that was made in the segregated Army and Navy, but not trying to "bring those advances about" more quickly than they were offered.[41] It was Garvey who, after the death of Booker T. Washington was to rock the boat by seeking the solution of the Negro problem outside the bounds of white society.

THE INTERNATIONAL MEANING OF GARVEYISM

The preceding is a crude schema and a tentative attempt to put some perspective on the rise and recurrence of nationalist movements like Garveyism among the blacks. It remains to analyze the actual thoughts of Garvey and the distinctive contribution he made to black self-consciousness, which is inextricably related to the African background. The subject is so vast and of such magnitude and complexity that only the most general suggestions can be attempted. In America the unparalleled success and continuity of capitalism produced no movement geared to the interests of the masses of working people, whether black or white. Black nationalism was and still is a reaction against the peculiar ideology of the Americans, which induces a bizarre and absurd (but in reality, effective and explicable) form of hegemony that tells all the classes in society that the system is good and that there is abundance for all who are willing to exert themselves; this despite its failure to deliver the goods for the working man in general, and for blacks in particular.

Several explanations have been offered as to what caused the rise and fall of Garvey, and most of these are mechanistic, ahistorical and unstructural. The utopian nature of Garvey's Back to Africa has been overplayed and not fully understood as a result of the black's lack of integration into the economic, social and political institutions of the country which gives him a pariah status. Max Weber observes that "even pariah people who are most despised are usually apt to continue cultivating in some manner that which is equally peculiar to ethnic and status communities: the belief in his own specific 'honor'."[42] This is the case with nationalists among the blacks. While Garvey spoke of "Africa for the Africans," he was quite cognizant of what was happening in the rest of the world.

> There is now a world revival of thought and action which is causing peoples everywhere to bestir themselves towards their own security, through which we hear the cry of Ireland for the Irish, Palestine for the Jew, Egypt for the Egyptians, Asia for the Asiatic, and thus we Negroes raise the cry of Africa for the Africans, those at home and those abroad.

> Some peoples are not disposed to give us credit for having feelings, passions, ambitions and desires like other races; they are satisfied to relegate us to the back-heap of human aspirations, but this is a mistake . . . We feel that we, too, are entitled to the rights that are common to humanity.[43]

He appealed to race pride and race courage. "We have died for five hundred years for an alien race. The time has come for the Negro to die for himself."[44]

Students of the black problem have disputed the actual paid membership of the Universal Negro Improvement Association, but all have admitted as incontestable fact that Garvey had the largest following of any known black movement. In 1920 some 50,000 marched in a mass UNIA rally in Harlem. When one bears in mind the slenderness of Garvey's resources, the vast material forces and the pervading social conceptions which automatically sought to destroy him, his achievement remains one of the propagandistic miracles of this century.[45] Garvey spoke the language of the harassed and sorely tried, and he moved them as never before. Throughout the world wherever black masses lived, the name of Garvey became a household word. "The British and French Governments took actual exception to Garvey's agents in their Colonies by barring Garvey followers."[46]

Garveyism came as a flash of hope to the doubly exploited and oppressed black American masses in particular, and the black world in general. Its militancy was a repudiation of the sycophancy of Washington. Even DuBois, James Weldon Johnson, and Eugene Jones were seen in comparison as "weak kneed and cringing . . . sycophant to the white man . . . the 'Uncle Tom' Negro."[47] A white commentator described the enthusiasm of Garvey's followers: "The bands of black peasants flock to Garvey. They worship him. They feel he is saying the things which they would utter were they articulate. They swarm to hear the fiery rhetoric. They pour their money into his coffers. They stand by him through thick and thin. They idolize him as if he were a black Demosthenes."[48] The NAACP and the Urban League, confusing influence with power, bovinely and uncritically accepting white America's glorification of itself as the ultimate in human development, could never reach the masses of the blacks in the way that Garvey did, particularly since they regarded those masses with fear.

The basic program of Garvey's Universal Negro Improvement Association was worked out in a Charter with a Preamble and a Declaration of Rights in 54 Articles.[49] The program was militant and encompassed national and international issues affecting all black people in Africa and of African descent in diaspora. The Preamble declared that "The European nations have parceled out among themselves and taken possession of nearly all the continent of Africa and the Natives are compelled to surrender their lands to the thieves and are treated in most instances as slaves." Strong protest was also made against inhuman conditions of life among the blacks in the West Indies and other colonial areas. The Preamble denounced lynching, Jim Crow, race riots, discrimination in jobs and wage rates, inadequate education, denial of the right to work, lack of justice in courts and the general state of terrorism under which black people were compelled to live.

The political center of the Declaration of Rights was contained in points 13 and 15 which declared:

> We believe in the freedom of Africa, in Europe for Europeans and Asia for Asiatics, we also demand Africa for the African at home and abroad . . . we strongly condemn the cupidity of those nations of the world whose aggression or secret schemes, have seized the territories and inexhaustible material wealth of Africa, and we place on record our most solemn determination to claim the treasures and possessions of the vast continent of our forefathers.[50]

In line with this general argument all blacks, no matter where they lived, were declared full citizens of Africa; and the right of self-determination for blacks, wheresoever they form a community among themselves, was affirmed. Such communities should be given the right to elect their own representatives to represent them in legislatures, courts of law or such institutions as may exercise control over that particular community. The Declaration insisted upon the right of black people to full recognition internationally, and it condemned the League of Nations as being null and void, so far as the Negro is concerned, in that it seeks to deprive the Negroes of their Liberty. This sentiment is a far cry from that expressed by the Pan-African Congress held in Paris during the deliberations of the League of Nations. In Garveyism there is no philistinism or narrowness, but rather a first attempt to create a hegemonic force. Its demands are shorn of all the middle-class respectability and paternalistic appeals that characterize the second Pan-African Congress, which was laughed at by the *Chicago Tribune* as an Ethiopian Utopia. Garveyism was the first seriously-conceived challenge to white hegemony.

The central political ideology of the Garvey Movement was not Back to Africa, but freedom for black men to create their own destinies. In the Madison Square Garden speech quoted above he further stated:

All men should be free—free to nationally build by themselves for the up-bringing and rearing of a culture and a civilization of their own. Jewish culture is different from Irish culture. Anglo-Saxon culture is unlike Teutonic culture. Asiatic culture differs greatly from European culture; and, in the same way, the world should be liberal enough to allow the Negro latitude to develop a culture of his own. *Why should the Negro be lost among the other races and nations of the World and to himself?* Did nature not make him a son of the soil? Did the Creator not fashion him out of the dust of the earth? Out of that rich soil to which he bears such a wonderful resemblance? A resemblance that changes not, even though the ages have flown? *No! the Ethiopian cannot change his skin*; and so we appeal to the conscience of the white world to yield us a place of national freedom among the creatures of present-day temporal materialism. (My emphasis)

The inclusion of the African Communities League in Garvey's Association and his use of Universal in the title showed the Association's stated interest in drawing the peoples of African races together. Its manifesto, drawn with great care, warned of the universal disunity existing among the people of Negro or African race"; and it called upon all people of Negro or African parentage to join in a great crusade to rehabilitate the race. Garvey itemized the ambitions and the general objects of the association:

> To establish a universal confraternity among the race, to promote the spirit of race pride and love, to reclaim the fallen of the race, to administer to and assist the needy, to assist in civilizing the backward tribes of Africa, to strengthen the imperialism of Independent African states, to establish commissionaries or agencies in principal countries of the world for the promotion of all Negroes, irrespective of nationality, to promote a conscientious Christian worship among the Native tribes of Africa, to establish universities, colleges, and secondary schools for the further education and culture of the boys and girls of the race and to conduct a world-wide commercial and industrial intercourse.[51]

White rule and hegemony bear on the black in a specific historically-determined way. A combination of structural and conjunctural factors in the contact between blacks and whites produced a denial of the validity of African culture. A new mythology was being created in the form of trusteeship which said that black people were a childlike race and needed the guidance of whites for their own good. Garvey rejected this assumption and demanded a government of the black people by the black for the black people:

> From our distinct racial group idealism we feel that no black man is good enough to govern the white man, and no white man good enough to rule the black man; and so of all races and peoples. No one feels that the other, alien race, is good enough to govern or rule to the exclusion of native racial rights. *We may as well, therefore, pose the question of superior and inferior races. In twentieth century civilizations there are no inferior and superior races. There are backward peoples, but that does not make them inferior.* As far as humanity goes all men are equal, and especially where peoples are intelligent enough to know what they want . . . It is true that economically and scientifically certain races are more progressive than others; but that does not imply superiority. For the Anglo-Saxon to say that he is superior because he introduced gun powder to destroy life, or the Teuton because he compounded liquid gas to out-do in the art of killing, and that the Negro is inferior because he cannot kill then he is open to the retort of 'thou shall not kill' as being the divine law that sets the moral standard of the real man. (My emphasis)[52]

Garvey's Back to Africa call must be understood in light of is entire philosophy:

> The Universal Negro Improvement Association represents the hopes and aspirations of the awakened Negro. Our desire is for a place in the World; not to disturb the tranquility of other men, but to lay down our burden and rest our weary backs and feet by the banks of the Niger and sing our songs and chant our hymns to the God of Ethiopia. Yes we want rest from toil of the centuries, rest of political freedom, rest of economic and industrial liberty, rest to be free and unmolested, rest from lynching and burning, rest from discrimination of all kinds.[53]

This type of black nationalism was denounced by certain circles of black intellectuals. Their position was later described by DuBois in these terms:

> The upper class Negro has almost never been nationalistic. He has never planned or thought of a Negro state or a Negro school. This thought and solution has always been a thought upsurging from the masses, because of the pressure which they could not withstand and which compelled racial institution or chaos.[54]

Such attitudes were fostered by the structural position of this particular class. Its sociological moorings enhanced its value as an intermediary between the white group and the masses of blacks.

Garvey held, like Delany, that it was impossible for the masses of blacks to get justice in countries where they formed a minority; and that with Africa subject to foreign rule, they lacked, above all, a place in the world which could make their opinions significant and actions effective. History seems to confirm his views.

> The end of the Second World War marked the beginning of the liberation of Africa and of racial integration in the United States. Although there is no causal connection between these two momentous developments, they are interrelated and they influence each other. That they occurred at approximately the same time has profound implications for Negro Americans, all of whom are aware that they are "of African descent."[55]

Whether or not one takes literally the appeal that black people must return to Africa, their traditional homeland, the undeniable fact remains that notwithstanding the numbers of blacks who fought and died during World War I (to make the world secure for democracy) anything would have been better than the treatment they too often received at the hands of crazed white mobs. W.E.B. DuBois, in a *Crisis* editorial of May 19, 1919, expressed this bitter disillusionment:

> We sing: this country of ours, despite all its bitter souls have done and dreamed, is yet a shameful land. It lynches. It disfranchised its own citizens. It encouraged ignorance. It steals from us ... This is the country to which we soldiers of democracy return. This is the fatherland for which we fought. But it is our fatherland. It was right for us to fight. The faults of the country are our faults. Under similar circumstances we would fight again.

> But by the God of Heaven, we are cowards and jackasses if now that the war is over we do not marshal every ounce of our brain and brawn to fight longer, more unbending battles against the forces of hell in our own land.

> We return: We return from fighting. We return fighting. We make way for democracy. We save it in France, and by the Great Jehovah, we will save it in America or know the reason why.[56]

Such heartfelt appeals made no impression on those who claimed to be "Lords of Humanity." Garvey revealed a surprising awareness and understanding that such appeals only showed black helplessness and impotence. How were the black masses to respond to their tribulations? Karl Mannheim has described experiences similar to the Garvey movement in the following words:

> Chiliasm joined forces with the active demands of the oppressed strata. The dawn of a millenial kingdom on earth contained a revolutionary tendency. Longings, which up to that time had been either unattached to a specific goal or concentrated upon the worldly objects, suddenly took on a mundane complexion. They were now felt to be realizable— here and now—and infused social conduct with a singular zeal. This is the "spiritualization of politics" which accounts for more or less conscious participation of all strata of society in the achievement of some mundane purpose, as contrasted with fatalistic acceptance of events as they are or of control from above.[57]

Marcus Garvey went beyond the verbal sloganeering and chastizing and actually set up in the United States a miniature replica of the governmental regime that he hoped to create in Africa. In 1921, he also began organizing an armed force which was to be used to liberate Africa from white usurpers. (In 1935, when Italy launched an attack on Ethiopia, a black brigade was formed, so that Garvey's idea was after all not too far-fetched.) The governmental structure which he proposed to establish in Africa was based on British feudal forms and on the organizational principles of American fraternal societies. There was to be a Potentate, a supreme Deputy Potentate, and a nobility which was to include "Knights of the Nile, Knights of Distinguished Service, the Order of Ethiopia, the Dukes of Nigeria and Uganda."[58] A flag of Black, Red and Green was adopted as colors—"Black for the race, Red for their Blood, and Green for their hopes." These are the same colors that Kenya adopted at independence. Ghana also named its shipping line *The Black Star*, a name adopted from Garvey.[59]

Garvey had the kind of political philosophy which could exert a strong attraction upon the black masses. It fitted with the trend I traced in Chapter Four: a tendency among the Afro-Americans to emigrate out of the South to the North, to Africa, to the West Indies, to Canada, to the West and to the East—anywhere to escape from the hell of southern racism and ghetto existence with all its debilitating effects.

> Race pride and African nationalism were inextricably woven together in the Garvey philosophy . . . and the program of the universal Negro Improvement Association centered around these two complementary objectives . . . Garvey's unparalleled success in capturing the imagination of the masses of the Negroes throughout the world can be explained only by recognizing that he put into words—and what magnificent inspiring words they were—what large numbers of his people were thinking.[60]

Toward the end of the 19th century some attempts had been made to translate African consciousness among the blacks into practical programs of service in Africa through the work of black missionaries. Black institutions of higher learning had joined in this service by training church personnel as well as by financially supporting Africans studying in their institutions. Thus, Garvey's attempt at African redemption was no Minerva sprung full-fledged from the head of Jove, for while its immediate inspiration lay in the conditions of the 1920s, its roots went back to earlier colonization and missionary efforts. Garveyism was a dramatic reformulation of this earlier consciousness in more dynamic sociopolitical terms.

One of the most important programs in the Garvey scheme for regenerating Africa was the sending of educational and technical assistance. About 1920, Garvey launched a drive for a $2 million construction project in Liberia aimed at rehabilitating that country. He told UNIA members that the purpose of the loan was to "start construction work in Liberia, where colleges, universities, industrial plants and railroad tracks will be erected, where men will be sent to make roads and where artisans and craftsmen will be sent to develop industries." A technical mission consisting of a surveyor, a pharmacist, an agriculturalist and a builder was dispatched to Liberia. By 1921, $137,458 had been raised for the construction loan and $4,440 of that amount was used for purchase of a sawmill intended for use in Liberia.[61] In this Garvey differed substantially from run-of-the-mill missionaries who were interested in spreading the word while reaping temporal benefits.

Saunders Redding has observed that:

> The Garvey movement cannot be dismissed merely as the aberration of an organized pressure group. The least that can be said of it is that it was an authentic folk movement. Its spirit of race chauvinism had the general sympathy of the overwhelming majority of the Negro people, even those who opposed its objectives, for this was the potent spirit of race consciousness and race pride that informed the "New Negro."[62]

Garveyism was both a nationalist movement and a kind of Black Zionism. Though Garvey emphasized race consciousness, to stop there would be to miss the greater import of his movement, which had definite political goals and which expressed with greater clarity the desire for nationhood. Living together with white people had proved oppressive and injurious to the blacks' manhood. This fact underlay the meaning of his whole notion of an African empire. Garvey stated: "The Negro must have a country and a nation of his own."[63] He declared that 400 million Negroes were determined to solve their problems by redeeming their Motherland Africa from the hands of alien exploiters, and to "found there a government, a nation, a force strong enough to lend protection to the members of our race scattered all over the world." Garvey was expressing a nationalist sentiment also when he said: "This is the Negro's job—that of remodeling our present civilization."[64]

Garvey gave a dress rehearsal of the nationalist aspirations of American blacks and African peoples at a time when even the thought of their ability to govern themselves was considered a utopian dream. The whites meeting at Versailles had decided, despite the fact that Africans had fought and died to save democracy, arrogantly to assume trusteeship over them. Opposed to this was Garvey, who hoped to develop black people commercially, industrially and politically. Earlier a Mr. Booth, an English missionary in Central Africa, had visions similar to those of Garvey about Africa and people of African descent. The Rev. F.B. Bridgeman wrote about Booth:

> In this quarter Ethiopianism received an impetus from a most unexpected source. It was in 1896 that Joseph Booth, an English missionary from Central Africa, appeared as a promoter of a scheme called the "African Christian Union." His prospectus was remarkable for its visionary proposal coupled with consecrated ignorance. Mr. Booth's idea was to induce all of African extraction the world over to unite in the organization of a semi-benevolent joint stock company for the commercial occupation of Africa. Commercial power he predicted would eventually mean political control also. He estimated that if one-sixth of the civilized blacks of Africa and America did their duty by giving one penny a day there would be available 3,000,000 annually. This sum invested yearly for ten years was to purchase and work with large profit, great plantations of sugar, coffee and other cotton, it was to buy and operate steamers, not only in the African lakes and rivers, but also ocean lines to England and America. Mr. Booth said: "Let the African be his own employer, develop his own country, establish his own manufacturers, run his own ships, work his own mines and conserve the wealth of his labor and his God given land for the uplifting of the Glory of God. Let the call be long and loud and clear to everyone with African blood coursing in his veins." The heading for the appeal was "Africa for the Africans."[65]

The idea of a Black "Manifest Destiny," had also been expressed by Bishop Turner, and the Rev. Morris, a black missionary on leave from Africa in 1900, sounded again the theme of Bishop Turner and Mr. Booth:

> I believe that God in His providence has been intending and preparing the American Negro to assume a large place in the evangelization of Africa. He not only has lack of formality and color prejudice. He is immune from fever . . . So, when I see the Negroes of our Southern States, people who came here naked savages, having no word of the language and no idea of God, and who today, are four million in number, redeemed, regenerated, disenthralled, I believe that God is going to put it into the hearts of these black boys and girls in the schools of the South to go with the message to South Africa and the rest of Africa and vindicate American Slavery as far as it can be vindicated by taking across the ocean the stream of life.[66]

Whether or not one agrees with the sentiments expressed by the missionary, there is one indisputable fact; people with foresight seemed to agree at least on one thing—and the course of historical development seems to have confirmed it—that Africans and peoples of African descent by losing their homeland, whether through enslavement or through imperial conquest, also lost the basis of their freedom and respect. By planning to create a great black state in an industrialized Africa, Garvey was speaking not in vague, indefinite terms, but in the concrete and definite political concepts of black nationalism.

Garvey had originally hoped to come to the United States as an admirer of Booker T. Washington, but Washington had died before his arrival. The transition by which Garvey became a propagator of black nationalism is one of the most important examples of the development of human thought. Garveyism, freed from its circus aspects and taken as an ideology of black man's liberation in the light of the conditions prevailing at the time, is the most significant statement of the hopes of black people. We know of the contemptuous remarks which were made about Garvey and of the notion of Pan-Africanism. The ideology of Europeans conceived of the blacks as childlike and the League of Nations trusteeship system was an affirmation of this belief. But Garvey demanded full independence.

The doctrine of nationalism as propounded by Garvey, particularly if taken in its entirety, left ample room for the most diverse and corrupt manipulations. In the name of black nationalism charlatans could mislead poor people and inveigle from them their meager resources. But nationalism as an alternative view to that of the dominant hegemonic class can also be used as a tool to break through the monopoly of consciousness which in any period belongs to the most powerful group.

What do blacks themselves think of their problems and the attitudes of the world towards them? Could we dismiss Garvey's venture as only escapist theatricals? These are very important questions and there is no single answer to them. I have merely suggested that for a long time there had been a growing awareness among the darker races of the unity of their common problems and the common solutions to them, and that this awareness was inspired and stimulated by the flagrantly specious assumptions and insults of Europeans. Garvey spoke to this awakened sensibility, this need for unity:

> We have reached the time when every minute, every second must count for something done, something achieved in the cause of Africa. We need the freedom of Africa now. At this moment . . . it falls to our lot to tear off the shackles that bind Mother Africa. Can you do it? You did it in the Revolutionary War. You did it in the Civil War. You did it in

Mesopotamia. You can do it marching up the battle heights of Africa. Climb ye the heights of liberty and cease not in well doing until you have planted the banner of the Red, the Black and the Green upon the hilltops of Africa.[67]

Perhaps all the verbal belligerency was only a gesture. The resolution condemning the League of Nations and stating flatly that its deliberations, insofar as they affected the division of Africa, were null and void, was also perhaps a gesture. Neither the American blacks nor the Africans had the machinery with which to secure a foot of African soil. To most white people Garvey seemed to be a figure in vaudeville or in the poetic words of the *New York World,* "the eternal child playing 'let's pretend.' "[68] But for Africans and Afro-Americans, he expressed their feelings and articulated their dreams. Essien-Udom said that the more than two million Africans who belonged to the Garvey Movement genuinely believed that Garvey would come to expel the Europeans, especially in such places as the Union of South Africa.[69] This explains why every nation ruling in Africa took notice of Garveyism. It probably would have been easier for the proverbial camel to go through the eye of the needle than for a professed Garveyite to have entered Africa at this time. Indeed, it was difficult for any American black to visit his Motherland! Garvey understood this:

For the cult of race is a real thing. And those who are holding the land by conquest, who squeeze the orange and hand the Native the rind, may legitimately feel a little nervous when across the ocean, in the richest country in the world, a stock blackman, dressed in robes the colors of which symbolize race, blood and hope, speaks to an illimitable multitude of black men saying: "We cannot allow a continuation of these crimes against our race." As four hundred million men, women and children, worthy of the existence given us by the Divine Creator, we are determined to solve our problems by ridding our Motherland Africa from the hands of alien exploiter, *and found a government, a nation of our own, strong enough to lend protection to the members of our race scattered all over the world* and compel the respect of the nations and the races of the earth.[70] (My emphasis)

The truth of this statement is quite obvious, and it structures our perspective of the relationship between the African and the American blacks. By and large it can be said that the one distinctive and coherent ideology which has taken root among the Africans and lower-class black movements in this century has been the various brands of the Garvey philosophy.[71] The NAACP and the Urban League have articulated their programs not in ideological terms but through institutional channels, and in the rhetoric of accommodation and love. While this may be helpful, the positive posture of these respectable organizations falls short of the expectations of the masses. Though outwardly they criticize the nationalist movements, at the subjective level they encourage and give support to these radical movements. Perry Anderson in his analysis of the history of the English working class stated that any movement of a subject class involves the dialectics of radicalism and constitutionality. "Clearly the reality in any historical situation involves a dialectic of both movements, pure positivity, the working class would be immobilized in its own fullness, incapable of launching any project of total social change. Pure negativity, it would be in permanent suicidal insurrection."[72]

Among blacks in the United States, the positive philosophy has been dominant, but now and again this position of respectability has been shaken out of its complacency by the radicalism propounded by the dispossessed. Black Nationalism is the language of this class. The intellectuals might renounce its parochial aspects, and it might embarrass the respectable leaders, but recently they have found it difficult to condemn. This has produced a group solidarity which cuts across class lines in the black community. The solidarity thus engendered then becomes an effective tool to facilitate the blacks' integration moves. Roy Ottley has stated that: "Concretely the [Garvey] Movement set in motion what was to become the most compelling force in Negro life—race and color consciousness which is today that ephemeral thing that inspires 'race loyalty,' the banner to which Negores rally; the chain that binds them together. It has propelled many a political and social movement and stimulated racial internationalism. It is indeed a philosophy, an ethical standard by which most things are measured and interpreted. It accounts for much constructive belligerency today."[73]

In this chapter I have sought to rescue, as one might say, a man and the movement he led from enormous scorn and condescension. Garvey's hostility toward white people might have seemed reactionary and his hatred of the mulattoes unjustified. His Back to Africa call may have been fantasy and his business ventures foolhardy; but he and his followers lived through times of acute social disturbance and disappointment. Their aspirations were valid in terms of their own experience, and if they are to be condemned, it must be understood that the society which was responsible for producing them was suffering from a pervasive sickness of which they were only a symptom. Samuel Lubell writes that Garvey's movement holds lasting significance:

In truth, it has never died out of the Negro consciousness. He was the voice of alienation which somehow managed to bring together into one package the main ideas that surge through the mind of the Negro when he feels spurned by white society. Much as the NAACP has symbolized the struggle to gain the white man's respect and acceptance, Garvey stands for the frustration of that goal.[74]

Our criteria of judgement should not be only whether or not a man's actions are justified in the light of subsequent evolution. In movements like Garveyism and the Nation of Islam we may discover insights into social evils which we have yet to cure. There is at least one compelling reason to turn our attention to the era during which Garveyism flourished. It was a time in which the peoples of African descent called with ever greater consistency for the independence of Africa as a condition for world peace. Today more than ever,

> If you want to understand the present in order to direct the future, you will have to grasp not only what great men did and how men lived, but also what all men hoped for . . . there were many things which men in the past hoped for . . . there were many things which men hoped to do. That hope is an explanation of the difference in what we now do, often because what our forefathers dreamed of has come true after they had passed away. The present was in the past as a hope, a longing and an ideal.[75]

That is, Garvey's genius lay not in the logic of his political philosophy, but in his ability to dramatize the historic mission of Africa and the African peoples. In his churches, and fraternal orders, in his cultural centers and business ventures, Garvey expressed the hopes of millions in a period of great trials for the black man. Thomas Hodgkin, in his *Nationalism in Colonial Africa*, notes that "the impact of Garveyism can be trced in British and French West Africa as well as in South Africa, particularly during the period of unrest and revolt immediately following the First World War"; referring to the growth of African independent churches, he writes:

> Probably the most important single outside stimulus was the American-born Garvey movement, in which the strands of Ethiopianism and Pan-Africanism were closely interwoven. Marcus Garvey . . . was successful in spreading the idea of Independent African churches as an instrument of African liberation.[76]

It now remains to see what the role of independent Africa as an ally in the freedom push in this country and in places like South Africa is going to be. In the next chapter we shall examine yet another facet of the freedom movement.

Notes

[1]Claude McKay, *Harlem: The Negro Metropolis*, New York, 1940, p. 168.

[2]St. Clair Drake, "Hide my Face?—On Pan-Africanism and Negritude," in *Soon, One Morning: New Writings by American Negroes, 1940-1962*, selected and edited with an introduction and biographical notes, by Herbert Hill, Alfred A. Knopf, New York, 1963, pp. 8-105.

[3]C.L.R. James, *The Black Jacobins*, Vintage Books, New York, 1963, p. 397.

[4]*Journal of Negro History*, Vol. 25, No. 40, 1940, pp. 590-92.

[5]Maxim Gorky, *Culture and the People*, International Publishers, New York, 1939, p. 7.

[6]Karl Marx, *The German Ideology*, International Publishers, New York, 1960, p. 14.

[7]*Negro Digest*, p. 57, April, 1963.

[8]*Crisis*, Vol. 15, No. 6, April 1918, p. 269.

[9]*The Messenger*, January 1918, Quoted in Jack D. Foner, (1974). *Blacks and the Military in American History: A New Perspective*, Praeger Publishers, New York, p. 110.

[10]W.F. Elkins, "Marcus Garvey, The Negro World, and the British Western Indies: 1919-1920." *Science and Society*, Vol. XXXVI, No. I, Spring 1972, p. 63.

[11]Richard Wright, *American Hunger*, Harper and Row, 1944, p. 28.

[12]George Padmore, *Pan-Africanism or Communism*, Doubleday, New York, 1972, p. 283.

[13]Mannheim, *Ideology and Utopia*, p. 195.

[14]Willard B. Satewood, Jr., "Black Americans and the Quest for Empire, 1898-1903," *The Journal of Southern History*, Vol. XXXVIII, No. 4, November 1972 p. 37.

[15]Saunders Redding, *They Came in Chains*, J.B. Lippincott, Philadelphia, 1950, p. 259.

[16]Quoted in Everett Hughes, "Race Relations and Sociological Imagination," *Race*, Vol. 5, No. 1, January 1964, p. 6.

[17]Gunnar Myrdal, *The American Dilemma*, McGraw Hill, New York, 1964, p. 724.

[18]*Ibid.*

[19]The denunciations of the Student Non-Violent Coordinating Committee (SNCC) and the Congress of Racial Equality (CORE) because of their advocacy of Black Power is an example of this. Financial support was withdrawn from CORE and SNCC because they did not seek to maintain white good will, but strove to develop black support.

[20]Lerone Bennett, Jr., "The Negro Establishment," *Negro Digest*, April 1964, p. 80.

[21]Vincent Harding, *No Other American Revolution* The University of California Press, Los Angeles, 1980, p. 88.

[22]Booker T. Washington, "The Atlanta Exposition Address, September 1895," from *Up From Slavery*, Page and Company, New York, 1901, pp. 219-225.

[23]W.E.B. DuBois, "The Talented Tenth" in Booker T. Washington and others, *The Negro Problem: A Series of Articles by Representative Negroes Today*, James Pott and Company, New York, 1903, pp. 33-75.

[24]Bennett, *op. cit.*, p. 9.

[25]Vincent Harding, *op. cit.*, p. 91.

[26]Ralph Bunche, quoted by Bennett Jr., *op. cit.*, p. 90.

[27]*Ibid.*

[28]Mannheim, *Ideology and Utopia*, p. 207.

[29]Quoted in Gwyn H. Williams, "Gramsci's Concept of Egomania," *Journal of the History of Ideas*, Vol. 21, No. 4, 1960, p. 590.

[30]Quoted in Gwyn H. Williams, "Gramsci's Concept of Egomania," *Journal of the History of Ideas*, Vol. 21, No. 4, 1960, p. 590.

[31]Vincent Harding, *op. cit.*, p. 109.

[32]*The Complete Works of Shakespeare*, George Lyman Kittredge, editor, Ginn and Company, Boston, 1936, p. 11.

[33]Vincent Harding, *op. cit.*, p. 109.

[34]Joseph S. Schechtman, *Fighter and Prophet*, Thomas Yoseloff, New York, 1966, p. 21.

[35]Williams, *op. cit.*, p. 592.

[36]*Ibid.*, p. 593.

[37]Quoted in Edmund D. Cronan, *Black Moses*, University of Wisconsin Press, Madison, 1964, p. 38.

[38]Anderson, "The Origins of the Present Crisis," p. 25.

[39]Quoted in Richard B. Moore, "Africa Conscious Harlem" in *Harlem, U.S.A.*, edited by John Henrik Clarke, p. 64.

[40]Ronald R. Hopkins, "To Kill an Image: The Social Function of Imagination," *Negro Digest*, March 1966, p. 35.

[41]Quoted in Era Bell Thompson, "How the Race Problem Embarrasses America," *Negro Digest*, November 1950, p. 53.

[42]Gerth and Mills, *op. cit.*, p. 190.

[43]/Marcus Garvey Speech before Negro citizens of New York at Madison Square Garden, March 16, 1924.

[44]Quoted in Redding, *op. cit.*, p. 261.

[45]James, *op. cit.*, p 396.

[46]*Journal of Negro History*, Vol. 25, No. 40, 1940, p. 592.

[47]*Ibid.*, p. 260.

[48]*The Independent*, 3 January, 1925.

[49]Raymond Leslie Buell, *The Native Problem in Africa*, Vol. 2, Archon Books, New York, 1927, p. 965.

[50]*Ibid.*

[51]Cronan, *op. cit.*, p. 117.

[52]*Ibid.*

[53]*Ibid.*

[54]DuBois, *Dusk of Dawn*, p. 305.

[55]Drake, *op. cit.*, p. 78.

[56]This editorial article was used by Byrnes, a Congressman from South Carolina, in an appeal to then Attorney General Mitchell Palmer to start espionage proceedings against DuBois on the pretext that it was such editorializing in the negro Press which caused race riots and which according to the Congressman aimed at establishing a "Bolshevik state."

[57]Mannheim, *Ideology and Utopia*, p. 212.

[58]McKay writes that "It is interesting to observe that some of the titled personages of the dream empire came from the elite of Afro-Americans. The Duke of the Nile was Emmett S. Scott, a light mulatto, Registrar of Howard University, Former Secretary of Tuskegee Institute, close associate of Booker T. Washington and friend of some high, ranking leaders of the Republican Party. Lady Henrietta Kinton Davis was one of the finest elocutionists of the Negro group and a very sensitive interpreter of Shakespearean roles at home and abroad." Claude McKay, *Harlem: Negro Metropolis*, E.P. Dutton, New York, 1940.

[59]H. Hayward, *Negro Liberation*, International Publishers, New York, 1948, p. 200.

[60]Cronan, *op. cit.*, p. 171.

[61]For a fuller discussion see E.U. Essien-Udom, "The Relationship of Afro-Americans to African Nationalism," *op. cit.*, pp. 391-407.

[62]Redding, *op. cit.*, p. 261.

[63]Cronan, *op. cit.*, p. 18.

[64]*Ibid.*

[65]*The Christian Express*, Vol. 33, No. 397, October 1, 1903, pp. 150-152.

[66]Quoted in "Ethiopianism and African Nationalism," by Shepperson, *Phylon*, Vol. 14, No. 1, 1953, p. 15.

[67]Quoted in Mary Ovington, *Portraits of Color*, Viking, New York, 1927, p. 18.

[68]*Ibid.*

[69]Essien-Udom, "The Relationship of Afro-Americans to African Nationalism," *op. cit.*, p. 397.

[70]Ovington, *op. cit.*, pp. 29-30.

[71]For instance it is intriguing to note how many themes of Garveyism as a rejection of white-society persist in black thinking and feeling: The glorification of the color black, the emotional identification with African independence, efforts to organize black-owned and operated business, drives to "buy black,;; retreats into your-segregation, "black power" and rejection of Western civilization, all echo Garvey's ideas who exhorted blacks to "erase the white gods from your hearts" and "worship God through the eyes of Ethiopia." Quoted in Samuel Lubell, *White and Black—Test of a Nation*, Harper and Row, New York, 1964, p. 42.

[72]Anderson, "The Origins of the Present Crisis," p. 38.

[73]Roy Ottley, *New World A-Coming*, Houghton Mifflin Company, Boston, 1943, p. 81.

[74]Lubell, *op. cit.*, p. 38.

[75]Quoted in Mukwungo Okoye, *African Responses*, Arthur H. Stockwell, Ltd., Bristol, 1964, p. 145.

[76]Quoted in Drake, *op. cit.*, p. 98.

CHAPTER SIX
Pan-Africanism:
An Aspect of the American Black's Perception of Africa

We cry among the skyscrapers
As our ancestors
Cried among the palms in Africa
Because we are alone
It is night
And we are afraid.

—Langston Hughes in "The Weary Blues"

We have seen that Garveyism was mostly a proletarian movement. Garvey's epigrammatic call, Back to Africa, was more a spiritual and psychological emancipation from the pervasive racism which afflicted the black proletariat at every turn, than an actual effort to get blacks to emigrate. In contrast, the Pan-African movement represented certain black intellectuals, most of whom could be described as farsighted fighters for black emancipation. It is true that many of those who took part in the Pan-African movement were not always clearly aware of the nature of the struggles they were waging, but all of them were conscious of one fact—the worldwide domination of white supremacy. Pan-Africanism can, in the final analysis, be reduced to a challenge to that supremacy, not only in the United States, but globally. By the turn of the century the capitalist division of the world was complete. As Walter Rodney noted: "It was a division which made capitalists dominant over workers, and white people dominant over black. At that point, everywhere in the world, white people held power in all its aspects—political, economic, military and even cultural."[1]

Ideas and concepts like Back to Africa did not develop, therefore, in a philosophical and sociological void; but in the scholarly confusion that has since surrounded them, they have usually been analyzed apart from the

127

historical context which would give them meaning. Consciousness, as E.B. Thompson once suggested,[2] ties together bundles of discrete phenomena, but it is an abstract concept not subject to statistical analysis. Pan-Africanism and Garveyism were active socio-historical processes, owing much to the agencies of time and place. And Pan-African consciousness in our definition was an historical phenomenon, unifying a number of seemingly unconnected peoples and events, both in the raw material of experience and in awareness.

One cannot overemphasize the fact that the idea of Pan-Africanism entailed notions of the historical relationship between blackness and Africa. Like any other relationship this has a fluidity which evades analysis if we attempt to immobilize it in order to dissect its structure, and can be fully comprehended only as embodied in real people in real contexts. Thus DuBois, analyzing his own gradual adoption of Pan-Africanism, wrote of the life experiences of a black boy growing up in American. Born in America of American-born parents, grandparents, and great-grandparents, speaking the American tongue, reading American history and newspapers, the child is nevertheless made to think of himself as a peculiar kind of American.[3] DuBois's consciousness began to change with his growing realization that the problem was not simply an academic one or a matter of attitudes and dislikes.

> But when it becomes an economic problem, a stark matter of bread and butter, then if this young, black American is going to marry and live a life, he must calmly face the fact that however much he is an American there are interests which draw him nearer to dark people outside of America than to his white fellow citizens. And those interests are the same matters of color caste, of discrimination, of exploitation for the sake of profits, of public insults and oppression, against which the colored people of Mexico, South America, the West Indies and all of Africa, and every country in Asia, complain and have long been complaining.[4]

Pan-African consciousness emerged when some black folks, because of common experiences (inherited or shared), felt and articulated the identity of their interests—as between themselves and as against other men whose interests were different from theirs. Africans at home and abroad were victims of the European-developed system of racism, which ruthlessly exploited them as a group. Pan-Africanism was one way in which these experiences were translated into terms understandable to people who, because of their experience in diaspora, had been deprived of common traditions, value systems and institutional forms.

There is a strong temptation today, in deference to an academic god, to be preoccupied with statistical correlations and with representative samples of who shares what ideas among the different strata in society. Pan-African consciousness cannot be so determined. Pan-African consciousness arose at different times, in different places, and manifested itself in different ways. The leaders of the Pan-African movement in 1900 appealed to the monarchs and sovereigns and were ignored; between 1919 and 1927 they appealed to the goodwill of the decent-minded people of Europe and America and to the intellectuals; in 1945 they appealed to the masses of black people.

One of the virtues of dialectical and historical thinking is that it conceives as important not that which at a given moment seems durable, although it may be in actuality entering a stage of deterioration; but that which is arising and developing, even though at the time it may not appear to be durable. To understand the rather hesitant and uncertain beginnings of the movements for African emancipation one must understand that the ability to grasp the meanings of a whole historical epoch, especially, when one was a part of it, needed sophisticated educational and intellectual consciousness which was hard to come by in the circumstances. To perceive the similarity in the positions and interests of such widely-dispersed groups was to make a discovery against overwhelming obstacles. Travel was difficult, there was a lack of communication and there was, above all, white hegemonic rule which determined what the Africans and those of African descent were to know and how much they were to know. The mass media were in hostile hands, responding only with ridicule to the efforts of the blacks, while educational facilities were notable chiefly for their inadequacy.

The post–1900 Pan-African consciousness among dark people in the Western world may be viewed from two angles. On the one hand there was a consciousness of the identity of interests that dark peoples of diverse nationalities had. This was expressed in the famous DuBois prophecy, "The problem of the 20th century is the problem of the color line," which was to receive organizational expression at the Bandung Conference of non-Western nations in 1955. On the other hand, there was the consciousness of the specifically African interests of the African people and the peoples of African descent, which was focused on the notion of African regeneration and independence. But the final definition of this consciousness was in large part to be the consequence of the role of the black masses. Garvey believed in the black masses, while the intellectuals still believed and had faith in rational arguments. It has been the peculiar feature of black political development that where one would expect to find a nationally conscious middle-class leadership, with the black masses behind it, the latter has proceeded by independent agitation to set the pace for the former.

It is quite true that, initially, consciousness of Africa was confined to a relatively small section of the black intelligentsia, and that therefore it is unfair to assume that the masses of blacks ever thought in those terms. DuBois in an article in the *New Republic* of December 7, 1921, showed an awareness of this when he wrote about the Third Pan-African Congress as follows:

> Europe asked: What do these hundred, more or less, persons of near and far Negroid ancestry really represent? Is this the real Pan-Negro movement or the work of individuals or small groups enthusiastic with an idea but representing little?[5]

These questions (which of course ignored the Garvey movement) are by our time irrelevant, or have at least been answered. Pan-Africanism has grown and flourished as an ideological concept, and has finally emerged as a political force of enormous consequences for all of Africa despite many setbacks. The obvious questions now are: How did it find acceptance as a guide to action? And who among its adherents did most to make it acceptable? Of the first Pan-African Conference called by Mr. Sylvester Williams in 1900. DuBois observed:

> This meeting had no roots in Africa itself, and the movement and the idea died for a generation. Then came the first World War, and among the American Negroes at its close there was a determined agitation for the rights of Negroes throughout the world, particularly in Africa.[6]

It might help my future analysis to say something at this point about the men who spearheaded the Pan-African Conferences in particular, to discuss their values and assumptions. There is a moral or religious, as well as a material, environment which sets its stamp on the individual, even when he is least conscious of it, and which influences his perception of problems and of methods for their solution. This was never more true than in the efforts of the early Pan-Africanists. In an article already quoted, DuBois stated: "We are undoubtedly an intelligentsia—a small group of intellectuals interpreting to a certain extent, but more certainly seeking to guide the public opinion of our groups."[7] But we cannot just accept this statement; we have to examine its implications further. The peculiar value attached to whiteness had produced a social and political philosophy which determined black exclusion and regulated conditions of black admission to society. This philosophy was expressed in a proposition passed rather hurriedly at

the 1921 Brussels meeting of the Pan-African Conference. The sponsor of
the proposition was a Mr. Atlet, a white Belgian, the father of the League of
Nations. According to his proposition, "Negroes susceptible" of advancement from their present backward condition and who by their development
would help rid humanity of the weight of 200 million ignorant incompetents,
"should be encouraged," and this task was to be done through "collaboration
between races on a basis of equality as an urgent duty today."[8]

During slavery blacks were owned by white Americans; after emancipation they existed in America but not as a part of it, a situation which reached
its most extreme form in the southern states. Now that blacks sought more
than just a peripheral existence in the nation, they found that they had
always to pay with personal misery for admittance into white society.
Assimilation, integration and equality, in other words acceptance by white
society, was granted them only as long as they were clearly distinguishable
exceptions from the black masses—though they still had to share with the
masses many restricted and humiliating social conditions. DuBois observed
that "individual Negroes became exhibits of the possibilities of the Negro
race, if once it was raised above the status of slavery."[9] These exceptions
were usually mulatto, and by the perverted standards of whiteness were
black and yet presumably not Negroes—which sometimes opened the
doors to the sanctuary of whiteness. Thus if they desired this kind of
intercourse, they had to try to both be and not be black, the result of which
was to give rise to the notion of the spoiled Negro and the assumption that
education turned the black into a hybrid and despicable creature. Small
wonder, therefore, that unable to rid themselves of some of their innate
qualities like "blackness," they were made to hate themselves. This
seeming paradox had an experiential basis, for wherever and whenever non-
white people came into contact with the white man, they were accorded
recognition as equals only to the extent that they were able to imitate the
white model—an ultimately unattainable goal since it included not only
acquirable characteristics but genetic ones as well.

Many advocates of black emancipation called for assimilation: adjustment to and reception by a society which itself was not prepared to make
adjustments and compromises with any other culture; that is, a society
which could tolerate only the reflection of its own culture from other people.
The growing school of cultural pluralism may be a belated admission, in the
era of self-assertion by black people, that perhaps the earlier assimilationists'
arrogance was wrong; because cultural pluralism is nothing more than an
attempt at justifying cultural co-existence. DuBois is his *Souls of Black
Folk*, perceptively argued for the blacks' cultural identity:

The history of the American Negro is the history of this strife—the longing to attain self-conscious manhood, to merge his double-self into a better and true self. In this merging, he wishes neither of the older selves to be lost. He would not Africanize America, for America has too much to teach the world and Africa. He would not bleach his Negro-blood for it has a message for the world.[10]

I have already referred to DuBois' elitist period, when in the last century and the early part of this one he saw the problem of black emancipation as one of education. It was taken for granted that the vanguard in both camps would consist of specially educated, tolerant, cultured persons. Therefore, it seems, the particularly tolerant, educated and cultured whites could be bothered socially only with exceptionally educated blacks. As a matter of course, the demand among the educated for the abolition of racial prejudice became very quickly a rather one-sided affair, until only the blacks finally were urged to educate themselves.

It is important to understand that the Pan-African movement was born into this atmosphere, because for a long time its ideology was overlaid with an exaggerated sense of goodwill for the Westernized educated black and Africans. One can hardly overestimate the disastrous effects this had on the masses of blacks. It also explains why the masses flocked to the Garvey movement, while they remained barely affected by the Pan-African congresses. While the Pan-African intellectuals realized the importance of an independent Africa, they were not prepared to take those measures which would have led to this logical and necessary goal, since it would have disturbed the harmonious coexistence of groups. The problem for this group was how best to condition the whites to accept the genuine grievances of the blacks. In the *New Republic* article quoted above DuBois showed clearly this awareness.

This awareness on the one hand, and the demand on the other that these self-appointed leaders of worldwide Black Unity be exceptional blacks or be exceptionally qualified, created all the pathologies of the early Pan-Africanists' attempts. DuBois tells the story of one session in which a Haitian delegate tried to play a game of paying platitudes. " 'We are a little France,' cried the Haitian Minister. 'Yes, but France did not give freedom to Haiti—Haiti took it,' answered the Americans amid the wild applause of young Haitians, and they added that when America seized Haiti it was not France but Black America which made the only effective protest,"[11] But more than anything else, the Pan-African Conference at the end of the First World War was haunted by the specter of Garvey and his Africa for the Africans movement. DuBois complained: "It was not easy to explain at first that this Congress was a meeting for conference and acquaintanceship, for organization and study, that it did not as yet represent any completely settled and adopted policy, but that its members almost unanimously repudiated any policy of war, conquest or race hatred."[12] In their appeals (with the exceptions of a few), the Pan-Africanists recognized and gave deference to the sharp differences between themselves and others (the imperialists). In fact, they asked that such differences be also legalized by the various colonial governments. The first Pan-Africanist appeal to the Mandates Commission was specific on this issue. And since this sycophancy constituted the true ticket of admission into the cultured European society, what else could the future generations of blacks do but develop a suspicious hatred for the educated black leaders?

In the early decades of contact between blacks and whites, when the educated blacks were few, the ideology of assimilation worked well for both groups. The whites could, through philanthropy, promote the gifted black, who could enter Harvard and Cambridge and be used as an example of what the black masses should be like. Hence DuBois and others like him, for example the Senegalese deputy, Blaise Diagne, had established many close connections with white people of influence, and sometimes of power. These connections enabled them to get funds and to organize meetings, not as a right but as a privilege. The relationship with famous and influential people became a mark of prestige on the part of the black leaders and a condition of liberal involvement in black affairs. Prominent white liberals used these relationships for non-personal, non-ideological or even non-political purposes. It is not surprising that so much of the controversy between Garvey and DuBois was to involve the role of white liberal friends of the blacks. Garveyism was a challenge to the very nature of the educated leadership and this controversy has not yet ceased. Any real alliances between educated leaders and the masses of the blacks are opposed by their very nature to token integration: they are in fact revolutionary because it would be impossible to accommodate the black masses without effecting radical structural changes. Of the early Pan-African movement Broderick wrote:

> The Pan-African movement that emerged in Paris was a curious international revival of the Niagara Movement, a handful of self-appointed spokesmen challenged a staggering problem by passing resolutions. Even the principal techniques were similar, periodic conferences to rectify the platform, refresh personal contacts and exchange enthusiasm and information and the manifestoes designed to rally colored support and convert white opinion. In the end the congresses accomplished, if anything, less than Niagara.[13]

Pan-Africanism evolved as DuBois' ideas evolved. It reached a point after 1940 where it merged with the best in Garvey's teachings, and it was this complementary union of the two strains which produced the dynamism of Pan-Africanism. If my treatment of the early efforts of Pan-Africanism seem extremely harsh and unfair, I may point out that in my opinion the history of ideas requires constant reinterpretation. What ideas mean changes with place, time and circumstances, and what they meant also changes with new socio-historical perspectives. Pan-Africanism is a living activity and not a fossilized doctrine. It is and was men of Africa and of African descent finding their place in a world which defined them negatively and excluded them from the community of nations. Pan-Africanism was born and grew in circumstances where the black and the African had no status and no country they could call their own. The only black-ruled countries were Ethiopia, Liberia and Haiti, and these were stunted, underdeveloped and provided a confirmation for those who believed Africans incapable of self-government. In the rest of the world blacks were either social rejects, as in the case of the Afro-Americans in the United States, or British, French or Portuguese colonial subjects. DuBois quotes Sir Harry Johnson:

> This is the *weakness* of all the otherwise grand efforts of the coloured people in the United States to pass on their own elevation and education and political significance to the Coloured Peoples of Africa. They know *little about real Africa*.[14] (Emphasis in original.)

It was a new historical situation which Africans faced. Their cultural and technological development did not provide the necessary experience to face the New World. They had to create for themselves in the exigencies of the moment a theory and an ideology which would enable them to challenge white hegemony. It took the eminent genius of a W.E.B. DuBois to chart the tortuous course of Pan-Africanism. Its weakness appears to have been less the result of its own assumptions than of the time in which the whole idea was born. A sociological understanding of the various manifestations of an idea in periods so different from our own demands a patient sifting through masses of controversial material where fact and legend have lain closely comingled for decades. It requires separating the probable from the impossible, the truth from fancy.

By contemporary standards the first four Pan-African Congresses were small not only in numbers, but also in influence. The constituent members were mainly American blacks and West Indians, with a few Africans who happened to be studying abroad. These conferences produced a whisper rather than an echo among the black masses. Yet from our perspective, which is structured by the later etiology of these ideas, their achievements were considerable. By the time its chief instigator had died, the movement for Pan-Africanism had returned to Africa and had become a profound ideology for continental unity. Initially it had brought together from several countries people of African descent and had attempted to create for the first time a lasting alliance between these peoples regardless of geographic boundaries. The simplest, surest and possibly the only criterion of the significance of an idea is its lasting influence; as the time recedes in which it was first propounded, does it leave behind a residue of truth and beauty?

The present attempts at African unity owe much to the historical experience of those peoples of Africa and African descent who, because of their common misfortunes, conceived of their problems as one. That the birth of Pan-Africanism took place 20 years after the collective dismemberment of Africa by Europe, and 25 years after the political expulsion of the black from the democratic process in America, is important. It is further important that this movement conceived the emancipation of Africa from white rule as a prerequisite to the emancipation of the black in America and wherever foreign rule was perpetrated on the African. There was also an awareness that white rule wherever it was perpetrated on the African led to the inequitable distribution of wealth. For instance, the London Conference of the Second Pan-African Congress stated in its Manifesto:

> If we are coming to recognize that the great modern problem is to correct maladjustment in the distribution of wealth, it must be remembered that the basic maladjustment is in the outrageously unjust distribution of world income between the dominant and suppressed peoples; in the rape of land and raw materials; the monopoly of technique and cultures. And in this crime white labor is *in particeps criminis* with white capital. Unconsciously and consciously, carelessly, and deliberately the vast power of the white labor role in modern democracies has been cajoled and flattered into imperialistic schemes to enslave and debauch black, brown and yellow labor, until with fatal retribution, they are themselves today bound and gagged and rendered impotent by the resulting monopoly of the world's cruel and irresponsible few.[15]

The late Dean Inge once cynically observed that ideas passed through three phases: What they proposed was first denounced as impossible; then it was denounced as immoral, and then people explained that they had said just the same things themselves. The Pan-African Congress was denounced by the *Chicago Tribune* of December 30, 1918, as an Ethiopian Utopia, one that "had less than a Chinaman's chance of getting anywhere in the Peace Conference." The Tribune allowed, however, that "it is nevertheless interesting. As 'self-determination' is one of the words to conjure with in Paris nowadays, the Negro leaders are seeking to have it applied, if possible, in a measure to their race in Africa."

Although Pan-Africanism primarily desired a free and independent Africa, it also developed another strand. It looked to "yellow Asia and the Islands of the Seas" for allies. In 1915, in his article "The African Roots of War," DuBois asked:

> Whence comes this New wealth and on what does its accumulation depend? It comes primarily from the darker nations of the world—Asia and Africa, South and Central America, the West Indies and the Islands of the South Seas . . . Chinese, East Indians, Negroes and South American Indians are by common consent for government by white folk and economic subjugation to them. To the furtherance of this highly profitable economic dictum has been brought every available source of science and religion. Thus arising the astonishing doctrine of the natural inferiority of most men to the few . . .[16]

Pan-Africanism, insofar as it conceived of black unity for the African and peoples of African descent, embraced a notion of what Hannah Arendt calls "an enlarged tribal consciousness."[17] All peoples of similar folk origins, independent of history and no matter where they happened to live, were felt to be responsible for one another's fortunes. The interest of India, after 1947, in the treatment of peoples of Indian origin in South Africa was an extension of this consciousness, just as the world Jewish communities' interest in the State of Israel is another example and the airlift of whites in the Congo in 1964, in which Britain, the United States and Belgium collaborated, was a cynical projection of this same consciousness.

Pan-Africanism, like Garveyism, starting with a much closer affinity to race concepts, enthusiastically absorbed the tradition of race thinking, in particular its social definitions. The race consciousness in Pan-Africanism was ideological in its basis because of the authentic experience of living under a white racist system. The intellectual sideline of Pan-Africanism was the romantic glorification of the past. In this phase it held that men of African descent born and raised in another country, without any knowledge of African customs or ancestral tribal connections, would be born African, thanks to color identification. One may call this chauvinistic and impractical;

but like nationalism it points to something which is supposed to have existed in the past, and merely tries to elevate it to a realm beyond human control.

Writing of colonial tribal minorities, Nadine Gordimer observed:

> You can assure yourself of glory in the future, in a heaven, but if that seems nebulous for you—and the Africans are sick of waiting for things—you can assure yourself of glory in the past. It will have exactly the same sort of effect on you in the present. You will fill yourself in spite of everything, worthy of either your future or your past.[18]

The proponents of Pan-Africanism found themselves hemmed in by enemies. The enemy in every case was absurdly jealous of his prestige and was puffed up with a mystique which exaggerated his sense of white glory and frustrated the ambitions of those who lived under his domain. This enemy had fashioned an ideology which, in the words of Hannah Arendt,

> Can be easily recognized by a tremendous arrogance, inherent in its self-concentration, which dares measure a people, its past and present by the yardstick of exalted inner qualities . . .[19]

Pan-Africanism was initially an expression of pariah status by educated blacks. They could, in the New World, show no country, no state and no historic achievement, except their achievements in Western institutions of learning. The hallmark of their origin was to be reasonable. The first Pan-Africanists desired emancipation, but only after the Native could shoulder responsibility. They accepted Western idealism, and only regretted failure to live up to these ideals. In contrast to Garveyism, with its demand for the expulsion of imperial interests in Africa, the early Pan-Africanists pleaded, sent deputations and did not offend. Fanon spoke scornfully of this tendency:

> The colonialist bourgeoisie, in its narcissistic dialogue, expounded by the members of its universities, had in fact deeply implanted in the minds of the colonized intellectual that the essential qualities remain eternal in spite of all the blunders men may make: the qualities of the West of course. The native intellectual accepted the cogency of these ideas, and deep down in his brain you could always find a vigilant sentinel ready to defend the Greco-Latin pedestal.[20]

This made them hope and look to the future when the natives would be like themselves and when the whites would eventually unshoulder the white man's burden. The *Chicago Tribune* explained:

> Dr. DuBois sets forth that while the principles of self-determination cannot be applied to uncivilized peoples, yet the educated blacks should have some voice in the disposition of the German colonies. He maintains that in settling what is to be done with the German colonies, the Peace Conference might consider the wishes of intelligent Negroes in the colonies themselves and the Negroes of the United States and of South America and the West Indies, the Negro Governments of Abyssinia, Liberia and Haiti, the educated Negroes in French West Africa and Equatorial Africa, and in British Uganda, Nigeria, Basutoland and Bechuanaland and in the Union of South Africa.[21]

The social character of the black intellectuals and their political physiognomy were determined by their origin and their structural place in white society. Thus the historical aspects of Pan-Africanism (1900-1945) reveal a fascinating reciprocal relationship between ideas, men and events. Peter Berger and Stanley Pullberg, writing about the social phenomenon called reification, distinguish between three levels of consciousness:

> First there is direct and pre-reflective presence to the world. Secondly, founded on the latter, there is reflective awareness of the world and ones presence in it. Thirdly, out of this second level of consciousness, there may in turn arise various theoretical formulations of the situation. We may then distinguish between the pre-reflective, the reflective and the theoretical level of consciousness. Reification may occur on the last two levels. It is important, however, that the foundations of theoretical reification lie in the pre-theoretical reification of the world and oneself.[22]

Social situations provide occasions in which certain expressions are alienated from the expressive intentions of their performer and are changed into reifications. For instance, the black in America has put forth a number of programs for the alleviation of his oppression and that of his fellow Africans, programs which have then been labeled utopian or racist by the white community. With such designation the program is alienated from the active process of history. It becomes a utopian or racist dream. The movement is thus fixed in an inert objectivity available to all, with a significance conceived as belonging to it intrinsically rather than as expressive of something else. The aspirations of the blacks as expressed in such movements as Garveyism and Pan-Africanism have been thus distorted from the historical time and experience of their human sources. "Societies have histories in the cause of which specific identities emerge; these histories are, however, made by men with specific identities."[23]

THE GROWTH AND DEVELOPMENT OF PAN-AFRICANISM

I have said that Pan-Africanism is a living idea which as it has grown has shed its utopian assumptions. It is, moreover, a living idea with a long history. It arose in diaspora where groups of Africans from many parts of the continent were brought together, and where black men and women had acquired the language of the enslavers and could thus articulate and organize for freedom.

I cannot go here into a detailed analysis of the historical threads which led to the development of the concept of Pan-Africanism. Nevertheless, it is at least worth mentioning the two strands of intellectual development in the 18th and 19th centuries which were the immediate antecedents of its development.

Among the forerunners and creators of Pan-Africanist thought was Ottobah Cugoano, who in 1787 published in London his *Thoughts and Sentiments on the Evil and Wicked Traffic of Slavery and Commerce of the Human Species*. Cugoana not only demanded freedom for slaves, but also predicted universal calamity for the criminal nations that profited from enslavement. Across the ocean in the US in 1829, David Walker published a pamphlet called *Walker's Appeal . . . to the Colored Citizens of the World But in Particular and Very Expressly to those of the United States of America*. Walker's *Appeal* was the first Pan-African-oriented call to struggle against slavery and racism. Predicting divine assistance in the struggle, Walker urged the children of Africa in the US to commit themselves to active struggle for freedom.

Martin Robinson Delany has been described as the most important proto-Pan-Africanist and is credited with the formulation of the slogan Africa for the African. He dedicated his life to black self-regeneration and the redemption of Africa. Another figure in the pantheon of Pan-Africanism is Edward Wilmot Blyden who Hollis Lynch describes as "the most articulate and brilliant 'vindicator' of black interests" in the 19th century. His aim was to create among black people pride, confidence and cultural identity. Lynch calls Blyden "the most important historical progenitor of Pan-Africanism."[24]

It was characteristic of the proto-Pan-Africanists that they placed their own struggle in diaspora in the larger context of the struggles by African peoples against colonialism and imperialism. That is, the idea of Pan-Africanism arose as a manifestation of fraternal solidarity among Africans and peoples of African descent who had come under the yoke of European hegemony.

At the turn of the century, Europe was at the pinnacle of its power, and European liberals and abolitionists saw black peoples everywhere as objects of philanthropy rather than agents in their own struggles. Typifying this objectification was the World Races congress held in London by leading anthropologists and sociologists to discuss American race problems. It was in response to this objectification that Pan-Africanism was born. Among the organizers of the first Pan-African Congress held in London in 1900 were Bishop Walters, Sylvester Williams from Trinidad, George James Christian from Dominica, and Dr. W.E.B. DuBois. At the races conference, George James Christian had led a discussion on the subject: "Organized Plunder vs. Human Progress Has Made our Race a Battlefield." In his talk, Christian pointed out that in the past Africans had been kidnapped from their land, and he also referred to the events in South Africa and Rhodesia where slavery was being revived in the form of forced labor.

It was in 1905 that the African Aid Association formed in 1861 was merged into a new Pan-African Association. The new association defined its charter as follows:

1. To secure to Africans throughout the world true civil and political rights.

2. To meliorate the conditions of our brothers on the continent of Africa, America and other parts of the world.

3. To promote efforts to secure effective legislation and encourage our people in educational, industrial and commercial enterprise.

4. To foster the production of writing and statistics relating to our people everywhere.

5. To raise funds for forwarding these purposes.

The conference unanimously adopted an "Address to the Nations of the World," to be sent to the heads of those states in which people of African descent were living. Signed by Walters, Williams, DuBois, and the Rev. Henry B. Brown, this document contained the lapidary phrase, "The problem of the 20th century is the problem of the color-line," which DuBois was to use three years later in his book, *The Souls of Black Folk.*

"Let not the cloak of Christian missionary enterprise," the address declared, "be allowed in the future, as so often in the past, to hide the ruthless economic exploitation and political downfall of less developed nations, whose chief fault has been reliance on the plighted troth of the Christian Church." Demanding an end to color and race prejudice, the address called on Britain in particular to give, "as soon as practicable, the rights of responsible government to the black colonies of Africa and the West Indies."[25]

A petition was sent to Queen Victoria on the situation of black people in South Africa and Rhodesia, which drew attention to the forced labor, the indentured system whereby black men, women and children were placed in legalized bondage to white settlers, through the pass system and various kinds of segregation.

The year 1919 was a milestone in the history and tragedy of Africans. In remembrance of the infamous anniversary of the coming of the first African to the Virginia colony, W.E.B. DuBois wrote in *The Crisis*:

> In sackcloth and ashes . . . we commemorate this [year], lest we forget; lest a single drop of blood, a single moan of pain, a single bead of sweat, in all these three, long, endless centuries should drop into oblivion.
>
> Why must we remember? Is this but a counsel of Vengeance and Hate? God forbid! We must remember because if once the world forgets evil, evil is reborn; because if the suffering of the American Negro is once forgotten, then there is no [guarantee], down to the last pulse of time that Devils will not again enslave and murder and oppress the weak and unfortunate.[26]

It was in 1919 that the second Pan-African Congress was held. As in 1884-5, European statesmen were meeting at the Peace Conference of Versailles to decide on the fate of the German colonies. With the benefit of hindsight it is quite obvious that both Garvey and DuBois had finally understood what Marxists had been saying since the end of the 19th century, that "the specific political features of imperialism are reaction everywhere and increased national oppression." The US foreign policy of expansion and conquest developed in parallel with a reactionary attack of black rights. Garveyism and Pan-Africanism intuitively understood this connection. DuBois' article "The African Roots of War" anticipated much of Lenin's theory of imperialism. In other words to understand the growth and development of the social phenomena one must understand the nature of these unusual historical developments—in particular the contradictions which they produced.

It was on the enslaved and colonized people, without means of defense, that the rising capitalist mode of production and its offspring, imperialism, shifted its contradictions and practiced its fascist arts. In his memorable article, "The African Roots of War," DuBois made the following observation:

> The Colored Peoples will not always submit passively to foreign domination. To some this is a lightly tossed truism. When a people deserve liberty, they fight for it and get it . . . Colored people are familiar with this complacent judgement. They endure the contemptuous treatment meted out by whites to those not 'strong' enough to be free. These nations and races composing as they do a vast majority of humanity, are going to endure this treatment just as long as they must and not a moment longer.[27]

As a result of the destructive horrors of the war,[28] sentiments began to be expressed regarding the ethical imperatives of self-government for the colonial world. The victorious powers were faced with the problem of what to do with the former German colonies. They could not assume direct control over them as they had done at the Berlin Conference in 1884, so the next best alternative was the Mandate System. American black and African soldiers had fought on the side of the allies in a war cloaked as a fight against super-racism. Thus, momentarily, there was an uneasy unity of the most dissimilar elements, and groups who had arrayed themselves against the notion of white supremacy, each for its own reasons. These social forces defeated German racism, only to create further governance of the black world. This extraordinary combination of forces had grown up out of the whole previous unevenness of Western imperialistic development with its postponed and unsolved problems.

It was under these circumstances that the Second Pan-African Congress was held. The idea of one Africa uniting the thoughts and ideals of all peoples of African descent was a serious challenge to white imperial interests. The Pan-African Congresses after initial enthusiasm experienced much hostility and, in time, many left with only the enthusiasm of DuBois, which managed to sustain the movement until 1927, when it sank for a generation into the doldrums. Between 1927 and 1945, when the Fifth Pan-African Congress was held, the world had undergone radical changes. In the 1930s Mussolini's Italy had attacked Ethiopia while the Western world looked on. Apart from economic motives and the necessity for fascism to find a way out of the economic crisis, racial aspects loomed large. The Italian attack on Ethiopia was a further humiliation of the black world, as Padmore stated: "It is well known that the Ethiopians and the Japanese are the only two Colored Nations which have ever defeated white powers at arms."

> This has not been forgotten by the Italians, and, for that matter, by the white race. Not without reason the Rome correspondent of the London Times, in a dispatch, writes, "Mussolini is not only defending the rights of Italy, but he is upholding the prestige of the White race in Africa;" while Vernon Bartlett, the diplomatic editor of England's great liberal paper, News Chronicle, shouts that "Great Britain cannot afford to jeopardize her friendship with Italy simply in order to defend Ethiopia on the basis of abstract justice . . . If a small nation like Holland is threatened then that is different. Ethiopia is not a civilized nation."[29]

We shall see in our next chapter what Italy's attack on Ethiopia meant for the blacks of the United States. But we emphasize that because Ethiopia was a black country, the Western world was willing to let it serve as a pacifier to Italy's fascist ambition, just as Britain, before World War I, had tried to pacify Germany's imperial aims with Portuguese colonies.

DuBois' vision of Pan-Africanism and Garvey's vision of a free and independent Africa were both vividly prophetic of the world created by World War II. The post-World War II independence movement in Africa and Asia took place in a world charged with the atmosphere of black nationalism. The old guard had been replaced by a new and dynamic leadership which had been emancipated from the illusion of the white man's good will. The call of Africa for the Africans, which was anomalous in the world of the 1920s, was an acceptable slogan in the late 1940s and early 1950s. The prophetic words of DuBois about the problems of the color-line received their cogency in the mid-1950s with the meeting of the Afro-Asian Bandung Conference.

Today, and as a consequence of colonialism, the world recognizes the relationship between color and power on the one hand, and color and poverty on the other hand. The power we are speaking of is political, economic and social, and the poverty is economic, cultural and mental. Geographically, it is Europe and North America versus Africa, Asia and Latin America. The sociological, political and economic realities of this situation transcend cultural pluralism:

> For us, colonialism is not a theoretical evil, for its effects are seen everywhere in our countries. The development, physical and mental, of our people has been stunted by colonialism and colonialism is the off-

spring of capitalism. Therefore, for us socialism is an essential escape
from poverty of the Colonial heritage.[30]

The American blacks who initiated the idea of Pan-Africanism did so
because the cause of Africans and of peoples of African descent had been
neglected as unworthy of consideration in world politics. From 1900 on,
and more so from 1919 to 1925, they made African independence a part of
the political consciousness of the world, a consciousness which has grown
with time. Today we can define the motivation for this black preoccupation
with Africa. There are two important reasons. First, the American blacks
were Western educated and Western education confined the black people
to a small segment of social territory. Before they could see themselves as a
free people like all other groups who had made America their home, they
had to clear their minds of the stigma that everything African was inherently
inferior and unsavory, which *ipso facto* presupposed that their descent from
Africa carried its own degradation. Whether or not they were conscious of
this implication, a debased picture of Africa was their own debasement.
Therefore, for some, the road to black national identity and psychic peace
lay in the regeneration of Africa. Secondly, American blacks were
interested in Pan-Africanism because some of them were looking for an ally
from another part of the black world—and what better ally than the Africans
who were related to them by ancestry? The international importance of the
kith and kin notion is of great sociological significance and it has up to now
determined the applicability of the abstract notions of justice and peace.
The association of the American black with other rising colored peoples
might help to impress white America with the urgency of racial progress. It
is true that in the 1920s DuBois was like a voice crying in the wilderness
because the masses of the blacks were unaware of his programs and can be
said to have lacked a Pan-African consciousness.

The study of the black problem in the United States according to Carter
Woodson often failed to take into consideration the broader aspects of the
people of color in the world. But, as evidenced by the Garvey Movement
and DuBois' Pan-Africanism and various other nationalist movements, the
relationships were so close that the blacks themselves did not miss the
connections. "The Negro in our history had become the Negro in world
history."

This was due mainly as perceptive American Negroes know, to the fact
that the colored people of Asia, Africa and the islands of the seas
totalled two-thirds of the people of the world. These people could think
rarely about the United States without considering its 19 million darker

people. They could see that mainly on account of their color these black and brown people like themselves were denied a fair share of the nations' substance and opportunity.[31]

This fact, much more than the physical residence of the blacks in America, stood out and determined the internationalism of Afro-Americans.

Our analysis has attempted to overcome a vicious political and sociological analysis which ignored or considered peripheral the black's relationship to Africa. Pan-Africanism as an idea links the black's intellectual and emotional interest to Africa bindingly. No intellectual ever works in a social vacuum. His ideas are an embodiment of the murmurings in his social milieu. That is why I have tried to give some kind of a total picture where academic sociologists would have compartmentalized. It became imperative that I consider the black's structural position, for only in that way could I give an integrated picture of the blacks' relation to Africa past and present.

In summary, Pan-Africanism aimed at what I would call spiritual integration of the black people. The early expressions at least show that such an ideological integration was not an abstraction but one means of improving the condition of black people everywhere. The spirit of Pan-Africanism would free the African and bolster the Afro-American's efforts toward emancipation. Even at the present time some Afro-Americans and Africans are agreed that if in any part of the world a black is still subject to white domination through discrimination and prejudice, their own dignity and self respect cannot be viable and effective.

Unlike other pan-movements, Pan-Africanism does not aim at external conquest and suppression of other peoples. In this sense it is essentially progressive and humane in its objective. Though at its inception it was a reaction to global imperialistic conquest of the black and brown races by the whites, Pan-Africanism is not anti-other groups, but it is extremely sensitive to color-consciousness. It is important to recognize what Colin Legum calls "the unique historical position of the black peoples as a universal bottom-dog" which "led to a revolt against passive submission to this situation." Legum goes on to discuss the intellectualization of the emotions associated with blackness and the utilization of Pan-Africanism as a tool in the struggle for atuonomy. "But," he points out "though black skins were made into a shield for the battle, Pan-Africanism became a *race-conscious* movement, not a *racialist* one."[32] As a consequence there was no problem in cooperating with yellow Asia and the islands of the seas for instance. Since World War I the advocates of Pan-Africanism have met at periodic conferences, and efforts have been made to spread the idea of Pan-

African personality whose values were to upgrade blackness and reevaluate its importance. The digging up of African history was part of this effort.

Why, the white people have asked, did blacks go into these futile exercises, when it was quite obvious that the only meaningful culture was that of the West? Paul Bohannan has written:

> American Negroes toward the end of the nineteenth century, when they were being more systematically closed out from the dominant culture than they had ever been before, turned back to Africa in search of security. There were two reactions: one was to deny any kind of association with Africa. The other was to embrace it as a father-land. Pan-Africanism started as a movement among American Negroes, they were its driving force from the late nineteenth century until the end of World War II. Since then, they have been grossly disappointed because African aims are nationalistic and their own are equalitarian.

Further Bohannan goes on to state:

> American Negroes are as American as American Swedes and their African heritage has made great contributions to American culture. The American Negro myth of Africa is one of the most dominant—and one of the most false precisely because Negroes too were subject to the dominant myths about Africa.[33]

What Bohannan is saying, besides being an exercise in contradiction, misses the importance of Africa to the American black. In the first place, to compare the blacks to Americans of Swedish origin does not help, but confuses, because Swedes have been integrated into the social system while peoples of African descent are American Negroes. When they embraced Africa as a fatherland, it was to disprove and at the same time to eradicate the notion that the black man from Africa was uncivilized and therefore fit for all types of degradation. Why should blacks have these illusions about Africa? In Europe the national minorities fought for independence from the larger society, but in the United States the national minorities that came to this country fought for integration within the larger society. The immigrants, more or less succeeded, but the case of the blacks proved a stubborn exception. Surely it is not the blacks' doing. Here is a complex pattern that cannot be solved by abstract criteria as to what constitutes a nation. It is the black's special oppression, the deprivation of his political rights, the discrimination against him on the job, Jim Crowism and racial segregation that make him a problem. The fact that American blacks associated Africa with their own problems reveals both the frustration they felt at ever achieving full democratic rights in America, and the fact that their repression has international implications. Pan-Africanism at the same time rallied desperate individuals on the basis of their spiritual oneness. Hence the advertisement of Pan-Africanism and its contraposition to Western social and spiritual life. It acted as a counterweight to Western racism and the Western world's use of Christianity and the notion of "Western civilization" for exclusiveness and to justify their imperialistic aggression.

Pan-Africanism, with its emphasis on spiritual integration of the blacks is by no means a reactionary abstraction, it is an essential means for achieving Afro-American and African spiritual emancipation from the notions of whiteness. The Pan-Africanists say that the characteristic feature of awareness of peoples of African descent is their interest in their past and the close ties between the past and the present. Common historical experiences override cultural and linguistic barriers to a black community of interests, and determine a unity of black men on a spiritual level.

It now remains to look at the man who was the moving spirit behind the Pan-African Movement, and the various Congresses which he organized.

DUBOIS AND THE PAN-AFRICAN CONGRESSES

To analyze an idea like Pan-Africanism, which is a reaction to what Aimé Césaire called the influence of the colonial, semi-colonial or para-colonial situation,[34] is difficult indeed; particularly if one realizes the emotions behind the idea, and the dispersal of people of African descent. The feelings which went into the making of the ideology of Pan-Africanism arose from many sources. There were, for example, physical dispossession and slavery, social, economical and mental attitudes fostered by colonialism, loss of land, persecution, inferiority and discrimination. When an idea revolves around the life of one man, the difficulties are compounded. DuBois was, until his death, the moving spirit and the guiding light of the Pan-African movement, and an integrated history of Pan-Africanism cannot be adequately written without touching upon his activities. But the story of the life of W.E.B. DuBois is not the same as the story of Pan-Africanism. Outlining a factual historical background of an idea, though difficult, can be done with relative precision. The interaction between the personal and the historical ingredients in the history of an idea is extremely difficult to dissect. If either assumes ascendancy, there is confusion of the socio-historical analysis with the biographical. It is not my intention here to offer a great deal about DuBois. I am interested in DuBois only insofar as he makes understandable the historical development of the idea of Pan-

Africanism, in particular, his thoughts concerning its significance for the American black. I believe at the same time that ideas considered apart from the real men who developed them might stand lonely and forlorn, and might lead one to commit the mistake current in sociology; that is, to generalize without taking a proper account of individuals, the setting and the place, An enlightening study is one which attempts a proper balance between the advocates of ideas and their temporal and spatial context.

W.E.B. DuBois had an insatiable spiritual curiosity, boldness and tenacity which are nowhere more obvious than in his pursuance of the Pan-African ideal. Early in his life he wrote:

> I am glad I am living, I rejoice as a strong man to run a race, and I am strong—is it egotism, is it assurance—or is it the silent call of the world spirit that makes me feel that I am royal and that beneath my sceptre a world of kings shall bow. The hot dark blood of that black forefather born king of men is beating at my heart, and I know that I am either a genius or a fool . . . This I do know: be the truth what it may, I will seek it on the pure assumption that it is worth seeking—and heaven nor hell, God nor devil shall turn me from my purpose till I die. I will in this second quarter century of my life, enter the dark forest of the unknown world for which I have so many years served my apprenticeship—the chart and compass the world furnishes me I have little faith in—yet, I have none better—I will seek till I find—and die.[35]

He undertook this quest in conjunction with his total involvement in the struggle for equality for the black people in America. To him a great and true freedom was an integral whole which could not be split without killing its essence: half-truths are not partially true—they are all wrong—worse than complete lies. Possessing as they do some external forces of veracity, they are likely to be accepted as truths and can deceive whole nations. They must, therefore, be unmasked, debunked, and combated more ardently than obvious falsehoods. In his article, "The African Roots of War," DuBois asked:

> How can love of humanity appeal as a motive to nations whose love of luxury is built on the inhuman exploitation of human beings, and who especially in recent years have been taught to regard these human beings as inhuman? . . . If we want real peace and lasting culture . . . we must go further. We must extend the democratic ideal to the yellow, brown and black peoples.[36]

Just as with his notion of Pan-Africanism, these assumptions about peace evoked blank hopelessness and shocked reactions from his colleagues. DuBois was a man of courage and was able to see things as they are, as well as to see them as they ought to be or might be. In his autobiography, *Dusk of Dawn*, he expressed the limited objective of his initial ideas about Pan-Africanism:

> My plans had in them nothing spectacular nor revolutionary. If in decades or a century they resulted in such a world organization of black men as would oppose a united front of European aggression, that certainly would not have been beyond my dream. But on the other hand, in practical reality I knew the power and guns of Europe and America, and what I wanted to do was in the face of this power to sit down hand in hand with coloured groups and across the council table to learn of each other, our conditions, our aspirations, our chances for concerted thought and action. Out of this there might come, not race war and opposition, but broader cooperation with the white rulers of the world, and a chance for peaceful and accelerated development of the black folk. With this in mind, I started to organize and hold a Pan-African Congress in 1921, which would be better attended and more carefully organized than that in 1919.[37]

Even with this modesty, he exposed and combated every attempt to seek solace in half-truths. Although DuBois knew that the historical blight of racism had grown out of the attempt to justify slavery and imperialism, he still saw this as a result of the Western notion that mankind can only rise by walking on men. He was still prepared to pursue the emancipation of the black within the structural institutions of American society. Pan-Africanism as he saw it might be described as a perfect characterization of the epoch in which he lived:

> Since then the concept of race has so changed and presented so much contradiction that as I face Africa I ask myself: What is it between us that constituted a tie which I can feel better than I can explain? Africa is of course my fatherland. Yet neither my father nor my father's father ever saw Africa or cared over-much for it. My mother's folks were closer, and yet their direct connection in culture and race became tenuous; still my tie to Africa is strong. On this vast continent were born and lived a large portion of my direct ancestors going back a thousand years or more.

But one thing is sure and that is the fact that since the fifteenth century these ancestors of mine and their other descendants have had a common history, have suffered a common disaster and have one long memory. The actual ties of heritage between the individuals of this group, vary with the ancestors that they have in common and many others: Europeans and Semites, perhaps Mongolians, certainly Indians. But the physical bond is the least and the badge; the real essence of this kinship is its social heritage of slavery, the discrimination and insult; and this heritage binds together not simply the children of Africa but extends through yellow Asia and into the South Seas. It is this Unity which draws me to Africa.[38]

It is essential to develop a clear understanding of why and how DuBois and most blacks came to associate Africa with their own efforts. The road to Pan-Africanism might from the vantage point of today seem straight and simple. But to men and women who were part of the formulation of these ideas it must have been very difficult. Witness for instance Countee Cullen's "Heritage"—

What is Africa to me:
Copper sun or scarlet sea,
Jungle star or jungle track,
Strong bronzed men, or regal black
Women from whose loins I sprang
When the birds of Eden sang?
One three centuries removed
From the scenes his fathers loved
Spicy grove, cinnamon tree,
What is Africa to me?

The poet is grappling with an important psycho-emotional problem: his relationship to Africa, which to most blacks was not one of nostalgia but one of ambivalence. "I am not just sure when I began to feel an interest in Africa," wrote DuBois. "Some folks seem to assume that just as the Irish-Americans and Americans of Scandinavian descent look back to their parents, so in similar ways blacks should regard Africa."[39] What DuBois says and Countee Cullen sings, in fact, is that for many blacks there was until recently very little or no direct acquaintance, let alone any consciously inherited knowledge about Africa. Instead there was much recoil from and distaste for association with Africa. This prevalent attitude among blacks did not deter DuBois from pursuing his ideals and from trying to counteract the ignorance about Africa.

In May 1917, a conference of Negro organizations was called in Washington, and DuBois wrote one of the resolutions it adopted. This resolution is extremely important in the light of 1919 and other later Pan-African Conferences.

The resolution read:

> We trace the real course of this World War to the despising of the darker races by the dominant groups of men, and consequent fierce rivalry among European nations in their efforts to use darker and backward people for purposes of selfish gain regardless of the ultimate good for the oppressed. We see permanent peace only in the extension of the principle of government by the consent of the governed, not simply among the smaller nations of Europe but among the natives of Asia and Africa, the West Indies and the Negroes of the United States.[40]

In this resolution as in the assumptions of DuBois we see the connection of the black problem with the conditions of the Africans and Asians. The attitude of the American black, unlike that of the white liberals, envisaged Africa and the colored peoples of the world in its schemes. After World War I, what better program than Pan-Africicanism to give the black leaders the opportunity to interest their groups in the worldwide significance of color? In initiating these congresses, W.E.B. DuBois was well aware of the international nature of the race question, and his insights led him to play an important role in the four Pan-African Congresses.

The call for the First Pan-African Congress in 1900 was issued by Henry Sylvester Williams, a barrister from Trinidad who had made contact with African students in London. Thus was born the idea of a Pan-African Conference which "would bring into closer touch with each other the peoples of African descent throughout the world."[41] The First Pan-African Congress had only 11 delegates from the United States, 13 delegates from the West Indies, and Reverend Henry Box Brown of fugitive slave fame representing the community in Lower Canada. As chairman of the Committee on Address to the Nations of the World, DuBois submitted a discourse which observed the importance and international nature of race relations:

> The modern world needs remember that in this age, when the ends of the world are being brought so near together, the millions of blackmen in Africa, America and the islands of the sea, not to speak of the myriads elsewhere, are bound to have great influence upon the World in the future, by reason of sheer numbers and physical contact.[42]

This address was accepted by the First Pan-African Conference and sent to the sovereigns in whose realms were subjects of African descent. Further, a request was made that the "peoples of Africa should not be sacrificed to the greed of gold, their liberties taken away"; the British government was asked to award the rights of responsible government to the black colonies of Africa and the West Indies; and it was asked "that Negroes should be granted 'the right of franchise, security and property . . . ' " everywhere. The Address to the Nations of the World concluded with the following impassioned call:

> Let the Nations of the World respect the integrity of the independence of the free Negro State of Abyssinia (properly called Ethiopia), Liberia, Haiti, etc.; and let the inhabitants of these states, the independent tribes of Africa, the Negroes (peoples of African descent) of the West Indies and America, and the black subjects of all nations take courage, strive ceaselessly, and fight bravely, that they may prove to the World their incontestable right to be counted among the great brotherhood of mankind.[43]

It will be clear that whatever the motivation, conception or composition, all the Pan-African Congresses have been alike in their moderation and reasonableness. Their aim was reformist. They appealed to the moral conscience by using the idiom and philosophy of the West. The Second Pan-African Congress which convened in 1919, soon after World War I, during the period of great frustration among the Negro masses, carried its reasonableness to ridiculous proportions as seen from today. The League of Nations had talked a great deal about the rights of nations to determine themselves. The delegates to the Second Pan-African Congress used these declarations to advance the idea of the necessity for African independence. The political demands of the Second Pan-African Congress were contained in the following paragraph:

> To the World: The absolute equality of races, physical, political and social, is the founding stone of World and Human advancement. No one denies great differences of gift, capacity and attainment among individuals of all races, but the voice of science, religion and practical politics is one in denying the God-appointed existence of a super-race, of races naturally and inevitably and eternally inferior.[44]

The Second Pan-African Congress sent a committee led by DuBois to make representations to the officials of the League of Nations who were meeting in Geneva. DuBois's Committee met the Chief of the Mandates Commission, Mr. Roppard, and discussed with him the status of Africa. The following petition presented to the Mandates Commission was accepted as the League's official document:

> The Second Pan-African Congress wishes to suggest that the spirit of the World moves towards self-government as the ultimate aim of all men and nations, and that consequently the mandated areas, being peopled as they are so largely by men of Negro descent, have a right to ask that a man of Negro descent, properly fitted in character and training, be appointed as a member of the Mandates Commission as soon as a vacancy occurs.

The reasonableness of the political contents of the resolutions and petitions to the League of Nations was seasoned with a mild criticism of Belgium's colonial rule. That criticism, though giving Belgium the benefit of the doubt for future plans for reform, aroused bitter opposition in Brussels, and attempts were made to substitute a resolution full of platitudes concerning the goodwill of Belgium in its treatment of her African colonies. The Second Pan-African Congress nowhere in its lengthy resolutions spoke of the African's right to independence. In the other sections of its resolutions it proclaimed the need for international laws to protect the natives, for land to be held in trust on their behalf, for the prevention of exploitation by foreign capital, for the abolition of slavery and capital punishment, for the right of education; and finally it insisted that the Natives of Africa must have the right to participate in Government as fast as their development permits.

It is also significant that, though DuBois played an important role in the NAACP as secretary and editor of *The Crisis*, the white liberals who supported the organization did not accept the Pan-African movement and its goals. In this they were joined by some black members. DuBois explained the attitude of liberals in the NAACP thus:

> The older liberation among the white people did not (sic) envisage Africa and the Colored peoples of the world. They are interested in America and securing American citizens of all and any color their rights. They had no schemes for internationalism in race problems and to many of them it seemed quixotic to undertake anything of the sort. Then too, there were coloured members who had inherited the fierce repugnance towards anything African, which was the natural result of

the older colonization schemes where efforts at assisted and even forcible expatriation of American Negroes had always included Africa. Negroes were bitterly opposed because such schemes were at bottom an effort to make slavery in the United States more secure and to get rid of free Negroes. They resented and feared any coupling with Africa.[45]

The attitude of some blacks made DuBois realize quite early that to be a successful movement Pan-Africanism had to be more representative of the Africans themselves. Thus, for the assembling of the Third Pan-African Congress, DuBois and a number of his colleagues "went to work in 1921, to assemble a more authentic Pan-African Congress and movement. We corresponded with Negroes in all parts of the World and finally arranged for a Congress to meet in London, Brussels and Paris in August and September. Of the 113 delegates to this Congress, 41 were from Africa, 35 from the United States, 24 represented Negroes living in Europe and 7 were from the West Indies."[46]

The spirit of moderation which characterized the demands of the earlier Pan-African Congresses was still predominant, but instead of arousing sympathy from the colonial powers it evoked indifference tinged with hostility. The war had been over for about five years and the colonial powers began a long and successful counter-offensive. The harassment began. For instance, the Second Pan-African Congress would not have been held were it not for the influence of a Senegalese deputy, Blaise Diagne, who persuaded French Prime Minister Clemenceau to allow it to take place. The hostility toward the Pan-African Congresses was partly caused by fear of the Garvey movement, and partly by fear of revolutionary communism. The Brussels *Neptune* wrote on June 14, 1921:

> An announcement has been made . . . of a Pan-African Congress organized at the instigation of the National Association for the Advancement of Colored People of New York. It is interesting to note that this association is directed by personages who it is said in the United States have received remuneration from Moscow (Bolsheviks). The Association has already organized its propaganda in the lower Congo, and we must not be astonished if some day it causes grave difficulties in the Negro village of Kinshasa composed of all the ne'er-to-do-wells of the various tribes of the Colony aside from hundreds of laborers.[47]

To associate the NAACP with the Bolsheviks was nothing but a slander campaign. It is thus not surprising that DuBois himself had to get to Paris as a press correspondent, and William Monroe Trotter of the National Equal Rights League and editor of the *Boston Guardian* was denied a passport and had to disguise himself as a cook on a ship to France. The powers that be were free to harass and demoralize a cowed sullen black people as much as they wished. When M. Dantes Bellegarde of Haiti, in the Assembly of the League of Nations, condemned the bombing and massacre in May 1922 of Africans of Bondelswarts in South West Africa, an act which had been approved by Jan Christian Smuts, one of the architects of the Mandates System, M. Bellegarde was recalled by the United States, which was then in control in Haiti. The plea made by the Haitian representative has been recognized as "a courageous and impassioned appeal that even now stands as one of the models of eloquence in the Assemblies of the League."[48] This campaign of harassment was to culminate in the arrest of Garvey and his deportation.

There were two separate sessions of the Fourth Pan-African Congress which took place in 1923 in London and Lisbon. Repeating earlier resolutions, the most important political demands were still only for Africans to have a voice in their own governments. Up until the Fourth Congress the Pan-African idea was still American rather than African, but it was growing and experiencing a real demand for the examination of the African situation and a plan of treatment from the African point of view. Attempts were made to hold the Fifth Pan-African Congress in the West Indies. This never took place and it was only two years later, in 1927, that American women revived the Congress idea and a Fifth Pan-African Congress was held in New York. Thirteen countries were represented even though direct African participation lagged. There were 208 delegates from 22 American states and 10 foreign countries. Africa was represented sparsely by delegates from the Gold Coast, Sierra Leone, Liberia and Nigeria. After 1927 the impetus of the movement succumbed entirely and the Pan-African ideal survived only in DuBois' determined commitment. The failure of Garvey completed the process and the black community withdrew into the period of apathy which was to continue with few exceptions until after World War II. But, whatever else may be said, the years 1918 and 1927 were highly significant in directing and linking the American blacks' emancipation efforts with Africa.

I have attempted to outline what I consider to be the mental universe of the leadership of the early efforts at African emancipation. The second major effort by the American blacks to do something about Africa came in the 1930s with the attack on Ethiopia by Italy, to be dealt with in the next chapter.

In conclusion, we may point out that DuBois and Garvey, in different

ways, have withstood the test of time. In their advocacy of African
nationalism and independence both can be classed in the exclusive race
of those to whom their own age paid little heed, but who have proved
in the judgement of future generations to be the timeless ones. The
message which Garvey and DuBois drummed so patiently and indefatigably
into the often deaf ears of their own generation, has become accepted
nowadays. Many of the famous figures in Afro-American life have passed
from history spiritually childless. Garvey and DuBois alone have left
political schools. In the Pan-Africanism of an Africa of emerging independent states, strong traces of the two great black leaders remain. Both found
the cause of Africans and of people of African descent deemed unworthy of
consideration; in a little less than 10 years they had made them part of the
political consciousness of the world. When DuBois and Garvey began to
advocate African independence, and when they spoke about African
history and achievements, the Western world was amazed. Africa was to
the West a dark continent, its history commencing only with the advent of
the white man. DuBois and Garvey recognized that before they could see
themselves as free and independent people they had to rid their minds of the
stigma that anything African was inherently inferior and degraded. The way
to the black man's freedom and national identity in the New World lay
through Africa. Pan-Africanism was the political expression of this
awareness.

Notes

[1] Walter Rodney, *The Groundings with My Brothers*, Bogle-L'ouverture
Publications, London, 1970, p. 17.
[2] E.B. Thompson, *The Making of the English Working Class*, Vintage Books,
New York, 1966, p. 9.
[3] Dr. Blyden expressed this reality in these words: "All our traditions are
connected with a foreign race. We have no poetry or philosophy but that of our last
masters. The songs that live in our ears and are often on our lips are the songs which
we heard sung by those who shouted while we groaned and lamented. They sang of
their history, which was the history of our degradation. They recited their triumphs
which was the history of our humiliation. To our great misfortune, we learned their
prejudices and their passions, and thought we had their aspirations and their power.
Quoted in Colin Legum, *Pan-Africanism: A Short Political Guide*, Praeger, New
York, 1961.

[4]W.E.B. DuBois, "Pan Africa and the New Radical Philosophy," *The Crisis*, Vol. 40, No. 11, November 1933, p. 247.

[5]DuBois, "A Second Journey to Pan-Africa," *New Republic*, Vol. 29, No. 377, December 7, 1921, p. 42.

[6]DuBois, *The World and Africa*, International Publishers, New York, 1946, p. 8.

[7]DuBois, "A Second Journey to Pan-Africa," p. 42.

[8]*Ibid.*, p. 40.

[9]DuBois, *Black Reconstruction, op. cit.*, p. 14.

[10]DuBois, *Souls of Black Folk*, p. 17.

[11]DuBois, "A Second Journey to Pan-Africa," *op. cit.*, p. 41.

[12]*Ibid.*, p. 21.

[13]Broderick, *op. cit.*, p. 130.

[14]W.E.B. DuBois, "My Second Journey to Pan Africa," *op. cit.*, p. 42.

[15]DuBois, *Ibid.*, 1921, p. 41.

[16]W.E.B. DuBois, "The African Roots of War," *Atlantic Monthly*, Vol. 115, No. 5, 1915, p. 709.

[17]Arendt, *Origins of Totalitarianism*, p. 223.

[18]Quoted in *Race*, Vol. 5, January 1964, p. 6.

[19]Arendt, *Origins of Totalitarianism*, p. 227.

[20]Fanon, *op. cit.*, p. 37.

[21]*Chicago Tribune*, January 19, 1919.

[22]Peter Berger and Stanley Pullberg, "The Concept of Reification," *History and Theory*, Vol. 4, No. 2, 1965, p. 204.

[23]Peter L. Berger and Thomas Luckman, *The Social Construction of Reality*, Doubleday, Anchor Books, New York, 1967, p. 173.

[24]Hollis R. Lynch, *Edward Wilmot Blyden: Pan-Negro Patriot, 1832-1912*, Oxford University Press, New York, 1967, pp. 248, 250, 252.

[25]Peter Fryer, *Staying Power: The History of Black People in Britain*, Pluto Press, London, 1984. (Four years earlier, colonial secretary Joseph Chamberlain had written privately that black people in the West Indies were "totally unfit for represenatative institutions." (Quoted, *Ibid.*)

[26]Quoted Harding, *op. cit.*, 1980, p. 101.

[27]DuBois, "African Roots of War," p. 714.

[28]"During the first year of the war 70,000 black troops were raised in French West Africa. By 1918 Black Africa had furnished France 680,000 soldiers and 238,000 labourers in all. We have seen what we have never seen before, what enormously valuable material lay in the Black Continent." General Smuts, quoted by Padmore, *op. cit.*, p. 98.

[29]Padmore, "Ethiopia and World Politics," *Crisis*, Vol. 42, No. 8, 1935, p. 157.

[30]Roeslan Abdulgani, "Ideological Background of the Asian African Conference," *United Asia*, No. 7, 1955, p. 43.

[31]Woodson, *The Negro in Our History*, p. 732.

[32]Legum, *Pan-Africanism*, p. 33.

[33]Paul Bohannnan, *Africa and Africans*, The Natural History Press, New York, 1964, pp. 7-8.

[34]Aime Cesaire, "Culture and Colonization," (3 part series), *Presence Africaine*, Nos. 8, 9, 10, 1956.

[35]Quoted in Bernard Fonlon, "The Passing of a Great African," *Freedomways*, Vol. 5, No. 1, Winter 1965, p. 1965.

[36]DuBois, "The African Roots of War," p. 112.

[37]DuBois, *Dusk of Dawn*, pp. 274-75.

[38]*Ibid.*, p. 115.

[39]DuBois, in *Battle for Peace*, Masses and Mainstream, New York, 1952, p. 15.

[40]W.E.B. DuBois, *Dusk of Dawn, op. cit.*, 1940, p. 248.

[41]Walters, *op. cit.*, p. 253.

[42]*Ibid.*, p. 258.

[43]*Ibid.*, p. 259.

[44]For full treatment of this and the documents mentioned below see Legum, *Pan-Africanism*, especially Appendix I.

[45]DuBois, *Dusk of Dawn*, p. 75.

[46]Padmore, *Colonial and Coloured Unity*, p. 66.

[47]Quoted in DuBois, *The World and Africa*, p. 237.

[48]Quoted by Richard B. Moore in Clarke, *op. cit.*, p. 181.

CHAPTER SEVEN
The Significance of Ethiopia in Afro-American Consciousness

What happens to a dream deferred?
Does it dry up
Like a raisin in the sun?
Or fester like a sore . . .

—Langston Hughes

In the last two chapters we dealt with two ideas, Garveyism and Pan-Africanism. To determine the significance of these ideas was not as simple a matter as might be supposed. The black had been told that he was an American (which of course he was) and that Africa was as foreign to him as it was to white Americans. This, however, was certainly not borne out by historical events. One is therefore faced with the problem of treating doctrines which, though often dismissed as the emptiest of superstitions, have revealed an unsuspected vitality. Such ideas cannot be judged by the criterion of representativeness, although to admit this is to raise problems which are eternal. We can assure ourselves of contributing to knowledge if we remember that the study of a thought which has persisted, even if with little success, may prove today not wholly without instruction. In the second half of the 20th century the old ideas seem indeed to have acquired a new actuality. Though American blacks and Africans have been physically separated for a long time they have shown that their fortunes cannot be separated as easily. The Italian-Ethiopian War demonstrated this more clearly than any other event that ever identified Afro-American and African interests.

Before I proceed with my discussion of the Italo-Ethiopian War I would like to point out that I do not intend to give it an exhaustive treatment. I have

159

only tried to understand its significance for the further development of certain ideas which "flowered" among some black intellectuals after World War I. The Italo-Ethiopian War is considered here as a social basis for the divergence and convergence of ideas; there arose and withered with it certain tendencies and beliefs about the nature of black-white relations. In the totality of our historical experience certain events act as catalysts and bring to the foreground emotions and feelings deeply imbedded in the recesses of our consciousness. Only those ideas and emotions which in some respect mark the nodal points in the development of African consciousness are dealt with here. The existence of the Kingdom of Ethiopia in normal times could not be said to have meant much to the ordinary man in the street; but the threat to its existence posed by a white nation brought about certain definite reactions among black people everywhere.

Among the various manifestations of black African consciousness there exists an important historical dialectic which has never been understood by students, let alone treated sympathetically. So long as the interest of American blacks in Africa was considered alien and chauvinistic it was unreasonable to expect any total treatment of the mood in the period 1918 to 1940. Yet an adequate understanding of the movements current among black people during that time must confront and illuminate all the related themes which dominate this era, and which together constitute the essential matrix of any interpretation in depth.

When Ethiopia was threatened, Afro-Americans put up a most inspired and concerted agitation for African freedom and independence, and raised African consciousness to a point where it became a force in the world.

During the peace conference following World War I, the National Association for the Advancement of Colored People in a pamphlet, *Africa in the World Democracy* (1919), expressed great concern over the future of Africa. The main object of the NAACP in injecting the future of Africa into the peace conference was to place on the international agenda the just claims of blacks everywhere. The concern of the NAACP for the betterment of the conditions in Africa was evidenced in the adoption of a program which stated, among other things, that while the principle of self-determination which had been reappraised as fundamental by the Allies could not be applied wholly to semi-civilized peoples, the NAACP felt it could be partially applied. The NAACP felt that the public opinion which should have a decisive voice in deciding the fate of the German colonies should be composed of the chiefs and intelligent Africans among the twelve and a half million natives of German Africa (especially those trained in the Government and in mission schools), the twelve million civilized blacks of the United States, and educated persons of African descent in South America and the West Indies.

After 1919 the white world was, for the first time, confronted with the task of managing a strong and coherent black movement within the arena of political democracy. The situation was potentially dangerous, particularly since World War I had unleashed revolutionary communism which had succeeded in Russia, one of the backward countries in Europe. The only time an all-black movement ever mustered enough self-confidence to look dangerous came with the inspiration of Garvey's Back to Africa Universal Negro Improvement Association. Add to this the Pan-African Congresses, and the potential dangers to those who were exploiting the blacks become real indeed. After a few years the heart went out of both the Garvey Movement and the Pan-African Congress. Be this as it may, no serious historical study of Pan-Africanism and the mobilization among Afro-Americans in defense of Ethiopia can omit the contributions of Garvey. But this is what in fact has happened. Historians have blurred the salient points in the Garvey movement and have praised what we have called the compromising attitude of the Pan-African Congresses. This approach takes no account of the international appeal of Garveyism which caused great disturbance in the colonial world. There were constant scares in the 1920s (without much justification) that Africans might rally around Garvey, and every effort was made to bar his followers from travelling to Africa.

Following the failure of Garvey and the Pan-African Congresses, consciousness of Africa was bolstered by the campaign of the American Negro Labor Congress for the liberation of the colonial peoples of Africa and Asia. The International Congress Against Colonial Oppression and Imperialism held in Brussels in August 1927, was cosponsored by the American Negro Labor Congress. The significance of the Brussels Congress as a forerunner of the Asian-African conference held at Bandung in April 1955, is widely recognized, as President Sukarno of Indonesia noted: "At that Conference many distinguished delegates who are present here today met each other and found a new strength in the fight for independence."[1]

The resolutions prepared and adopted by the Brussels Congress Against Imperialism stated:

> For five hundred years the Negro peoples of the world have been the victims of the most terrible and ruthless oppression. The institution of the slave trade as a consequence of the commercial revolution and expansion of Europe was the beginning of a regime of terror and

robbery that is one of the most terrible in the history of mankind. As a result of this traffic Africa lost a hundred million of her people. Four out of every five of these were killed in the bloody business of capture and transport, the survivors being consigned to a most cruel slavery in the New World.

The resolution went on to deal specifically with the position of American blacks:

> In the United States the twelve million "Negroes" though guaranteed equal rights under the Constitution, are denied the full and equal participation in the life of that nation. This oppression is greatest in the Southern States where the spirit of chattel slavery still predominates. Segregation, disenfranchisement, legal injustice, debt and convict slavery and lynching and mob violence degrade and crush these peoples. This vicious system of suppression operates to reduce this race to an inferior servile caste, exploited and abused by all other classes of society . . . [2]

In the cause of emancipation of the black peoples of the world the Congress pledged to work for the complete liberation of African peoples, the restoration of their lands, and for several other measures including the establishment of a university at Addis Ababa in Ethiopia for the training of candidates for leadership in the unions and cultural and liberation movements of the oppressed people of Africa.

We need to emphasize here that these movements, with all their justifiable demands, could be said to have been confined to a small group of blacks who were radical in orientation and politically conscious. An attempt to judge the prevalence of an idea that is so limited in its overt manifestations, and on which there is scant data, could be idle exercise. Yet what impresses me most today is the conviction and the persistence that those who were politically conscious showed in relating the black emancipation efforts to the freedom of Africa; and this may prove, despite the paucity of evidence, not wholly without significance. At the present time, when the importance of Africa for the American black is accepted, it must be remembered that this was not always the case. The previous chapters have demonstrated, I trust, that relationships which ought to have been buried by the accretion of centuries (as happened in the case of other nationalities) have shown in our own day that they were not dead but sleeping. I have examined the forms which they have assumed and the phases through which they have passed. At time I have had to limit myself to the activities of individuals.

One of the forms in which African-consciousness expressed itself among American blacks was in the defense of Ethiopia after it was attacked by fascist Italy in the spring of 1935. The name Ethiopia has had more than one significance in the life of Afro-Americans. It had long been—as in the Bible and in Shakespeare—the broad and nearly generic term for the whole universe of dark-skinned people. Many black people felt that the day when "Ethiopia's hand shall stretch forth unto God, would be the day for liberation of all dark-skinned people everywhere who had been submerged under white mastery for so long."[3] Furthermore, for a people whom history had deliberately starved of all legend, Ethiopia linked the African (contrary to the pervasive myth that Africans were prehistoric and that their history began with European conquest) to the glory of ancient classical times. The fact that the Iliad speaks of the gods feasting among the blameless Ethiopians, and Homer elsewhere praised Memnon, King of Ethiopia, and Eurybates

> Of visage solemn, sad but subtle hue
> Short, wooly curls, o'er fleeced his bending head . . .
> Eurybates, in whose large soul alone,
> Ulysses viewed an image of his own.

gave a great deal of vicarious pride and satisfaction to the Afro-American. They were after all not prehistoric if even the Greek historian Diodorous Siculus of the first century B.C. could write that:

> The Ethiopians conceived themselves to be of greater antiquity than any other nation, and it is probable, that, born under the sun's path, its warmth may have ripened them earlier than other men. They supposed themselves to be the inventors of Worship, of festivals, of solemn assemblies, of sacrifice, and every religious practice.

Surely here was evidence that a black skin and kinky, woolly hair were not after all signs of inferiority and primitiveness, but of pride and maturity. This kind of evidence based on such ancient sources provided a sort of "believe-it-or-not" about black achievements which, far from being bounded by the cotton fields of the American South, stretched back thousands of years beyond Christ. A typical work of this kind is a pamphlet by J.A. Rogers entitled *100 Amazing Facts about the Negro*. In this pamphlet Rogers writes: "Ethiopians, that is, Negroes, gave the world the first idea of right and wrong and this laid the basis of religion and all true culture and civilization." Historically and sociologically Ethiopia has played a signifi-cant role in the black's self-conception. "The Old Testament, whose historical reliability is being validated more and more by the findings of archaeology, provides perhaps the best evidence of the role the black men played in the development of civilization."[4]

Thus to the emotions of masses of black church-goers the Ethiopia of today is the wonderful Ethiopia of the Bible. In a religious sense it is far more real to them than the West African lands from which most of their ancestors came. Even among black intellectuals, Ethiopia assumed great prominence:

> Black writing is replete with references to Ethiopia's legacy. The brilliant Pan-Africanist Edward Wilmot Blyden (1832-1912) called the Ethiopians of antiquity "the most creditable of ancient peoples" and claimed that they had achieved "the highest rank of knowledge and civilization." J.A. Rogers [who was to serve as a correspondent in Ethiopia in 1935-6], the lecturer, columnist, traveler, and chronicler of Negro achievements, asserted categorically that the Ethiopian royal family was the "most ancient lineage in the world." He maintained further that at least eighteen rulers of ancient Egypt were unmixed Negroes or Ethiopians. And W.E.B. DuBois wrote of Ethiopia as the "sunrise of human culture" and the "cradle of Egyptian civilizations."[5]

By reason of a combination of circumstances in which oversight cannot be excluded, Ethiopia was allowed to remain independent, the only spot on the African continent besides Liberia, and Haiti in the Caribbeans that could still call its political soul its own. From time to time efforts were made to remedy the lapse from the natural law, as for example, the first Battle of Adowa in 1896. But they were never crowned with the success that attended similar European efforts elsewhere in Africa. Italy in 1935 was making a final effort for an auspicious conclusion of things. All Africa would then serve as Europe's baggage as was predestined.[6]

When this historical significance was crystallized by the Italian assault on Ethiopia in the winter of 1935, a tailor-made issue arose for the expression of solidarity and for translating into action all the sentiments that the blacks harbored about Africa. Ethiopia, besides providing a link with the ancient world, was, on the contemporary scene, along with Liberia and Haiti, one of the few black-ruled countries in the world. Daniel Thwaite has observed:

> Ethiopia's prestige in Africa, consequent upon her triumphant success in repelling invasion and having remained unconquered throughout the centuries, is practically unfathomable. To the Africans in general, not

only to those who invoked her as a liberator, she stands as a granite monument, a living exponent and testimony of the innate puissance of the black race, the shrine enclosing the last sacred spark of African political freedom, the impregnable rock of black resistance against white invasion, a living incarnation of Africa's independence.[7]

Roy Ottley says that American blacks first became aware of the modern black nation in 1919 when Ethiopian dignitaries arrived in the United States on a diplomatic mission. The group included Dadgazmatch Nadou, later to be one of the signatories for Ethiopia when it was admitted to the League of Nations, and Belanghetta Herouy, the Mayor of Addis Ababa and later Minister of Foreign Affairs. While staying in New York at the old Hotel Waldorf Astoria they received a delegation of Harlem citizens. From the Waldorf the group journeyed to the Metropolitan Baptist Church in Harlem where they were welcomed, not only in the name of Harlem, but in the name of Black America. At the end of the ceremony the audience was assembled in front of the church where pictures were taken with the Ethiopian delegation in a nice show of racial unity.

In his parting message to Black America Mayor Herouy, through an attache of the Persian legation, had this to say:

On the part of the Ethiopian Empire we desire to express the satisfaction we have felt on hearing of the wonderful progress Africans have made in this century. It gives us great confidence in the government of the United States to know that through the independence given you by America, you have increased in numbers and developed in education and prosperity. We want you to remember us after we have returned to our native country.[8]

When Italy assaulted Ethiopia in the winter of 1935 a new wave of African consciousness was bound to spread through the black community. Here at last was an issue that evoked a deep indignation and which could be translated into tangible action. Organizations were set up to mobilize support; the executive director of the International Council of the Friends of Ethiopia, Dr. Willis N. Huggins, was commissioned to deliver an appeal on behalf of Ethiopia to the League of Nations in Geneva, Switzerland. Arden Bryan, president of the Nationalist Negro Movement, sent a petition to the League and protests to the British Foreign Office and the United States State Department against their failure to aid Ethiopia. The *Crisis,* the official organ of the NAACP, in such editorials as "Ethiopia Against the World" and "Ethiopia Thrown to the Wolves" in the 1935 issues, saw the conflict as a "sad spectacle of 'White civilization.' "*Opportunity*, the journal of the National Urban League, echoed *The Crisis* and declared in one of its editorials:

> Western civilization has come to Ethiopia out of the belching mouths of cannons, it has descended in clouds of poison gas, it has been borne on the bloody blades of bayonets. In the villages and towns, in the path of the conqueror lie the maimed and broken bodies of men and women and children. Courageous—yes—but of what use is courage against death that comes ripping out of machine guns or silently creeps through the quiet air or roars suddenly out of the sky?[9]

Both magazines suggested that the Anglo-French efforts to prevent the war were motivated by fear of the effect of the war on their colonies and the threat of a world-wide challenge to white supremacy.

On August 2, 1935, *The New York Times* reported that a petition urging the United States to take measures in defense of Ethiopia was presented to Acting Secretary of State Phillips by a delegation of seven Negroes and Italians. The delegation included Alleyne of the Provisional Committee for the Defense of Ethiopia, Dido Johnson of the League of Struggles for Negro Rights, and Clora Ashcraft of the Harlem branch of the American League Against War and Fascism. On August 4, 1935, *The Times* reported again that about 20,000 marched through Harlem. Among those at the parade were a group of uniformed, white-gloved Brotherhood of Sleeping Car Porters, a black trade union. A large contingent of Father Divine's followers was present and Ethiopian flags were on display.

> Besides delegations and parades a campaign was launched to boycott Italian peddlers, and there were reported incidents of smashing of shop windows owned by Italians. Riots continually erupted in adjacent neighborhoods of Italians and Negroes. Some blacks like Herbert Julian, the "black Eagle of Harlem" and John C. Robinson the "Brown Condor of Ethiopia" volunteered for service in Ethiopia.[10]

Indeed, a large section of the black population in the United States rallied to the cause of Ethiopia as they had never rallied before. Here was a black nation, a symbol for the black man's independence (however tarnished it might have been by its feudal institutions and backwardness), threatened with extinction. Membership in the debilitated nationalist organizations and in the remnants of the Garvey movement suddenly began to increase. These groups found themselves with a solid basis for organization and action, and when white liberals and radicals joined in condemning fascist aggression, they were given a solid boost in prestige.[11]

About their activities Roy Ottley made this rather insightful observation:

> White people wondered at the phenomenon of the Negroes being fiercely stirred by an affair abroad! Yet this was no new thing in Negro life. Once before Negroes had been aroused by the struggles beyond the borders of the United States, when the black men in Haiti struck for freedom in 1791 and the distant but heroic figure of Toussaint L'Ouverture, black leader of the revolt, fired the imagination of the sore-beset American Negroes. In those days only Jefferson among the white leaders seemed to understand what was happening. "The West Indies," he observed, "appears to have given considerable impulse to the minds of the slaves in the United States."[12]

Throughout 1935 and much of 1936, according to Professor William R. Scott, the Afro-American press overflowed with news relating to the Italo-Ethiopian crisis and war. "News reports, special features, editorials, letters to the editor, and photographs concerning the conflict appeared abundantly in the pages of the nation's leading black publications. In their coverage of the conflict, black newspapers demonstrated a strong sense of racial patriotism, which transcended the borders of the United States and extended as far as the distant shores of Northeastern Africa. By publishing a multitude of pro-Ethiopian articles, columns and editorials, the national black press promoted the general cause of Pan-Africanism in America and helped work thousands, if not millions, of Afro-Americans into a frenzy of support for the Ethiopians."[13]

Dr. Scott's summary of the speeches, editorials and sermons which appeared at the time gives a flavor of the depth of anger and indignation felt by the Afro-American community at this unprovoked attack on Ethiopia:

Felix H. Bretton of New Orleans urged blacks at an early stage in the crisis to find means of aiding their kith and kin in Ethiopia, "for the time is here for the Negro to begin to look for the higher things in life—a flag of his own, a government of his own and complete liberty." Joe E. Thomas, a physician from Cleveland, believed that "every son and daughter of African descent" should render assistance to their blood relatives in Ethiopia. "We must not desert our Race in Africa. We must stand, 'One for all, All for one.' " The African Patriotic League of New York City claimed it was "the solemn duty of every Race-loving Black Man and Woman to Fight in Defense of the Ethiopian Nation." A group of blacks from Fort Worth, Texas, considered going to Ethiopia as combat troops; expressing the volunteers' sense of racial identification with the Ethiopians, their leader, Walter J. Davis, wrote a letter to Emperor Haile Selasie informing him of the group's willingness "to spill their blood in behalf of our native land."[14]

Why this outpouring of emotion? The rape of Ethiopia if it had succeeded would have been the last nail in the coffin of black humanity. It was an attack on the principle of national rights for the African peoples everywhere. The defense of the principle of black nationhood was the primary motivating force. Dr. L.K. Williams, President of the National Baptist Convention, told a mass rally: "We do not want to see the black empire in Africa lose its independence and culture . . ."[15] The Fraternal Council of Negro Churches, with leaders from nine principal black church groups, passed the following resolution at its meeting in August 1935:

> Americans of African descent are deeply stirred in their attitude and sympathies for Ethiopia, a Negroid people, who represent almost the only remaining example of independent government by the black race on the continent of Africa. While by sympathy, principle and ideas we are Americans to the core we cannot be deaf to the cry that comes from a menaced nation in the land of our fathers' fathers![16]

It remained for the cool, dispassionate pen of DuBois to demonstrate the true meaning of the attack of Ethiopia; that is, to show the links between the aims of imperialism on the one hand and race and class on the other. From its birth, capitalism as a system resolved its internal contradictions by exporting them overseas to the Americas, Asia and Africa. Such was the dynamic that lay behind the dismemberment of Africa at the Berlin Conference in 1884-5, World War I, and now the destruction of the sole African country that had maintained its autonomy. Haiti, which had won its independence from France in the early part of the 19th century, had been occupied by the United States for 20 years, and even though it had gained nominal independence, it was at the price of shouldering an enormous debt which kept her in chains for many years. Liberia was practically mortgaged to the Firestone Rubber Company after being threatened with absorption by both France and Great Britain. But, DuBois pointed out:

> Ethiopia on the other hand, had kept comparatively free of debt, had preserved her political autonomy, had begun to reorganize her ancient policy, and was in many ways an example and a promise of what a native people untouched by modern exploitation and race prejudice might do.[17]

As to the morality of turning Ethiopia into Italy's colony, DuBois drew parallels from the southern part of the continent:

> In South Africa a small white minority of Dutch and English descent have already done much to reduce the natives to the position of landless workers. They propose to further this degradation by drastic means; to deprive of the right to vote even those few educated Negroes who now enjoy the franchise; and to continue to deny the colored population any representation in the legislature. Educational facilities for the blacks are to be increased very slowly, if at all. All this is to be done with the intention of forming an abject working class below the level of the white workers. This program the Union of South Africa is enforcing not only on its own black citizens but on those of its mandate, South West Africa. In order to make it uniform, the Union is trying to obtain control of the British colonies in Basutoland and the Rhodesias, thereby consolidating the serfdom of the black man in South Africa. Italy now proposes to do exactly what South Africa has done without the frank Italian statement of aims. South Africa rightly fears resentment and disillusionment among her own blacks, who are still being fed with the idea that Christianity and white civilization are eventually going to do them justice. For the more radical natives and the few with education, the Italian program merely confirms their worst fears.[18]

What South Africa was doing, the Jim Crow Laws in the United States had already accomplished for ten million former slaves, who formed a laboring class with the nominal rights of free laborers but in actual fact were subject to caste.

Early in 1936 a delegation composed of the officers of various organizations for the defense of Ethiopia was sent to the First Congress of the International Peace Campaign meeting in Brussels, with instructions to try to influence the Congress to take action in support of Ethiopia. The delegation interviewed Emperor Haile Selassie in London and requested him to send a representative to cooperate in the work of mobilizing the blacks in the United States, Dr. Malaku E. Bayen, cousin and personal physician to the Emperor, was appointed and received tumultuously at a great meeting at Rockland Place. Meanwhile money and medical supplies were raised and sent to Ethiopia.

Thus the Ethiopian crisis became a fundamental issue in black life in 1935-36. Emperor Haile Selassie I was hailed by some blacks as the new "messiah." One writer was quoted by Roy Ottley as describing the emperor as "a black edition of the pictured Christ."[19] The Ethiopians on their own had asked in a public letter to American blacks that "an independent Red Cross of colored people act with other groups for us." Ottley wrote that: "It was all but impossible for Negro leaders to remain neutral, and the position they took toward the conflict became a fundamental test. The survival of the black nation became a topic of angry debate in poolrooms, barber shops and taverns."[20]

When in 1936 Dr. Malaku Bayen arrived as the official representative of the Emperor, a much more inclusive organization, the Ethiopian World Federation Incorporated, with much broader political objectives, was formed. The Emperor's gesture of racial solidarity was not lost on American blacks, and a weekly organ was established by this new federation called *The Voice of Ethiopia* which was militantly pro-black as well as pro-Ethiopian. There is no doubt that the attack on Ethiopia by a white Italian nation helped to whip up wild currents of racial solidarity and identification. It spotlighted more than anything the white exploitation of a darker people; and when these people began grumbling loudly and convincingly about white imperialism and oppression, their charges could not be disputed. Selassie was quoted as saying, "We cannot cut up Ethiopia like a cake, handing sugared parts to this and that country just to win their smile and satisfy their sweet tooth."

Besides Garvey's UNIA there is no other phenomenon that stirred the rank and file of the Afro-American as did the Italo-Ethiopian War. Doctor Huggins is quoted as having said that it marked Ethiopia's return to the black race. Garvey, in his London exile, began organizing in defense of the motherland of Ethiopia. In meetings at Hyde Park he denounced the Italian dictator for his attempt to despoil Africa and made appeals to the crowds around the Marble Arch for support of the beleaguered Abyssinians.[21] Garvey called on black people everywhere to unite in defense of their ancestral home and he gave fair warning to *Il Duce* in a bit of angry poetic verse entitled "The Smell of Mussolini":

> We'll march to crush the Italian dog
> And at the points of gleaming, shining swords
> We'll lay quite low the violent Roman hog.[22]

However, Garvey's enthusiasm was not to last long, for when the Ethiopian Emperor Haile Selassie fled to London he was unwilling to have contact with Garvey, leading Garvey to launch his bitterest attack on the "snobbish Lion of Judah." Haile Selassie, he proclaimed, is "the ruler of a country where black men are chained and flogged. He will go down in history as a great coward who ran away from his country."[23] Garvey called upon the Ethiopian people to forget the cowardly flight of their ruler and instead wage fierce guerrilla warfare in defense of their country.

American blacks, dissatisfied with the reporting of news from Ethiopia in the white press, sent J.A. Rogers to Ethiopia as a war correspondent for the *Courier*. When Rogers returned to the United States he published an illustrated brochure, "The Real Facts about Ethiopia," devoting an entire section to the subject, "Of What Race are the Ethiopians?" This little pamphlet was one of the best sellers of the times.

The major effect of the war on the American blacks was that for the first time they became involved in a realistic way in a major African issue. The Garvey movement had involved the lower-class blacks emotionally, but the Italo-Ethiopian War gave them their own handle to world affairs, and it opened the door on the world for many who had hitherto hardly known it was there. *The Crisis* in one of its many editorials asked: "What is to be done?"

> The peoples of African descent in America, as well as elsewhere, have a great moral duty to perform in this hour of danger. How can this best be done? Personally we think that the NAACP (or some other organization, it does not matter which) representing and enjoying the confidence of Afro-Americans should convene a national conference of all Negro organizations—religious, political, educational, social, fraternal, etc., for the purpose of organizing common action on behalf of Ethiopian people. Such a coordinated effort can achieve tremendous results, and demonstrate to the people of Africa that their descendants in the New World have not forgotten their ties of blood and race with them. For when all is said and done, the struggle of the Abyssinians is fundamentally a part of the struggle of the black race the world over for national freedom, economic, political and racial emancipation.[24]

Harold Isaacs, who interviewed a group of Afro-Americans on their attitudes toward Africa, quotes one of his panelists as saying: "There were glimmerings of these things before . . . but it was around the Ethiopian affair for the first time that there was the crystallizing of attitudes among American Negroes toward colored people outside the United States."[25] John Hope Franklin has put the matter even more strongly. With Italy's attack on Ethiopia, "almost overnight, even the most provincial among American Negroes became international-minded."[26]

A sobering aspect of the events unleashed by fascist Italy's attack on Ethiopia is the spotlight it cast on the fears of the white world. The Italo-Ethiopian War revealed rather starkly white fears and suspicions about black people everywhere. *The New York Times*, of September 7, 1935, quotes Mr. Thompson: "In these modern times of rapid communication the native population educated during the last quarter of a century of white rule will learn quickly of the causes of war. In Africa it is black against white and a crushing defeat of whites at any point may be the sequel for a general uprising." A dispatch from Aden, Arabia, voiced the fear of the white people in East Africa that Mussolini and his fascist legions might prove inadequate to the task of conquering Ethiopia. Their uneasiness was caused by the undoubted loss of prestige the white race would suffer by a defeat in Africa, to say nothing of the danger of such a defeat spurring black colonies to action against white overlords. "No one in full possession of his faculties can imagine such uneasiness being voiced in a newspaper dispatch if the infallibility of Il Duce's worries could be taken for granted," commented *The Crisis* of August 1935. Booker Carter was even more specific:

> The British are fearful that victory of the Abyssinians or a long drawn-out war, in which the Italian's arms actually lose prestige, may be the spark which will inflame the African blacks against their white rulers. If ever such a thing happened, it would mark the end of the British empire. There are 330,000,000 blacks in the empire, ruled by 70,000,000 whites of whom 40,000,000 are in England.[27]

Thus did the Italo-Ethiopian War cause to arise, on both sides of the color-line, age-old fears—on the blacks' side there was identification with the blacks across the sea, and on the white side there were fears that the Africans who were ruled by a comparative handful of whites would set fires of nationalism ablaze. In an article, *The New York Times* correspondent of the *Carrier della Sere* interpreted for his Milanese readers what he considered to be American opinion:

> Because of America's large Negro population and its many years of experience with the "primitive psychology of the colored races". . . America more than other countries in the world could appreciate the reason for Italy's policy in Ethiopia.[28]

He even suggested that Ethiopia's admission to the League of Nations in 1923 corresponded to the emancipation of the black following the Civil War: if 70 years of freedom in civilized America has not altered the "semi-barbarism" and "incurable immaturity" of American blacks, how could one expect that a mere decade in the League of Nations would do so for Ethiopia? The correspondent concluded that:

America knows the Negro well and understands how to treat him (by keeping him in his place). How many Americans are curious to know if, as would be logical, one could institute a Jim Crow diplomatic car on the international train which leads to Geneva.[29]

But the prize goes to the fascist paper *Affair Esteri*, which published the following appeal:

It is true that the white nations of Europe should abandon their long suffering toleration towards the only African state which is still autonomous, and proceed to settle all questions connected with the Abyssinian problem. Abyssinia is a danger to the white race. The young Abyssinians are inspired with the idea of "Africa for the Africans," and are already combining with Japanese immigrants in the country to combat the white man's influence in Africa.[30]

As a result of the Italo-Ethiopian War, the political horizons of Afro-Americans were lifted even further. From now on it would be difficult to deny the view held by Garveyites and Pan-Africanists, that the black struggle was part of a world struggle by those damned by European imperialism. The impulse of the black community to identify its own fate with events and situations outside the borders of the US, and especially in Africa, after the fall of Ethiopia to Italian fascism was now carried on by the Council on African Affairs.

The Council on African Affairs was planned in London in 1939 by Paul Robeson, the black American singer. Robeson's efforts were stimulated by his contact with Mr. Max Yergan, a black YMCA secretary who had just returned from a long and trying service in South Africa, and who became a member of the Council. This organization was both a welfare agency for collecting money and clothing to help destitute Africans in South Africa, and an agency of inestimable importance in forwarding the efforts of Africa's liberation from white rule. In recognition and appreciation of the efforts of the Council on African Affairs, Robeson, its chairman, was selected as one of three recipients (the others were Kwame Nkrumah, first president of Ghana, and Nnamdi Azikiwe, first president of Nigeria) of the award of "Champion of African Freedom" bestowed by the National Church of Nigeria at ceremonies attended by 5,000 at Aba, Nigeria, on January 29, 1950.

The Council on African Affairs for many years stood alone as the one organization in the United States devoting full time and attention to the problems and struggles of the peoples of Africa. With the cooperation of

Frederick V. Field, a fine African library and a collection of African art, along with offices for the new organization, were secured. A monthly fact sheet devoted to developments in Africa was issued. Though the dissemination of information was central to its work, the Council was not content to function simply as an information agency, but sought also to translate knowledge into action. From 1944, when the shape of post-war African policy was under consideration, to 1955 and Bandung, the council organized assemblies ranging from conferences of community leaders to a Madison Square Garden rally for the purposes of hammering out and enlisting public support for the programs of action in the interest of African people's welfare and freedom. When the United Nations was formed the Council took a strong interest in the policies of the world organization pertaining to Africa, and it tried to influence what it considered the pro-imperialist and compromising stand of the United States delegation on such issues as the status of South West Africa. "The knowledge that we have friends on the other end of the Atlantic is comforting and inspiring in our struggle for freedom from want and heartless exploitation," wrote a Nigerian trade union leader to the Council's officers.[31]

Another facet of the Council's work was providing direct help and assistance for Africans in emergency situations, as they did with a special campaign of behalf of South Africa in 1945. Dr. Z. K. Mathews of the African National Congress in South Africa acknowledges the help of the Council in these words:

> Africans in this country have benefited directly from its practical interests in their affairs. As far back as 1945 when a severe drought struck the Eastern Cape Province of the Union of South Africa, hundreds of Africans . . . had cause to be thankful that such a body as the Council on African Affairs was in existence . . . The Council made available financial aid and food supplies of various kinds collected in America to be forwarded to the area for distribution among the needy. Many African women, children and older people in the area concerned owed their lives to the assistance given by the Council.[32]

In 1945 the Council was branded as "subversive" by the Attorney General, and though it continued until 1955 its effective usefulness was greatly reduced after the denunciation. W.E.B. DuBois later commented:

> Nothing illustrates more clearly the hysteria of our time than the career of the Council on African Affairs. It had been the dream of idealists in earlier days that the stain of American slavery would eventually be

wiped out by the service which American descendants of African slaves would render Africa. Most of the American Negroes who gained their freedom in the 18th century looked forward to a return to Africa as their logical end. They often named their clubs and churches, their chief social institutions "Africa." But the Cotton Kingdom and Colonial Imperialism gradually drove this dream entirely from their minds until the Negroes of the post Civil War era regarded Africa as a remedial of Color Caste and Slavery. They regarded the colonization and "Back to Africa" movements of Lincoln and Bishop Turner with lackluster eyes and when in 1918 I tried to found a social and spiritual Pan-African movement my American Negro following was nil.[33]

The period between the two World Wars therefore saw a number of organizations and activities which fostered and heightened the trend linking the American blacks' struggle for freedom with that of the Africans. The Italo-Ethiopian War merely defined the issues. A white nation attacked a black nation for the glory of Italy—i.e., for imperialistic stealing of the black kingdom's territory for the sole reason that Italy wanted it.[34] What greater evidence did one need to indicate that white people were not willing to protect the interests of the black people? World War I and the Italo-Ethiopian War were to affect the structure and mythology of white supremacy. They brought to the Africans and the Afro-Americans a moment of existential truth, and the result was a feeling of historical liberation. George Padmore later wrote of this period:

> The brutal rape of Ethiopia combined with the cynical attitude of the great powers convinced Africans and people of African descent everywhere that black men had no rights which white men felt bound to respect. Not only did the Western powers turn a deaf ear to the emperor's appeal to the League of Nations for help, but actually connived at Mussolini's gassing of defenseless Ethiopians by selling oil to the dictator . . . With the realization of their utter defenselessness against the new aggression from Europeans in Africa the blacks felt it necessary to look to themselves.[35]

Thus did colonialism and white rule over blacks stand exposed morally after 1935-36. Questions of principle and rhetorical morality had been sacrificed to brilliant opportunism. The 19th century moral certainties of the imperial mission and the "white man's burden" never recovered from the shell-shock of this period. In World War I black and white for the first time stood side by side in the trenches to save the world for democracy; yet the Africans had to be betrayed. Colonial rule was from now on no longer such a benign and selfless mission. This was to be brought home with a singularly traumatic effect by the Italo-Ethiopian War. Despite the fact that Britain, France and America had been saved with the help of black soldiers in their hour of need, a country which was the example of black hopes and aspirations was sacrificed.

The attitude of the sponsors of the first Pan-African Congresses was changed from reasonable appeasement to great militancy. There had been a short, sometimes frustrating, flirtation between the leaders of the black movements and revolutionary communism which had its appeal to the oppressed everywhere. The nexus between the educated elite which in the period from 1919 to 1925 was loose, was strengthened by the circumstances of the 1930s. Black intellectuals were becoming more and more disenchanted with their lot, because after all the sweet talk about the rights of nations to self-determination, the white imperial powers were still bent upon retaining the status quo. The self-doubts characteristic of the war period, which had led to the talk of the rights of nations to determine themselves, were shelved and replaced by a vulgar pomposity of trusteeship. When World War II came, the imperial crisis of confidence became a profound moral malaise.

World War II produced a qualitative change in the attitude of the blacks toward their servile status. Issues and choices became clear—even stark. The dark people everywhere no longer felt hostage to events beyond their country and beyond even their comprehension. When the Fifth Pan-African Congress met in Manchester in 1945, its resolutions showed the effects of the events of the preceding 20 years. Political demands and ideologies were as much a part of their intellectual furniture as of their political conceptions, reflecting the changed position of the bearers of the ideas. The historical situation of American blacks has been the most potent force in giving character to their African consciousness. To examine the blacks' ideas about Africa is not to indulge in vain curiosity but to stand at the source of rivulets which are now a flood. Pan-Africanism grew in the post-World War II era and changed in character from dominance by American blacks to dominance by Africans, because African independence, despite external stimulation, had to be nourished by indigenous forces.

The Manchester Congress of the Pan-African movement reflects this changing mood. For the first time we find the forthright challenge: "We demand for black Africa autonomy and independence, so far, and no further, than it is possible in this One World for groups and peoples to rule themselves subject to inevitable world unity and federation." A new note of militancy was struck which bade a farewell to patience and the acceptance of suffering:

We are not ashamed to have been an age-long patient people. We continue to sacrifice and strive. but we are unwilling to starve any longer while doing the world's drudgery, in order to support by our poverty and ignorance, a false aristocracy and a discarded imperialism.[36]

The Fifth Pan-African Congress was conducted under the direction of W.E.B. DuBois, who at the age of seventy-seven had flown across the Atlantic to be present at Manchester. The meeting of this Congress was a personal triumph for DuBois, now called the "Father of Pan-Africanism." For fifty years he had worked patiently for the advancement of this idea. Returning from the Congress in 1945, DuBois openly declared:

We American Negroes should know . . . until Africa is free, the descendants of Africa the world over cannot escape their chains . . . The NAACP should therefore put in the forefront of its program the freedom of Africa in work and wage, education and health, and the complete abolition of the colonial system.[37]

He offered this counsel when it was quite obvious that the leadership of the Pan-African Congress had been taken over by the younger Africans. In 1945 his words sounded something like the words written in 1925 by James Weldon Johnson, the celebrated black poet: "It may be that the day is not far off when the New Negroes of Africa will be demanding that their blood brothers be treated with absolute fairness and justice." Almost half a century has passed since the Congress and in that time most African states have become independent. Has the hope of Johnson and DuBois been fulfilled? That is to be the subject of our next chapter.

Notes

[1]Quoted in Richard B. Moore, "Africa Conscious Harlem," in Clarke, *op. cit.*, p. 68.

[2]For full text of the resolutions see *Crisis*, Vol. 35, No. 5, July, 1927, p. 165.

[3]Harold Isaacs, *The New World of the Negro American*, Viking Press, New York, 1964, p. 149.

[4]Charles E. Silberman, *Crisis in Black and White*, Random House, New York, 1964, p. 172.

[5]Robert Weisbord, *Ebony Kinship,* Westport, CT: Greenwood, 1973, p. 89.

[6]For fuller treatment see Nathaniel Pfeffer, "R.I.P. Ethiopia," *Opportunity* Vol. 14, No. 1, January 1936, p. 19.

[7]Daniel Thwaite, *The Seething African Pot*, Constable and Company, London, 1936, p. 207.

[8]Ottley, *op. cit.*, pp. 106-7.

[9]*Opportunity*, p. 19.

[10]*The New York Times*, July 13 and 14, 1935.

[11]Ottley, *op. cit.*, p. 105.

[12]*Ibid.*

[13]William R. Scott, "Black Nationalism and the Italo-Ethiopian Conflict, 1934-1936," *The Journal of Black History*, Vol. LXIII, No. 2, 1978, p. 120.

[14]*Ibid.*

[15]Scott, *Ibid.*

[16]*Ibid.*

[17]W.E.B. DuBois, "Inter-racial Implications of the Ethiopian Crisis. A Negro View," *Foreign Affairs*, Vol. 4, No. 1, October 1935, pp. 85-6.

[18]*Ibid.*, p. 85.

[19]*Ibid.*, p. 109.

[20]*Ibid*

[21]For Garvey's activities in London with regard to Ethiopia see Cronan, *op. cit.*, pp. 162-64.

[22]*Ibid.*, p. 162.

[23]*Ibid.*

[24]*Crisis*, Vol. 42, No. 8, July 1935, p. 214.

[25]Isaacs, *op. cit.*, p. 151.

[26]John Hope Franklin, *From Slavery to Freedom*, Alfred A. Knopf, New York, 1965, p. 561.

[27]Booker Carter, *Black Shirt, Black Skin*, Telegraph Press, Harrisburg, Pennsylvania, 1935, p. 161.

[28]Brice Harris, *The United States and the Italo-Ethiopia Crisis*, Stanford, California, Stanford University Press, 1964, p. 44.

[29]*Ibid.*

[30]George Padmore, "Ethiopia and World Politics," *Crisis*, Vol. 42, No. 8, 1935, p. 157.

[31]Paul Robeson, *Here I Stand*, Othello Associates, New York, 1958, pp. 126-128.

[32]*Ibid.*, p. 128.

[33]DuBois, *In Battle for Peace*, p. 16.

[34]*Crisis*, Vol. 42, No. 8, August 1935, p. 241.

[35]George Padmore, *Pan-Africanism or Communism*, Rory Publishers, New York, 1956, pp. 146-147.

[36]Padmore, *Pan-Africanism or Communism*, p. 148.

[37]*Ibid.*

CHAPTER EIGHT
Afro-Americans' Response to Africa's Independence

At the beginning identity is a dream;
At the end, it is a nightmare.

—Larry Rivers and Frank O'Hara in
"How to Proceed in the Arts"

In the past few years several studies have appeared examining what is called the American black's "identity crisis." These studies tell us that the black man is in psychological disarray because of social disorganization in his communities and cultural deprivation. In their book *Mark of Oppression*, Kardiner and Ovesey wrote:

> He had no culture, and he was quite green in his semi-acculturated state in the new one. He did not know his way about and had no intra-psychic defenses—no pride, no group solidarity, no tradition. This was enough to cause panic. The works of his previous status were still upon him—socially, psychologically and emotionally. And from these he has never freed himself.[1]

Essien-Udom described what he called the tragedy of the Negro thusly:

> The tragedy of the Negro in America is that he has rejected his origins—the essentially human meaning implicit in the heritage of slavery, prolonged suffering, and social rejection. By rejecting this unique group experience and favoring assimilation and even biological amalgamation, he thus denies himself the creative possibilities inherent

179

in it and his folk culture. This dilemma is fundamental; it severely limits his ability to evolve a new identity or a meaningful synthesis, capable of endowing his life with meaning and purpose.[2]

In his study, *The New World of Negro Americans*, Harold Isaacs reaches the same conclusions as Essien-Udom:

> The flight from blackness and the yearning to be white have had a major part in shaping the Negro group identity down through the generations. It involved the more or less total acceptance of the white man's estimate of the black man, the more or less total rejection of self. This was a widely shared experience which took on many forms.[3]

Continuing the same theme, Charles E. Silberman writes:

> It is in the United States, in short, and only in the United States, that the American Negroes will be able to resolve their problem of identification. To be sure, Negroes must recapture their African past, because denying them a place in history has been one of the means whites have used to keep them down; and they must find some basis on which to relate to Africa, because denying that relationship has been central to Negro self-hatred. But building a bridge to Africa past and Africa present is simply a means of erasing the old stigma of race; it is not a base on which Negroes can erect a new identity. For American Negroes have been formed by the United States, not by Africa; Africa gave them their color but America gave them their personality and their culture. The central fact in Negro history is slavery, and Negroes must come to grips with it, must learn to accept it—to accept it not as a source of shame (the shame is the white man's) *but as an experience that explains a large part of their present predicament.* (My emphasis) Only if they understand *why* they are *what* they are, can Negroes change *what* they are. Identity is not something that can be found; it must be created.[4] (Emphasis in the original)

A fundamental principle underlying anthropological thought is that culture is always learned and never biologically inherited. This general sociological axiom must be understood and its implications appreciated. Between the American black and his African past stand 300 years of attempts to de-Africanize him in terms of culture, language, religion, identity, vision and philosophy of life through deliberate falsification in the furnaces of American slavery. This so-called non-man was then freed minus references, history or archtypes. That some black men hate themselves and reject their past must be understood as expressive of the historical perspective so well stated by Malcolm X: "The white man's heaven is the black man's hell." This can be interpreted as meaning that psychological phenomena in their totality reflect a part of social-historical consciousness. Inasmuch as social consciousness is a reflection of the social being, that part of it which is psychological cannot help but be a reflection of social existence. Self-hatred would thus be nothing more than a reflection of the blacks' historical reality in a white society. The "flight from blackness" would be a flight from the negative status of the black man in the era of colonialism and imperialism. But we cannot be satisfied merely with an awareness of this historical truth. We must also show the structure of the experience. When one begins to analyze people's empirical experience and to define the forms it takes, one arrives at the conclusion that it is made of at least two parts: knowledge and ideas, both acquired through direct contact with nature and other people. In the Western world knowledge, ideas and social values proclaimed the exploits of the white races, including the conquest and enslavement of the black races. Such exploits, while comforting to the whites, disfigured black people.

Social-psychological reality may be perceived by the experienced eye in layers of greater or lesser depth, and these layers of course interpenetrate and influence one another. Such levels of social-psychological phenomena may roughly be said to form units of four types. On the first level of experience are feelings, inclinations, attitudes and tastes. The basic feature of this level of social-psychological reality is that it represents unconscious emotional expressions of a person's attitudes toward certain phenomena, events and objects that exist in reality. The extent to which the present experience coincides with the past experience of a person, and the extent to which what is perceived at the given moment corresponds with the ideological orientation, habits and immediate subjective experience of persons, is reflected in tastes, attitudes, etc., at this first level. The social-psychological phenomena of the second level include the character traits and features of an individual; the specific psychological make-up. The second level also represents unrealized unconscious reflections of conditions of experience in a form typical, in modes of expression, of individual attitudes, opinions, tastes and manners in intercourse with other people. The third category consists of opinions and values, which differ essentially from the phenomena of the other two levels: the basic difference being that the immanent conditions of existence are not reflected immediately, but are consciously and fully thought out in the form of judgments, conclusions and results of comparison. Therefore, they can be said to be intellectually evaluated. Depending on a given individual's evaluations, opinions and judgments, one can judge how much he considers himself a representative of a certain class or social group, and how much his personal views coincide with the social views typical of that class or group. The final category consists of habits, traditions and rites, which are specific reflections, over a long period, of the elements operating in the immediate conditions of people's existence.

A characteristic common feature of many social-psychological phenomena is that they arise under the influence of two factors—personal experience and mediated experience or ideology. The fundamental question for the American black's identity and his conception of Africa is: By what social-psychological phenomena can he be characterized, and, further, what distinctions exist between the various strata?[5] As Marx pointed out:

> Since he comes into the world neither with a looking glass in his hand, or as a Fichtian philosopher to whom "I am I" is sufficient, man first sees and recognizes himself in other men. Peter only establishes his own identity as a man by first comparing himself with Paul as being of a like kind.[6]

The descriptions of the superficial social-psychological manifestations of oppression by Kardiner and Ovesey, Essien-Udom, Isaacs and Silberman may be correct at the first two levels of social-psychological experience. To limit the psychological experiences of black folks to those two levels is erroneous, however, because it does not conceive of each group or even each experience of a group as "total phenomena." One can explain self-hatred and a desire to be white on these levels, but, for our purpose, it is the third domain of experience which is of particular interest. Here people reflect upon their experiences, judgments are made and alternatives investigated. It is at this level that movements like Ethiopianism, Pan-Africanism, Garveyism, and Black Nationalism arise.

Granted that slavery severed the black man from his social roots and identities, which ordinarily sustain regular intercourse with family and significant others; he has, over the years, through reflective evaluations of alternatives, created and propagated ideas which have since become viable alternatives to white supremacy in culture and historiography. When Africa was in chains, the American blacks pleaded her cause to the world and produced her major ideology—Pan-Africanism. Chief among those who introduced the idea of the existence of ancient Africa are black American historians. The individuals we have quoted above may be right in terms of experiences at the first and second level, but all the levels of social reality interpenetrate. Isolated from one another, they would cease to be elements of social reality. If we analyze small human peculiarities without taking into account the historical reality of the groups concerned, we will be led astray. The "self-hatred" of the black is not a personal and psychological matter only, but the result of an objective social-historical reality. It can only be understood by disclosing the actual conditions of life, and the actual growing crisis in people's existence. In this way we can depict all the problems of popular life which lead up to the historical crisis which the black has represented in White America. In his essay "Our Strange Birth," Richard Wright draws our attention to the historical roots of Afro-American alienation, and what he said is worth quoting at some length:

> Each day when you see us black folk upon the dusty land of the farms or upon the hard pavement of the city streets, you usually take us for granted and think you know us, but our history is far stranger than you suspect, and we are not what we seem. Our outward guise still carries the old familiar aspect which three hundred years of oppression in America have given us, but beneath the garb of the black laborer, the black cook, and the black elevator operator lies an uneasily tied knot of pain and hope whose snarled strands converge from many points of time and space.

> We millions of black folk who live in this land were born into Western civilization of a weird and paradoxical birth. The lean, tall, blond men of England, Holland, and Denmark, the dark, short, nervous men of France, Spain, and Portugal, men whose blue and gray and brown eyes glinted with the light of the future, denied our human personalities, tore us from our native soil, weighted our legs with chains, stacked us like cord-wood in the foul holes of clipper ships, dragged us across thousands of miles of ocean, and hurled us into another land, strange and hostile, where for a second time we felt the slow, painful process of a new birth amid conditions harsh and raw. . .

On the next page Wright made the important observation:

> Captivity under Christendom blasted our lives, disrupted our families, reached down into the personalities of each one of us and destroyed the very images and symbols which had guided our minds and feelings in the effort to live. Our folkways and folk tales, which had once given meaning and sanction to our actions, faded from consciousness. Our gods were dead and answered us no more. The trauma of leaving our African home, the suffering of the long middle passage, the thirst, the

hunger, the horrors of the slave ship—all these hollowed us out, numbed us, stripped us, and left only physiological urges, the feelings of fear and fatigue.[7]

Louis Lomax in his study *The Negro Revolt*, in arguing against those who had lost faith in the US, wrote that "whatever else the Negro is, he is an American. Whatever he is to become—integrated, unintegrated or disintegrated—he will become it in America."[8] Muhammed Ali may state publicly that this is not his nation. It is possible for any given individual black to change his alliance; it is not possible for the blacks as a people to do so. A group cannot shop around for a more amiable national identity. Like it or not, the American black is an American, not an African. There is no African nationality. As a Ghanaian, or a Nigerian or Egyptian, one can share a general African culture. One can be an African if one is something first—a Ghanaian, a Nigerian, or an Egyptian. All this is quite true; yet it does not resolve the fundamental problem raised by Richard Wright elsewhere in his writing:

> The fortuity of birth has cast me in the "racial role" of being of African descent, and that fact now resounds in my mind with associations of hatred, violence, and death . . . To be of "black blood" meant being consigned to a lower plane in the social scheme of American life, and if one violated that scheme, one risked danger, even death sometimes.[9]

It seems therefore that more questions ought to be asked as to what the persistence and growth of African consciousness in the history of the United States say of the larger society itself; the expectations of its black citizens, the promises, practices and potential of its economic political apparatus, with regard to the realization of these expectations. What is the America the blacks want so much to flee from? What is the Africa, the Ethiopia—really the America, I think—they seek so hard to find? Most of the writers who constantly tell Afro-Americans that they are "as American as apple pie" never seem to get around to spelling this out in secular terms, or at least not clearly enough to be translated into policy or sociopolitical action.[10]

Silberman shows some awareness of the invidious nature of the black's African background and has written that "there is some evidence to suggest that Elijah Muhammed's claim that the black is original man may not be as wide of the mark as it sounds."[11] He urges whites to understand that the black does have a rightful place in mankind's history, asserting further that it is necessary for the black to reaffirm his tie to Africa and his cultural heritage if only for the sake of his own dignity.

Irresponsible sociological theories have a way of bending facts and creating misery. The fundamental historical reality of the American black then and now was influenced by his African origin. In fact, the basic concepts of Western development were predicated on his exclusion from full integration except only theoretically. Historically, the black has been part of an exploited and despised humanity. African consciousness was an expression of the dilemma posed by his racial origin. It was a groping for an ideology which would correlate the black's positions on the various issues of being black and go beyond the question of civil rights to the general problem of the dispossessed and alienated.

In the fourfold classification of social-psychological phenomena we can better understand the nature of black American-African relations. Some black leaders through the reflective and evaluative process reached the conclusion that it was impossible for the Afro-American to achieve freedom when the rest of his putative brothers were under white man's colonial rule. The obverse side of this argument could be extended: While the African world was dominated by the white world no black could have either solace or pride. Imperialism as a system of economic and political relations between the white world and the black world was reflected in the manner in which American blacks were denied the fruits of emancipation. Historically, we have tried to point out how the NAACP, Urban League, CORE and other traditional civil groups with their white liberal friends have helped the black petty bourgeoisie to establish a middle-class hegemony over the black masses. Disgusted with the failure of this approach and somewhat disdainful of the insult implied therein, the nationalists have tried (sometimes successfully) to step into the programmatic vacuum with an ideology which attempts to identify the undifferentiated white as the black's oppressor. In eschewing reliance on whites the nationalists have to use the psychology of nationalism as a tactical device to build black power centers in the ghetto. In their ideology they identify with the anti-colonial movement throughout the world,[12] but it would be stretching the argument too far to suggest that this identification is a rejection of the America their labor power helps build. The ghetto existence of the black is an existential fact, and the nationalists mean to recapture the power that rules over them.

> The nationalist does not insist that to be free the Afro-American must return to Africa, for he recognizes that culturally the vast majority of us are Americans, or potentially so. He does insist that he must, to be truly free, stop being masochistically blind to his history.[13]

I pointed out previously that DuBois felt that half-truths should be replaced by whole truths, lest they perpetrate widespread deception. Half-truths must therefore be unmasked and combated even more ardently than obvious falsehoods.

Politically conscious blacks saw the relationship between exploitation of blacks in America and in Africa and did not or could not disregard the oppression of their African kith and kin as irrelevant to their own endeavors. Certain white liberal circles and black leaders considered it not in the interest of the American black to concern himself with issues outside the United States, as this would impede him in his search for advancement. They admitted by this argument a sharp antithesis between the attitudes the white man held about the peoples of Africa and the practices which were meted out to the Afro-Americans. Does the idea of democracy involve different sets of standards to apply to black people? Such have been the issues posed by the emancipation of Africa from white colonial rule.

These questions are receiving prominent attention today, but I hope that in my study, with all its limitations, I have shown that the black has been asking them since his coming to America as a slave. The period after World War II saw a collision between the treatment of the black in America and the attitude America was to adopt toward independent Africa in particular and the black world in general. In understanding the present-day conflicts I have attempted to place myself at the point where these relations between Africans and American blacks began. The background consisted of notions and emotional consciousness which were the legacy of the pre-Civil War era. The black could not have a sense of security in a world that despised, degraded and rejected him, and the 19th century was marked by assumptions about the black man which placed him in just such a position. The blacks initially expressed their interest in Africa as a way to its regeneration, as the traces of this ideology in Garveyism and DuBois's Pan-Africanism attest. Ideas do, in fact, have pedigrees which if realized would often embarrass their exponents. By the very nature of their social situations American blacks showed an ambivalence toward Africa, and many blacks who were interested in Africa thought that they were engaged in missionary efforts in which they would "enlighten the Africans." The work of social conversion and social reconstruction thus became almost indistinguishable. In Ethiopianism, Pan-Africanism and Garveyism we find sentiments that can only be explained in terms of the nature of white hegemony over the blacks. These sentiments may be too simple, too elementary, cutting through outer layers of desperate social and political and cultural facts to the bare, brute residues of human existence. They were produced by racial oppression and despoliation of the black masses. The American blacks' identification with Africa was something extra-political, extra-social; it was sometimes selfless and sometimes self-interested but it never denied the blacks' American citizenship. Ethiopianism, Garveyism and the Muslim Movement taken literally can easily be misinterpreted, but given a historical dimension they then answer the question: What has the black American in common with the African?

The American black's thoughts and actions have been torn between two separated developments—liberal democratic thought on the one hand, and nationalism on the other. The significance or relevance of each of these two strands to the eventual amelioration of the black's position in the United States is relative to the particular frames of reference; and the judgment whether one or the other of the two strands expressed the true aspirations of the black is contingent upon the discovery of an absolute frame of reference. To take into account the national aspirations of some blacks provides another dimension to this monumental problem. Malcolm X pointed out the difference between the nationalist point of view and the civil rights point of view:

> Among the so-called Negroes in this country, as a rule the civil rights groups, those who believe in civil rights, they spend most of their time trying to prove they are Americans. Their thinking is usually domestic, confined to the boundaries of America, and they always look upon themselves as a minority. When they look upon the American stage, the American stage is a white stage. So a black man standing on that stage in America automatically is a minority. He is the underdog and in his struggle he always uses an approach that is a begging, hat-in-hand, compromising approach.

> Whereas the other segment or section in America, known as the nationalist, black nationalist, are more interested in human rights than in civil rights. And they place more stress on human rights than on civil rights . . . those so-called Negroes in human rights struggle don't look upon themselves as Americans. They look upon themselves as a part of dark mankind. They see the whole struggle not within the confines of the American stage, but they look upon the struggle on the world stage. And in the world context, they see that the dark man outnumbers the white man. On the world stage the white man is just a microscopic minority.

> So in this country you find two different types of Afro-Americans—the type who looks upon himself as a minority, and you as the majority, because his scope is limited to the American scene; and you have the type who looks upon himself as the majority and you as part of the

microscopic minority. And this one uses a different approach in trying to struggle for his rights. He doesn't beg. He doesn't thank you for what you gave him, because you are only giving him what he should have had a hundred years ago. He does not think you are doing him any favors.[14]

The importance of Africa is much more than a mere question of identity. The domination of the world by white people of the West was of immense importance for the failure of what is called the American dream, and the observation of Harold R. Issacs becomes even more relevant for our argument:

> The downfall of the white supremacy system in the rest of the world made the survival of it in the United States suddenly and painfully complicated. It became our most exposed feature and in the swift unfolding of the world's affairs, our most vulnerable weakness . . . When hundreds of millions of people all around looked in our direction it seemed to be all that they could see.[15]

Malcolm X pointed out an important distinction in the conception of the black problem, a conception which has deep historical roots and is predicated on the unity of American blacks with Africans, and even with all the wretched of the earth in their determination to destroy the common imperialistic foe which threatened them. As early as May 1917 DuBois had written, "We trace the real cause of this World War to the despising of the darker races by the dominant groups of men." Sociologists such as Myrdal, Rose, Allison Davis and others considered the black problem to be a moral issue in the heart of the white Americans; they thought it was a conflict between what they described as the values and the practices of white Americans. Their emphasis was on the nature of prejudice and they directed their efforts to creating situations which would reduce prejudice, and convince white people that blacks are just plain old humans. There was no examination of the structural factors nor of the whole system of black-white relations as they existed historically in the world.

I have maintained on the other hand that with the advent of colonialism and imperialism the black had to suffer all the indignities that became his lot. I assert that if he had been allowed to evolve to full citizenship, the whole basis of imperialism could have been questioned ideologically and could have become an inexplicable anachronism for the theorists of white supremacy. The historical decision of the Supreme Court with regard to desegregation had a significance far beyond the question of whether or not segregation was morally wrong. Rupert Emerson and Martin Kilson in an article, "The Rise of Africa and the Negro American" have written:

The judiciary reached its apogee in this sphere with the Supreme Court's decision on desegration of public schools in May 1954. Long cognizant of the social and political environment within which it functions, the Court's decision in *Brown v. Board of Education* was as much influenced by America's postwar circumstances as the decision supporting segregated schools in *Plessy v. Ferguson* in 1896 was shaped by the post-Reconstruction era. The supporting brief of the Justice Department in submitting the segregation cases to the Supreme Court in December 1952 indicated full awareness of the contemporary international atmosphere and pressures. It declared that "it is in the context of the present world struggle between freedom and tyranny that the problem of racial discrimination must be viewed. . . . Racial discrimination furnishes grist for the Communist propaganda mills, and it raises doubt even among friendly nations as to the intensity of our devotion to the democratic faith. . . . The segregation of school children on a racial basis is one of the practices in the United States which has been singled out for hostile foreign comment in the United Nations and elsewhere. Other people cannot understand how such a practice can exist in a country which professes to be a staunch supporter of freedom, justice, and democracy."[16]

At another point in the same article they quote Nehru, speaking at a private meeting with Negro and white American civil rights leaders which was organized at the behest of Ralph J. Bunche and Walter White:

Whenever I warn against acceptance of Soviet promises of equality because they are so frequently broken, I am answered quite often by questions about America's attitude toward dark-skinned people. The people of Asia don't like colonialism or racial prejudices. They resent condescension. When Americans talk to them about equality and freedom, they remember stories about lynchings. They are becoming increasingly aware that colonialism is largely based on color—and, for the first time in the lives of many of them they realize they are colored (p. 1059).

This, then, is the sobering aspect of Afro-American reality that has been missed or misinterpreted by the "identity-alienation" school of recent years. The emergence of Africa from colonialism and its juxtaposition and coincidence in time with the changing tactics of the integration movement have been assumed to be causally related. But this argument ignores the historical feelings among the blacks against their inferior status. They might have used different methods and tactics, but they did express in no uncertain terms their abhorrence of oppression. The black movement for self-assertion was the first to speak for black emancipation. It led and encouraged black nationalism everywhere—a nationalism which would mean the emancipation of the black man all over the world. The developments in Africa, while separate, are yet intimately and intricately interrelated with the developments here; just as the imperial conquest of Africa, though a separate and independent event, had its repercussions for the black in America. DuBois proclaimed the inevitability of the color problem and its implications for the American black. Dean Rusk, Secretary of State in the Kennedy administration, recognizing that the black was an albatross around the neck of America's foreign relations, confirmed DuBois's prophecy in 1961:

> The biggest single burden that we carry on our backs in our foreign relations in the 1960s is the problem of racial discrimination here at home. There is just no question about it.
>
> We are dealing with forty or fifty new countries that have become independent since 1945, and we are living through a decade when the white race and the non-white races have got to re-examine and readjust their traditional relationships.
>
> Our attitude on a question of this sort is of fundamental importance to the success of the foreign policy of the United States.[17]

In Chapter One we dealt with the meanings of white hegemonic dominance of the world for the black; and what the Secretary of State says, and what the "alienation-identity" school is trying to say, show the relevance of our argument. Hegemonic dominance and racial oppression mean much more than just self-alienation and loss of identity, they mean the stunting and destruction of black personality. The black man's contact with the white man everywhere brought with it disaster, curses and cudgelling in the name of civilization and Christianity. The irony and the tragedy, according to DuBois, was that:

> After all, these black men were but men, neither more nor less wonderful than other men. In build and stature, they were for the most part among the taller nations and sturdily made. In their mental equipment and moral poise, they showed themselves full brothers to all men—"intensely human"; and this too in their very modifications and peculiarities—their warm brown and bronzed color and crisp curled hair under the heat and wet of Africa, their sensuous enjoyment of

music and color of life; their instinct for barter and trade, their strong family life and government. Yet these characteristics were bruised and spoiled and misinterpreted in the rude uprooting of the slave trade and sudden transplantation of this race to other climes among other peoples. Their color became a badge of servitude, their tropical habit deemed laziness, their worship was thought heathenish, their family customs and government were ruthlessly overturned and debauched, many of their virtues became vices, and much of their vices, virtues.[18]

What the "identity-alienation" school failed to do was to determine the historical character of what they were trying to understand. Under white hegemony the black could not develop a coherent world view, but produced one that was disjointed to the point of being bizarre. Self-hatred among the blacks was partly due to this distorted vision. Because of their social and intellectual subordination, they as a group have borrowed a world view from other classes and assert this borrowed world view in words while manifesting in behavior a contradictory perspective. In normal times it is possible to work within the limitations of the borrowed world view, but in times of crisis the black has moved autonomously, not according to its borrowed ideas but according to its actual needs. Nationalism and identification with the Third World is expressive of needs rather than of the logic of the borrowed world view.[19] Gramsci pointed out:

> Critical understanding of one's self takes place through a struggle of political "hegemonies" first in the field of ethics, then in politics, to render a high understanding of reality. The consciousness of belonging to a given hegemony is the first phase of a further self-consciousness in which theory and practice are finally united.[20]

Historically, the ideas I have treated above reflected the strong efforts on the part of the black to create a distinctive world view and to resist becoming an image of someone else. The Ethiopian movement and the Garvey movement attempted to create images and "gods" which would be meaningful for black people. In 1918, DuBois wrote in *The Crisis*:

> This war is an End, and also a beginning. Never again will darker people of the world occupy just the place they had before. Out of this war will rise, sooner or later, an independent China, a self-governing India, an Egypt with representative institutions, an Africa for the Africans and not merely for business exploitation. Out of this war will rise, too, an American Negro with the right to vote and the right to work and the right to live without insult.[21]

Our argument does not deny the fact that a large part of the living energy of the black intellectuals in America has been expended in an attempt to break the hold of whiteness by way of integration. Some of the more radical black writers like W.E.B. DuBois, Richard Wright, and James Baldwin had to remove themselves physically from the American environment to escape the psychological enslavement which they experienced. The poor blacks, such as the followers of Garvey, because of their station, could only think unthinkable thoughts without realization. But the restlessness evident among blacks points to the truth that unless a person feels that he belongs somewhere, that his life has some meaning and direction, he must feel like a particle of dust and be overcome by his individual insignificance. He will not be able to relate himself to any system which might give meaning and direction to his life; he will be filled with doubt, and this doubt will eventually paralyze his ability to act—that is to live. As long as American blacks confined their struggle to the American scene they felt helpless and had to plead and beg, but those who looked beyond the narrow confines of America took pride in what was happening elsewhere.

Don Hopkins in his article "Black Nationalism, Black Nationalists," says that preoccupation with integration has led to what he calls "a masochistic compulsion, a veritable will to whiteness which obtains in direct proportions to the will not to be black." He then spells out what he considers the case for nationalism among the blacks.

> The consequence of the affirmation of an Afro-American as opposed to a "Negro" personality is the association of the black in this country with a past, or a history outside the context of the American experience. When one is referred to as a Negro in the sense that Americans know and use this term, he is being defined as an individual who, for all practical purposes, is nothing more than a manumitted slave, for it is only in terms of slavery and the struggle for full citizenship thereafter that the Negro personality takes on any dimension. The nationalists and those persons who define themselves as Afro-Americans on the other hand, have refused acquiescence in this sadistic and self-denying fixation on slavery. They regard it as a fixation tantamount to basing a reputation of damsel upon an unfortunate rape, an experience suffered without a word being said about how valiantly she fought off her attackers. The nationalist does not see the whole history of the black man in Africa as just a preparation for an orgy that was slavery, nor does he regard slavery as the swaddling clothes of the American black. To define the black personality only in terms of slavery has further consequences of reducing the American blackman to just another

artifact of this country. It is clear that an artifact can never, save humorously, aspire to humanity, and it is for this reason that without Africa the American "Negro" is a Pinnochio at best, a Frankenstein at worst, and bereft of legitimate claim to humane treatment. He is in a word, a figment of American imagination and a living monument of his guile.[22]

Essien-Udom, Harold Isaacs, Charles Silberman and Louis Lomax limit the historical experience of the black to slavery, and when they speak about identity and pride they ask the black to accept this shameful experience and to shape his identity accordingly. They emphasize that the black personality has been shaped by the American environment and because of their a-historical approach they do not see any real connection between the American black's personality and his African background. In other words, they confuse the recognition of this essential fact with either the desire to repatriate the American black to Africa, or with the ability to identify with the culture of the African which is quite different from that of the American black. Thus if a black visits Africa and feels strange in its cultural milieu this is considered an indication that he has nothing in common with Africa. (This argument assumes, of course, that when an Irish-American goes to Ireland he takes to the Irish culture like a fish takes to water, which is, of course, an absurdity too preposterous to be maintained.) These writers select arbitrarily isolated phases and fail to grasp the phenomenon of African consciousness among the American blacks in its totality, and in its systematic and inevitable interrelationship with African emancipation. Ethiopianism, Garveyism and Pan-Africanism of the early 20th century may have been poor efforts, small fissures and factures in the dry crust of white hegemony, but they revealed an abyss. Beneath the apparently solid surface of world domination by whites they showed oceans of liquid matter only needing expansion to rend into fragments the hold of white supremacy. Noisily and confusedly they proclaimed the emancipation of the blackman. Don Hopkins grasps more thoroughly the nature and meaning of the American black's relation with Africa.

The few American black intellectuals who became Africa-conscious, and who saw the relation between the position of the black in white America and the status of Africa in the world, did so after many years of unprecedented torments and sacrifices, painstaking research and study; testing in practice European assumptions and beliefs and facing, of course, the inevitable disappointments. When considering certain phases of this African conscious-ness, we must not forget that at times it was temporarily overshadowed and forced into the background, but that it was bound to assume prime importance in the further development of the conflicts and contradictions between the white man's interest and black interests in the Third World. When America helped in the Congo airlift these conflicts and contradictions became obvious. One must be able to view the development of a given phenomenon in perspective, to see the interrelations of all its parts, and at the same time distinguish the lynch-pin of each concrete situation. The complexity of human reality, and its contradictory nature and its flux and change is reflected in one's judgement of it. This constant state of flux imposes the necessity for finding clear and definite answers to the problems that arise at any given moment. We must distinguish the apparent contradictions in social reality, understand their significance and study their developments. The progressive development of black consciousness of Africa, properly understood, reflects the reality of the world situation. The Student Nonviolent Coordinating Committee issued a statement in 1966 which caused a great deal of upset in the civil rights movement and in the white press. The statement, which was characterized as counter-racism, disclosed and unmasked the source and dimensions of racism in the US:

> The foundation and consequence of racism are not rooted in the behavior of black Americans yesterday or today. They are rooted in an attempt by Europeans and white Americans to exploit and dehumanize the descendents of Africa for monetary gain. This process of universal exploitation of Africa and her descendents continues today by the power elite of this country. In the process of exploiting black Americans, white Americans have tried to shift the responsibility for the degrading position in which blacks now find themselves away from the oppressors to the oppressed . . .

> We reaffirm our belief that people who suffer must make the decision about how to change and direct their lives. We therefore call upon all black Americans to begin building independent political, economic, and cultural institutions that they will control and use as instruments of social change in this country.[23]

Adam Clayton Powell, formerly Harlem Congressman and Chairman of the House Committee on Education and Labor echoed the SNCC sentiments when he called upon black people in America to drop their self-shame and seek audacious power in their struggle for freedom and equal justice in the land their forefathers had contributed so much to making the mighty power it is today. He made his address to the 1966 graduating class of Howard University.[24]

Consciousness always strives to adapt itself to existential reality. It is therefore nonsensical to say that the blacks rejected Africa and rejected themselves during the era of enslavement, colonialism, and imperialism. A proper identification with Africa could not be realized until Africa freed itself from imperial rule and degradation. That historical situation of imperialism surrounded the black folks, producing all their ambivalent reactions. Change was slow. As Mannheim noted:

> Man's thoughts had from time immemorial appeared to him as a segment of his spiritual existence and not simply as an objective fact. Reorientation had in the past frequently meant a change in man himself. In these earlier periods it was a case of slow shifts in values and norms, of a gradual transformation of the frame of reference from which men's actions derived their ultimate orientation. [25]

Historical analysis has enabled us to understand how and why African consciousness grew. For a black man to be engulfed in a white society without the possibility of escape is both oppressive and suffocating. A restoration of pride and identity, whatever one might call it, is a painful process. Fanon says it is a replacing of "certain species" of men by another "species of men." The adoption of X's by the Muslims might be considered silly by some but it attests to the implications of Fanon's argument. [26] The drive toward mental "de-colonization" forces upon the individual a more intense examination of the values of oppressor groups. He comes to learn that he has been controlled not only by the physical forces of white rule, but that he has been the victim of a particular kind of psychological make-up. "The need for psychological equality," wrote Stokely Carmichael,

> . . . is the reason why SNCC today believes that blacks must organize in the black community. Only the black people can convey the revolutionary idea that black people are able to do things themselves. Only they can help create in the community an aroused and continuing black conciousness that will provide the basis for political strength. In the past, white allies have furthered white supremacy without the whites involved realizing it—or wanting it. [27]

THE INDEPENDENCE MOVEMENT IN AFRICA AND THE AMERICAN BLACK

I have touched upon a statement by the Secretary of State and the Supreme Court Decision of 1954; both events were to a large extent influenced by events in the Third World. The independence movement in Africa caused for the first time (even though still on a limited scale) direct knowledge of the Afro-American by the African and of the Africans by the Afro-American. The once utopian ideas became concretized; and exposure to Africa was said to have "confirmed the conviction of the Negro that he was an American rather than an African."[28] Whether this was true or not on the part of the American black is unimportant. What is important is how they regarded Africa's emancipation *vis-a-vis* their emancipation efforts. James Baldwin among others gives primary credit for the civil rights campaigns of the 1950s and 60s to the rise of Africa in the context of the Cold War:

> Most of the American Negroes I know do not believe that this immense concession would ever have been made had it not been for the competition of the Cold War and the fact that Africa was clearly liberating herself and therefore, had, for political reasons, to be wooed by the descendants of her former masters. Had it been a matter of love or justice, the 1954 decision (concerning school segregation) would surely have occurred sooner. Were it not for the realities of power in this difficult era, it might very well not yet have occurred.[29]

In our discussion of the rights of man and the lack of a place in the world to make opinions effective we made the statement that the loss of Africa's independence influenced in large measure the black's treatment here. In their article Emerson and Kilson seem to agree with that analysis. They wrote:

> For the Negro in particular it has been a unique and stirring experience to see whole societies and political systems come into existence in which from the top to the bottom, from president, through civil service to office boy, all posts are occupied by blackmen, not because of the sufferance of white superiors but because it is a sovereign right. In contrast to the Negro's experience of the American society, the control of the new African states and societies is in African hands and where white expertise is needed it is employed by African governments in African terms.[30]

There is of course the obverse side of the matter: When Ghana became independent in 1957 it was hailed by DuBois in these beautiful and poetic words:

I came to Africa
Here at last, I looked back on my dream
I heard the voice that loosed
The long-locked dungeons of my soul
I sensed that Africa had come
Not up from Hell, but from the sun of Heaven's glory.[31]

But the entry of Ghana into the world community of sovereign nations was to magnify the conflict in black/white relations in America. For the first time in its history America found itself compelled by world events to deal with black men on the basis of full equality.

The first problem that presented itself was a racial one. Was the prospective United States ambassador to the emerging state of Ghana to be Negro or white? America had seldom, if ever, sent its first-class citizens, whitemen, as ambassadors to black Africa, or for that matter to any country ruled by blackmen. Afro-Americans had always had, as their political "plum" the Liberian ambassadorship. This was understandable; both groups were "seventh sons" of America.[32]

In any complex situation many contradictions exist, and it is necessary to distinguish their varied manifestations. Since blacks were regarded as second-class citizens, could a young and proud African state legitimately accept one of them as an ambassador without "hurting" its own international standing? The Ghanaians, it is said, discretely let it be known that they would have none of this.

Rumors flew about that President Nkrumah himself would refuse to accept an American Negro as an ambassador. According to reports, he felt that since Negroes were regarded as second-class citizens in the United States, such an appointment would reflect an equivalent judgment of his country. Officially Ghanaians issued heated denials of these rumors but they had served their function: to warn America that emerging Africa would demand racial equality. Thanks in part to the Cold War, Ghana was to have its wish: a white, first-class American as its ambassador.[33]

Ghana's whispering campaign could be interpreted as paradoxical; it could be made to mean that Africans look down upon the American blacks; which is, in fact, what has been done. This construction however misses the salient points of the argument. For the Ghanaians to accept a black ambassador could make them accomplices to the degradation of the black people; but at the same time to accept a white ambassador would also insult their race, since he would represent a country that did not consider its black citizens worthy of a position in the foreign service. This problem of ambassadorial exchanges has been manifested more critically in South Africa's relations with the non-white world and America. Since America believes in equality, it has been asked why it has not appointed a single black man on its staff in South Africa? The only solution that has been suggested by Africans is for the United States either to suspend diplomatic relations with South Africa, or to send blacks to serve as full-fledged members of the American foreign service in white countries as well as black, and in particular in South Africa.

The racial problems at the diplomatic level become even more accentuated at the social level. How were the ever-increasing number of African diplomats in Washington and in the United Nations to be treated? How were the ever-increasing number of Africans studying in American universities to be distinguished from Afro-American students? There is nothing more fascinating than to enter a lily-white establishment and to be met with all the hostility imaginable; and then when your accent betrays your "non-Negro" origin to see the hostility melt away and be replaced by synthetic smiles. "Periodically, however, Africans did find that their presence was not appreciated by many white Americans, since color-conscious whites saw only a *black man* under exotic robes, and refused to rent apartments to Africans or to serve them meals in restaurants. Many a policeman found out too late that the black man he had beaten up and taken to the police station for being 'cheeky' was actually carrying a diplomatic passport. Of course the embarrassed city fathers tried to make amends, but Africans recognized the real source of their discomfort: the relations between Afro-Americans and white Americans."[34]

Since 1957 there have been 50 independent African states. What has been their reaction to the treatment of people of African descent in America? Samuel W. Allen in the introduction to the book *Pan-Africanism Reconsidered* has written:

> The unrealism of any attempt to compress the dynamics of Pan-Africanism within the logical confines of a definition was apparent in the contrast between the expressed concern over the plight of the Negroes in the Americas and the assertion of solidarity with the North Americans.[35]

Consciousness about the black plight in America, contrary to the popular notions expressed in popular daily papers and weeklies, was pin-pointed much more specifically by Alionne Diop, Director of the *Societe Africaine de Culture:*

> Whatever honors the American Negro community is, you can be sure, a source of pride for us—just as we are pained whenever this American Negro society is affected in one of its members. When a Negro somewhere in America is lynched or is the victim of injustice often the news reverberates throughout Africa and moving poems are written, poems of which many Americans are unfortunately unaware, poems of solidarity.[36]

Interest in the American black has been shown not only by African intellectuals who are conscious of the black's contribution to the struggle for African emancipation, but has been expressed by African leaders and heads of states. Dr. Nnamdi Azikiwe in his inaugural address as the president of the Federation of Nigeria stated:

> We regard all races of the human family as equal. Under no circumstances shall we accept the idea that the black race is inferior to any other race. No matter where this spurious doctrine may prevail, it may be in London or Sharpeville or Decatur, we shall never admit that we are an inferior race, because if we accept the Christian or Muslim doctrine that God is perfect, and that man was made in the image of God, then it would be sacriligious, if not heretical, to believe that we are an inferior race. We cannot concede that it is in our national interest to fraternize with such nations that practice race prejudice and we must not acquiesce in such outrageous insult on the black race. In fact, we must regard it as a mark of disrespect and an unfriendly act if any country with whom we have friendly relations indulges in race prejudice in any shape or form, no matter how it may be legally booked.

In a speech celebrating the 50th anniversary of the NAACP held in New York City in 1959, Dr. Azikiwe acknowledged that the NAACP had been an inspiration for him and his colleagues:

> This spirit of the American Negro as exemplified in the constitutional struggles of the NAACP has also fired the imagination of the sleeping African giant who is now waking up and taking his rightful place in the

community of nations. In Africa, the NAACP spirit of active resistance to the forces which are inconsistent with Democratic principles has fired our imagination. We have relentlessly fought any attempt to foist upon us the horrible stigma of racial inferiority.

After several racial incidents occurring during the civil rights "push," Jaja Wachuku, Nigerian representative to the United Nations, said before the 15th General Assembly on December 13, 1960: "Anybody who is not prepared to eradicate the humiliation that has been meted out to the people of African descent or the people of our racial stock cannot claim to be in love with us."

At the All-African People's Conference, held in Accra, Ghana, on December 13, 1958, Dr. Nkrumah, the president of this new African state, expressed his delight in seeing "so many people of African descent from abroad attending this conference." He went on to say:

It has warmed us to see here so many of our brothers from across the sea. We take their presence here as a manifestation of keen interest in our struggle for a free Africa . . . We must not forget that they are a part of us. These sons and daughters of Africa were taken from our shores, and despite all the centuries that have separated us, they did not forget their ancestral links.

Nkrumah reminded the delegates of the role of the American blacks in the struggle for African freedom:

Many of them made no small contribution to the cause of African freedom. Names which spring immediately to mind in this connection are those of Marcus Garvey and W.E.B. DuBois. Long before many of us were even conscious of our own degradation, these men fought for African national and racial equality. Long may the links between Africa and people of African descent continue to hold us together in fraternity. Now that we in Africa are marching toward complete emancipation of this continent, our independent status will help in no small measure their efforts to attain full human rights and human dignity *and* as citizens of their country.[37]

Africans were bitterly resentful of the inhuman treatment sometimes meted out to civil rights workers. In May 1963, for example, Gordon Cooper's dramatic space flight coincided with both the Birmingham riots and the meeting of the African Heads of States in Addis Ababa, Ethiopia.

As Cooper flew over Africa he beamed a message of good will to the conference on behalf of the people of the United States. This message was ignored and the African Heads of States in their final communiqué sent an open letter to President John F. Kennedy which stated:

> The Negroes, who, even while the conference was in session, have been subjected to the most inhuman treatment, who have been blasted with fire hoses cranked up to such pressure that the water would strip bark off the trees, at whom the police have deliberately set searching dogs, are our own kith and kin . . . The only offense which these people have committed are that they are black and that they have demanded the right to be free to hold their heads up as equal citizens of the United States.

The New York Times of May 1, 1963, published their special correspondent's report that the Foreign Minister of Nigeria rose "to denounce racial discrimination in South Africa and the United States." A later report stated further: "American observers have been dismayed to hear Alabama linked with South Africa in attacks on apartheid inside and outside the conference hall . . . American correspondents approaching members of the delegations frequently hear the question: 'What's the latest news from Birmingham?' "[38]

Essien-Udom quotes an event which he says took place 40 years ago. This involved the giving of a scroll to Roland Hayes, the outstanding black tenor, by 12 distinguished Africans and a West Indian, in honor of his accomplishments and especially his contribution in projecting the dignity of African peoples. Among those who signed the scroll were: Duse Muhammad Ali of Egypt; Henry M. Jones of Ghana; two Liberians, M. Massaquoi and Harold Friedrichs; Chief Oluwa of Lagos; Gage H. O'Dwyer, Ozimtola Sapara and D. Doherty from Nigeria; and John Alemdor from Trinidad, West Indies. The text of the scroll is significant:

To Roland Hayes, the Negro Tenor

We the undersigned, having closely observed your interesting rise to a pre-eminent and enviable position in the realm of music, and being members of the various races that go to make up the families who comprise the inhabitants of Africa as well as those who have descended from the same parent stock as yourself, beg to tender you our high felicitations and regards on this your visit to the seat of the British Empire.

We realize that your success is our success and that by proving that you are capable of higher musical culture you are rendering incalculable benefits to your race.

As blood of our blood, flesh of our flesh, and bone of our bone, we wish you continued success in all your undertakings, praying that all Wise Creator will graciously grant you health and strength to complete the task you have so nobly undertaken which must indubitably redound to His Glory to the amelioration and recognition of the undoubted mental capabilities and endowments of your brothers of the Negro race.

We therefore beg that you will accept this slight token of our undying admiration and esteem.[39]

It may be predicted that despite problems and difficulties Africans will continue to show interest in the fate of their kith and kin whether in the United States or in South Africa. In the case of the American black this interest will be fully realized as Africans come to know more and more about the efforts of their brothers across the seas on behalf of African emancipation, and as they realize that there is no rational or logical conflict between their own vital interests and the liberation of the Afro-American people. But just as the Afro-Americans realized that freedom and dignity are indivisible, Africans will realize their kinship with American blacks, will recognize that the infringement of Afro-American rights is a negation of their newly-acquired African pride, and will insist that black rights be respected.

Freedom and the full development of the human personality, therefore, requires independence for the African peoples as well as full citizenship rights with equal status and opportunity for the minority peoples of African descent wherever they now exist. An enlightened awareness of African lore and liberty is, and will continue to be, the inevitable expression of the indomitable will to self-knowledge, self-determination, self-realization, one's self-development in parity with all mankind.[40]

Most of Africa has now been independent for over 25 years. For some Afro-Americans the independent Africa offers many opportunities including a refuge from the race prejudice and from the status of being a minority. African states have welcomed business ventures by Afro-Americans as well. For organizations like TransAfrica, Africa and the Caribbean has provided a focus for meaningful political action. "It ha[d] served this function in the past for members of American Negroes who [were] interested in cementing intercultural ties or doing research."[41]

The "cult of Africa" which Drake says has always existed in the black community has grown in size and influence to include disparate groups of devotees ranging from ghetto Nationalists who support overtly African struggles, through middle class families that specialize in entertaining African dignitaries and are entertained by African representatives of the U.N., to African cultural enthusiasts who have together with their African counterparts held a number of cultural festivals in Africa. Africa is no longer a far-off but inescapable embarrassment or a negative stereotype. It is true that for some die-hard racists the aberrations of an Idi Amin or an Emporer Bokassa are still used to discredit blacks and their abilities to government. But then blacks can point to the Hitlers and the Verwoerds of this world that Europe has produced. As blacks gain political influence, they are becoming an important factor in the formulation of U.S. foreign policy.

Drake, in the above cited article, summed up the meaning of Africa's independence for Afro-Americans in these words:

> Because of the African friends they have made, or because they wish to be identified with the process of "poetic justice" now working itself out, or because of sentiments which became deeply imbedded in their youth, or because they smart under the continued impact of deprecatory definitions placed upon their own physical Negroidness, Africa will function as a "spiritual homeland." They will share the feelings which made a Nigerian who had studied in America, Mboni Ojike, write a book entitled *I Have Two Countries*. There is nothing "un-American" about this, for such identification has its parallel among the Poles and the Irish, the Jews and the Swedes, and numerous other groups who keep alive both memories and contacts with an "ancestral homeland."[42]

Notes

[1]A. Kardiner and L. Ovesey, *The Mark of Oppression*, World Publishing Company, New York, 1962, p. 385.

[2]E.B. Essien-Udom, *Black Nationalism—A Search for Identity in America*, Dell Publishing Company, 1964, p. 9.

[3]Isaacs, *op. cit.*, p. 22.

[4]Silberman, *op. cit.*, pp. 184-85.

[5]Professor Bernhard J. Stern, in speaking of the doctrine of integrative levels of culture, stated: "It does not negate the importance of the psychological processes underlying all cultural phenomena just as biological processes underlie all psychological phenomena. However, it stresses the fact that reduction to a psychological level cannot explain any specific aspect or pattern of culture, for each is a historical product; and that, to interpret properly the forms and functions of culture as they condition the behavior of humans, one must understand their historical backgrounds." Bernhard J. Stern, *Historical Sociology*, Citadel Press, New York, 1959, p. 16.

[6]Karl Marx, *Capital*, Vol. I, Kerr edition, p. 52.

[7]Richard Wright, *Reader*, (eds.), Ellen Wright and Michael Fabre with notes by Michael Fabre, Harper and Row, New York, pp. 149, 151.

[8]Louis Lomax, *The Negro Revolt*, Harper and Row, New York, 1962, p. 249.

[9]Richard Wright, *Black Power: An American Negro Views the Gold Coast*, Harper Brothers, New York, 1953, p. 5.

[10]Cf. Roy S. Bryce-Laporte, "The Rastas," *Caribbean Review*, Vol. 2, No. 2, 1970, p. 4.

[11]Silberman, *op. cit.*, p. 170.

[12]In "Malcolm and the Conscience of Black America," Lawrence P. Neal wrote that: Malcolm forced us to see—and we were very reluctant to see it—that our 'Negro leaders' were begging for entry into a system, a way of life which was *at its roots* corrupt and spiritually dead. Not only was there no room for us in this integrated dream; we came more and more to understand that integration meant joining with White America in the oppression of the rest of the non-White world. It means a world where a Roy Wilkins refused to take a stand against Black people participating in a war against other colored peoples. We came to understand that there were distinct orientations at work in the struggle. One identifies with America and its values; the other strives for a new more humane system of values. Malcolm stood for the new values, pride in self, the development of a strong Afro-American personality, and a revolutionary dynamic that was in synch with contemporary realities. (Liberator, Vol. 6, No. 2, February 1966, p. 10).

[13]Don Hopkins, "Black Nationalism, Black Nationalists," *Black Dialogue*, Vol. 1, Nos. 3,4, 1965, p. 74.

[14]Malcolm X, *Two Speeches by Malcolm X*, Pioneer Publishers, New York, March 1965, p. 10.

[15]Isaacs, *op. cit.*, p. 211.

[16]Rupert Emerson and Martin Kilson, "The Rise of Africa and the American Negro," *Daedalus*, Vol. 94, No. 4, Fall 1965, p. 1073.

[17]Quoted in *Ibid.*, p. 1063.

[18]W.E.B. DuBois, *John Brown*, International Publishers, New York, 1962, p. 17.

[19]Malcolm X has observed: "It is incorrect to classify the revolt of the Negro as simply a racial conflict of black against white or as purely an American problem.

Rather, we are today seeing a global rebellion of the oppressed against the oppressor, the exploited against the exploiter." *The Autobiography of Malcolm X*, Grove Press, New York, 1965, p. 133.

[20]Antonio Gramsci, *The Open Marxism of Antonio Gramsci*, translated and annotated by Carl Marzini, Cameron, New York, 1957, p. 30.

[21]*Crisis*, Vol. 16, No. 2, 1918, p. 60.

[22]Don Hopkins, *op. cit.*, p. 14.

[23]*National Guardian*, 28 May, 1966.

[24]*Muhammed Speaks*, 10 June 1966.

[25]Mannheim, *Ideology and Utopia*, p. 42.

[26]We may remind ourselves here that today's Women's Liberation Movement has discussed widely the pros and cons of bearing of one's husband's name. Indeed, some of them have already changed to their maiden names in their search for a separate identity from their husbands.

[27]*The New York Review of Books*, September 22, 1966, p. 6.

[28]Emerson and Kilson, *op. cit.*, p. 1066.

[29]James Baldwin, *The Fire Next Time*, Dial Press, New York, 1963, pp. 117-18.

[30]Emerson and Kilson, *op. cit.*, p. 1066.

[31]W.E.B. DuBois, *Freedomways*, Vol. 2, No. 1, Winter 1962, p. 71.

[32]Elliott P. Skinner, "American, Afro-American, White America," *Freedomways*, vol. 5, No. 3, Summer 1965, p. 387.

[33]Skinner, *Ibid.*, p. 386.

[34]*Ibid.*, p. 388.

[35]American Society of African Culture (ed.), *Pan-Africanism Reconsidered*, University of California, Los Angeles, 1962, pp. 12-13.

[36]*Ibid.*, p. 32.

[37]*All African People's Conference News Bulletin*, Vol. 1, No. 1, 1961, p. 2.

[38]*New York Times*, 23 May 1963.

[39]Essien-Udom, *Black Nationalism*, p. 406.

[40]Moore, *op. cit.*, p. 75.

[41]St. Claire Drake, "Hide My Face?—On Pan Africanism and Negritude," *op. cit.*, p. 103.

[42]*Ibid.*, p. 104.

CHAPTER NINE
Afro-Americans and the Struggle Against White Rule in South Africa

When one of African descent seriously studies racist South Africa and understands the continuum of suffering, the great loss of both life and freedom, the systematic destruction of human potential, and finally the absence of Southern Africa's own wealth for use by the African; one cannot escape a deep sense of personal loss, as well as the certain knowledge that when Africa is strong and free, Africans around the world will be a much stronger political/economic force and a more respected and protected people.

Al Mitchell, Editor, *Ground Level Magazine*

History has a way of throwing long shadows. The experiences of Afro-Americans and of the black people of South Africa share a great deal in common. The first African arrived on the shores of the "new world" as a slave in 1619 and the first European settlers arrived on the southern tip of Africa in 1652, to begin the enslavement of the African in his own land. As the capitalist mode of production grew, European expansion also developed in depth and breadth; and blacks in the US and South Africa bore its full brunt. The situation of both peoples today unmasks the nature of racism and its indissoluble link to capitalism.

Cecil John Rhodes who endowed the famous Rhodes scholarship is said to be "the first distinguished British statesman whose imperialism was that of race and not that of empire." His will is said to be color blind between the British Empire and the American Republic; that is, his will aimed at making Oxford University the educational center of the English-speaking race:

He specifically prescribed that every American State and Territory shall share with the British Colonies in his patriotic benefaction.[1]

207

The idea of the "imperialism of race" was also expressed by Andrew Carnegie, who expected that the Anglo-Saxon would one day reunite, undoing the rupture of 1776. According to James P. Sheraton:

> The need for unity among the Anglo-Saxons was accepted as urgent because it was assumed that the decline of Great Britain had become evident. America had now to grasp the sceptre of Anglo-Saxon world dominance or share in the British collapse . . . Ties of blood and kinship were similarly invoked to justify expanded American and British cooperation.[2]

In the spirit of Anglo-Saxonism an *extente cordiale* existed between the governments of the United States and Britain. Indeed between Joseph Chamberlain, Secretary of State for British colonies, and President William McKinley there was "similarity of thought."[3] The support the US administration gave to Britain during the Anglo-Boer War of 1900-02 is therefore understandable. In his study of American and British imperialism, Victor Kiernan wrote that:

> When Chamberlain's war in South Africa started late in 1899, and all Europe was anti-British, with Germany loudest, America was able to reciprocate the goodwill of the previous year [when the British had not criticized the American conquest of Samoa]. These two colonial wars had the same plausibly altruistic look, which allowed many progressives in America to approve of both, even though in South Africa a monarchy was attacking two small republics. Ostensibly Britain was fighting to protect its settlers from ill-usage by the Boers; harder-headed men in London had their thoughts fixed on gold and diamonds. The two contests resembled each other also in muddle and incompetence on the stronger side, and their opportunities for profiteering. But Britain had more prestige at stake, and the length of the struggle, protracted to 1902, made it feel uncomfortably isolated. John Bull's old maxim of *Oderint dum metuant*, let them hate so long as they fear, was out of date.

> America's attitude was therefore a great relief. Convinced that the vital principle of American foreign policy must be "a friendly understanding with England," Hay rejected a series of Boer requests for him to interpose, and showed a marked lack of sympathy, over the British use of concentration camps in particular. In the US an avid interest was taken in British heroes like Baden-Powell. True, there was still an opposite current of feeling, and a number of American volunteers

served with the Boers. One of them, surgeon-general with the force beleaguering Baden-Powell at Mafeking (which itself had some Americans in its composite population) wrote him a stiff letter of protest at the British employment of African soldiers, horror at "the idea of arming black against white," and called on him to "act the part of a white man in a white man's war." His letter is reminiscent of outcries by Americans in bygone days about the British employing Red Indians against them. They themselves had just been employing some Indians in Cuba against the Spaniards.[4]

Kiernan goes on to say that

Friendships between nations are most often, as Dr. Johnson said of friendships between individuals, partnerships in folly or confederacies in vice. Conservative Britain was always blind to the virtues that made America the hope of the 19th century, but was ready to encourage its worse proclivities; after looking with favor on the expansionist South, it was now looking with favor on Northern expansionism. The two countries encouraged each other in the work of suppressing their respective rebels, by what the British Liberal leader denounced in South Africa as "methods of barbarism." An American engaged in putting down colonial revolt could scarcely criticize Englishmen, or Frenchmen, or Dutchmen who were having to deal with nationalist movements in Asia, and could scarcely serve as a beacon to these movements. Senator Beveridge visited the Far East and was keen to learn about the British colonial system, which various Americans were setting themselves to study as a model. America besides, as now a force in the Far East, might be useful not only to keep Russia in check, but to help in putting pressure on China. A British businessman with Japanese connections wrote in 1898: "China will . . . seek regeneration at the hands of Britain—whom she will trust when she once more fears her wrath—of America, soon to be an Asiatic power, and of Japan, best fitted of all to undertake the task."[5]

Many other voices echoed this proffered partnership. "It is always a joy to me to meet an American, Mr. Moulton," said Sherlock Holmes solemnly, "for I am one of those who believe that the folly of a monarch and the blundering of a Minister in fargone years will not prevent our children from being some day citizens of the same worldwide country under a flag which shall be a quartering of the Union Jack with the Stars and Stripes." An admirer of the great detective must blush at the uses to which his blundering creator sometimes put him. A few years after this, an American actor was running a Sherlock Holmes play in the States, and Conan Doyle was writing a pamphlet to defend the Boer War and its methods of barbarism, which sold widely in the US as well as in Britain. All that was needed to make the US a friend and ally, Lord G. Hamilton said in 1903, was its entry into world politics. Kipling, summoning Americans to "take up the white man's burden," took it equally for granted that a US with a taste for colonialism must automatically find itself at England's side. His influence was far from insignificant. This was in the day when "high-school girls were poring over his 'Barrack-Room Ballads' with flaming cheeks in every nook and corner of the country . . . "

So it came about that in 1909, a constitution patterned on the American South was imposed on the people of South Africa by the British imperial administrator. As in the southern United States a white oligarchy was installed in power and was used to keep blacks in economic servitude. J.A. Hobson in his book, *The Crisis of Liberalism* pointed out that "a South African Union as is now established [is] a close replica . . . of the Southern States of the American Commonwealth, where the races subsist side by side in the same land in no organic spiritual contact with one another, each suffering the moral, intellectual and industrial penalty of this disunion."[6]

Anglo-Saxon chauvinism burdened not only the United States but the entire world. The study of the economic, political, civic, legal, and moral aspect of the Afro-American and African problem in the US and South Africa is of special interest under present circumstances. Their problems are not just of today; its roots extend back ever deeper. This chapter traces these linkages. At every point in their history of struggle against racism Afro-American leaders never failed to draw attention to the parallel situation in South Africa. The African Methodist Episcopal Church of Bishop Turner established one of its earliest branches in South Africa; some of the Africans who were the founding members of the African National Congress in 1912, studied in black colleges like Tuskeegee in Alabama, where they got their political inspiration. For waging nonviolent struggles against racism in the U.S. and South Africa four blacks, Dr. Ralph Bunche and Dr. Reverend Martin Luther King Jr. in the US, and Chief Albert Lutuli and Reverend Bishop Desmond Tutu from South Africa, have received Nobel Peace prizes.

At the first Pan-African Congress held in London in 1900, as we have seen, the situation in South Africa drew the special attention of the delegates. In 1923, the Pan-African Congress protested the slaughter in Namibia and drew attention to J.C. Smuts, asking:

What more paradoxical figure today confronts the world than the official head of this state [Smuts] striving blindly to build peace and good-will in Europe by standing on the necks and hearts of millions of Africans![7]

I have referred briefly to the activities of the Council on African Affairs (CAA) formed in 1937 by Paul Robeson and the Afro-American sociologist, Max Yergan. This organization did much to draw attention not only to the worsening racial situation in South Africa, but also to the growing support of the racist regime in that country by the US administrations. As early as 1937, the International Committee of the Council on African Affairs sponsored lectures by Professor D.D.T. Jabavu and Dr. Alfred Xuma, two prominent leaders of the All-African Convention formed in 1935 to oppose the Hertzog Bills that ultimately disenfranchised the Black population of their limited voting rights. In 1946, the CAA submitted a memorandum to the United Nations Commission on Human Rights, calling for an investigation of racism in South Africa, to be followed by appropriate action by the Security Council. On June 19, 1946, it organized a massive rally attended by 15,000 people in Madison Square Garden to denounce the racist regime of South Africa and oppose its plans for the annexation of Namibia.[8]

Later, in 1946, the Council hosted the first delegation of the South African Liberation Movement to the United Nations. This delegation consisted of Dr. Xuma, then President of the African National Congress of South Africa; Mr. H.A. Naidoo, a leader of the South African Indian Congress; and Mr. H.M. Bassner, a senator representing the Africans in the Transvaal and the Orange Free State. It organized many meetings in support of the African freedom struggle. In August 1946, the Council organized a large picket line in front of the South African Consulate to protest its racist laws and the brutal massacre of African miners during their historic strike.

Like the 1923 Pan African Congress resolution, the CAA tore the mask off the then Prime Minister of South Africa, so-called Field Marshall Jan Smuts, who was being paraded in the West as a liberal when he was in fact a racist. It denounced the hypocrisy of the so-called "Free World" which betrayed its professions and its promises, and allied with the racist regime of South Africa in its oppression of the black people of South Africa and Namibia. The CAA recalled the moves to limit the Atlantic Charter to the Caucasians, with the elimination from its scope of people across the color line throughout the world.

In 1952, when the South African people launched a "Campaign of

Defiance against Unjust Laws," the Council on African Affairs raised funds to support the liberation movement and organized petitions to the President of the United States.

In 1952, an editorial in the CAA Magazine, *Spotlight on Africa*, drew attention to the class basis of the Truman administration's policy toward South Africa:

> South Africa is part of President Truman's "free world." Yes, dozens of America's biggest auto, oil, mining and other trusts have highly profitable holdings in that country.

> Hence it is clear that in raising our voices against the Malan regime we simultaneously strike a blow at reactionary forces in our own land who seek to preserve here, in South Africa, and everywhere else the super profits they harvest from racial and national oppression. United support for our brothers' struggles in Africa is an integral part of our task in achieving freedom for all Americans and peace for the world.[9]

The sociologist Kevin Danaher points out that because of the anti-capitalist thrust of the CAA's work, it was put on the Attorney General's list of subversive organizations in 1948. "The group's fate was sealed by a cyclical process of government harassment, steady radicalization of its perspective, and defection of its more moderate members. The CAA folded in 1955 without having been more than an irritant to the policy apparatus."[10]

I have on many occasions referred to W.E.B. DuBois as the "Father of Pan-Africanism." Even more than his championing of Pan-Africanism and African independence, his hatred of racist oppression in South Africa was unequaled. Thus, DuBois used his pen to help to inform the world about the nature of apartheid and to criticize those who accorded respectability to the white minority state: "It is almost unbelievable that in the middle of the 20th century the Union of South Africa is widely recognized as a civilized nation."[11]

DuBois warned that corporate investments, bank loans and trade were helping to strengthen the system of white domination. He pointed out that economies so supported would call for

> larger and larger numbers of black workers who must be thrown more and more in competition with white skilled labor in and out of Africa, (so) they are trying to segregate workers by race and color, and to turn them into something as near slavery as modern conditions will permit.

DuBois' vision of Africa in general and South Africa in particular, was clear:

> Men of all races are welcome to Africa if they obey its laws, seek its interests and love their neighbors as themselves... But the white bigots of South Africa... are solemnly warned that they cannot win... We will be free... we will govern ourselves for our best good. Our wealth and labor belong to us and not to thieves at home or abroad. Black Africa welcomes the world as equals; as masters never; we will fight this forever and curse the blaspheming Boers and the heathen liars from Hell.
>
> Let the white world keep its missionaries at home to teach the Golden Rule to its corporate thieves. Damn the God of Slavery, Exploitation and War. Peace on earth; no more war. The earth of Africa is for its people. Its wealth is for the poor and not for the rich. All Hail Africa. [12]

Because of their travels and contact with black leaders from South Africa, Robeson and DuBois had a unique understanding of apartheid in South Africa and spoke with particular eloquence, but their views were shared by the broad masses of Afro-Americans.

During the inter-war years, and even more so in the post-World War II phase, the US made a decisive entry into Africa as an imperial power in its own right. The thrust of US foreign policy toward Africa in general and South Africa in particular reveals a tendency to undermine the interest of other imperial powers and to establish itself as the dominant imperial power. Washington's support of the racist regime went against the fundamental human rights advocated in the US Bill of Rights. In the early stages of the United Nations, India and a number of newly-free countries proposed a resolution requesting that the Union of South Africa report on the treatment of people of Indian origin in South Africa. The United States voted "no." When the UN proposed that negotiations take place between India, Pakistan and South Africa on the treatment of Asians in South Africa, the United States joined with South Africa to vote "no." On the same day when the General Assembly Resolution 616 (VII)A was passed to establish a United Nations Commission to study the South African government's policy of apartheid, the US abstained.

In September 1960, Krushchev, Chairman of the Council of Ministers of the USSR, proposed the adoption by the UN of the Declaration on the Granting of Independence to Colonial Countries and Peoples. In his speech

Chairman Krushchev stated that in order to adhere to the principles set forth in its Charter, the UN must declare its unequivocal support for the "immediate and complete elimination of the colonial system in all its forms and manifestations." The Declaration on Colonialism was prepared by 43 African and Asian countries. Resolution 1514 XV was passed on December 14, 1960, by a vote of 89 to 0, with the US among the nine countries that abstained. [13]

The year 1971 was proclaimed by the UN as the International Year Against Racism. On December 6, the General Assembly passed an extremely important resolution (2784 XXVI). Among the components of the resolution are the following:

> . . . Invites Economic and Social Council to request Commission on Human Rights to study policies and practices of racial discrimination, in particular, discrimination against peoples of African origins in all countries, and submit report to the General Assembly by its 28th Session. (US voted "no.")

> . . . Notes with appreciation the report of the Committee on the Elimination of Racial Discrimination. *(US voted "no.")*

> . . . Reaffirms Apartheid is a crime against humanity. (US abstained while 97 countries voted "yes," so it passed.)

It is unnecessary to mention every resolution passed by the UN on the question of colonialism and racism that was opposed by the United States. Suffice it to mention an *International Covenant on the Elimination of All Forms of Racial Discrimination*, which was adopted by the United Nations and went into effect on January 4, 1969, as part of the body of International Law accepted by the member states of the United Nations. Eighty nations have ratified this International Covenant. The US is among the few that has not.

This behavior of the United States toward the practice of racism and toward blacks in South Africa should not be a surprise. Early in its history the US ruling class, while casting off the chains of English colonial rule, shackled every fifth citizen whose roots were African to the chains of slavery. Many years later Frederick Engels drew attention to this flagrant contradiction of American democracy. "It is significant," he wrote, "that the American constitution, the first to recognize the rights of man, in the same breath confirmed the slavery of the colored races existing in America. Class privileges are proscribed, race privileges sanctioned." [14]

Jack O'Dell recently pointed to the same contradiction:

Born during the Industrial Revolution and the Age of Enlightenment in 18th century Europe, fully a product of the capitalist epoch in world history, the United States of America as a society has always expressed in exaggerated form all of the contradictions characteristic of the capitalist world order. The leaders of the U.S. Revolution of 1776 were the first to raise the enlightened, democratic demand of popular individual freedom which was crystallized in the Bill of Rights of the Republic's Constitution. Yet this was the last industrial country to abolish human slavery on its national territory. The United States was a sanctuary for millions of the poor from Europe who flocked to its shores, and at one and the same time a slave pen for millions of Africans dragged here in chains and a prison-house for the captive peoples of the Mexican Republic and the sovereign Indian nations conquered by the United States in wars of aggression.[15]

The brief resume of US voting on the question of colonialism and racism is inseparable from its treatment of peoples of African descent. Those who rule the US have never taken important social or political steps on the question of Africa or Afro-Americans unless the most crying necessity forced them to do so, and unless these steps promised immediate or long-term economic political and other dividends. I will discuss further the attitude of the US toward the issue of divestment.

The post World War II period saw a great mass upsurge for human and democratic rights in the United States and South Africa. To discredit this popular upsurge, the US government and the South African regime resorted to the anti-Communist scare. It could not be otherwise. The capitalistic mentality, when its domination is challenged, has no other way of diffusing the challenge to its exploitations and oppressive politics; it knows only one answer—anti-Communism. Paul Robeson drew attention to the use of anti-Communism by the white supremacist in the US South and in South Africa who were intent on suppressing the black struggles:

As in South Africa, where the notorious "Suppression of Communism Act" is used to attack the liberation movement, the enemies of Negro freedom in our country have accused the NAACP of being a "subversive conspiracy" and the organization has been outlawed in Louisiana, Texas and Alabama, and legally restricted in Georgia, Virginia, South Carolina and Mississippi. City ordinances, as in Little Rock, are also used for this purpose.

The indifference with which various other organizations viewed the suppression in 1955 of the Council on African Affairs, which was falsely labeled a "Communist front," should not be repeated now by any group in the case of the NAACP. The Red-baiting charges against that organization are utterly untrue, as the makers of such charges know full well; and those elements in Negro leadership who have in the past resorted to Red-baiting as a "smart" tactic should realize that such methods serve no one but our people's worst enemies.[16]

The meaning of racial oppression for blacks as a group in the US and South Africa is revealed. The collective historical experience of blacks in North America and South Africa is not incidental but central to the economic development and socio-political formations of the two white settler states. The capitalist foundations of the US and South Africa rested upon super-exploited black labor. Indeed, the pace and scale of early development of both societies would have been inconceivable without the dehumanized and super-exploited black labor. The use of anti-communism in the US and South Africa to discredit the human rights struggle of the black people therefore reflects consciously or unconsciously the awareness of the working-class character of black demands.

The divestment movement is built on a long established tradition. In 1962 Dr. Martin Luther King and Chief Albert Lutuli, President of the African National Congress of South Africa, issued a joint statement appealing for the imposition of international sanctions against the white minority regime of South Africa. They urged all people to "translate public opinion into public action . . . until an effective international quarantine of apartheid is effective." On December 10, 1965 (International Human Rights Day) Dr. King renewed his call for the international boycott of South Africa.

Dr. King's December 10th speech represented a major step and an example of his internationalist thinking which later shaped his stand against the war in Vietnam. It is worth quoting at some length. Dr. King began his call for sanctions against South Africa by recalling that:

We are in an era in which the issue of human rights is the central question confronting all nations. In this complex struggle an obvious but little appreciated fact has gained attention—the large majority of the human race is non-white—yet it is that large majority which lives in hideous poverty. While millions enjoy an unexampled opulence in developed nations, ten thousand people die of hunger each and every day of the year in the undeveloped world. To assert white supremacy, to invoke white economic and military power, to maintain the *status quo* is to foster the danger of international race war . . . What does the South African Government contribute to this tense situation?[17]

After criticizing Great Britain, France and other democratic powers for propping up the economy of South Africa, Dr. King came to the unconscionable role of the US in South Africa.

> Our default is all the more grievous because one of the blackest pages of our history was our participation in the infamous African slave trade of the 18th century. The rape of Africa was conducted substantially for our benefit to facilitate the growth of our nation and to enhance its commerce. There are few parallels in human history of the period in which Africans were seized and branded like animals, packed into ships' holds like cargo and transported into chattel slavery. Millions suffered agonizing death in the middle passage in a holocaust reminiscent of the Nazi slaughter of Jews. We have an obligation of atonement that is not cancelled by the passage of time. Indeed, the slave trade in one sense was more understandable than our contemporary policy. There was less sense of humanity in the world three hundred years ago. The slave trade was widely approved by the major powers of the world. The economies of England, Spain, and the U.S. rested heavily on the profits derived from it. Today, in our opulent society, our reliance on trade with South Africa is infinitesimal significance. No real national interest impels us to be cautious, gentle, or a good customer of a nation that offends the world's conscience.

Dr. King emphasized once again the special relation between Africa and Afro-Americans.

> For the American Negro there is a special relationship with Africa. It is the land of his origin. It was despoiled by invaders; its culture was arrested and concealed to justify white supremacy. The American Negro's ancestors were not only driven into slavery, but their links with their past were severed so that their servitude might be psychological as well as physical. In this period when the American Negro is giving moral leadership and inspiration to his own nation, he must find the resources to aid his suffering brothers in his ancestral homeland. Nor is this aid a one-way street. The civil rights movement in the United States has derived immense inspiration from the successful struggles of those Africans who have attained freedom in their own nations. The fact that black men govern states, are building democratic institutions, sit in world tribunals, and participate in global decision-making gives every Negro a needed sense of dignity.

As Garvey and DuBois had picked up the international spirit of resistance to white domination from the tradition laid down by David

Walker, Richard Allen, Bishop Turner and others, so it seems Malcolm X, Dr. King, Rev. Jesse Jackson and TransAfrica, carry forward the torch and continue to link Afro-American freedom and dignity to that of the people of South Africa.

Just as in his South Africa speech, in his speech on Vietnam in 1967, *"A Time to Break Silence,"* Dr. King had made a clear connection that any progressive future involving improvements in American society immediately rested upon substantial changes in the content and direction of US foreign policy. An editorial in *Freedomways* underlines this connection:

> It is difficult for many of the people of our country to face up to, but the stubborn fact is we inherit a terrible legacy of criminal-like behavior toward other nations of the world from the Truman Administration down to the recently disgraced Nixon-Agnew-Ford. The suffering caused by this foreign policy has been enormous, as the government of this country poured billions of dollars into propping up fascist-type dictatorships all over the globe because these governments promised to be "friendly" to US corporate investments. It is primarily this area of regressive foreign policy that earned Dr. King's condemnation when he said: "The American government is the greatest purveyor of violence in the world today." In a very real sense our large cities with their squalor, mass unemployment, declining social services and deteriorating public school systems are a mirror and a symptom of what US foreign policy has wrought in domestic conditions. The riches of the national treasury have been poured into the military while the peoples' needs go begging. Consequently, foreign policy is, in a very fundamental sense, a major domestic issue. The spiritual and economic waste, which every administration of the past three decades has sponsored by pursuing a foreign policy of national chauvinism and arrogance, has brought the nation to this point wherein a whole generation of young people are saddled with a way of life that offers less hope for a progressive future than has been faced by any generation of Americans in this century. [18]

In the 1950s the crisis of the colonial system continued to deepen. The imperialists, above all those of the United States, took measures to save the racist regimes in Southern Africa. The enormous investment of the capitalist countries in the Southern African region, the vast mineral resources which they extracted with almost slave-like labor, and hence the huge returns on capital investment determined the attitude of the capitalist countries to the South African problem. According to Dr. Kevin Danaher, with US trade and investment steadily increasing, the Commerce Department in 1953 began a new service for American business interests in South Africa. In addition to reporting on South Africa's impressive natural resources and rapid growth, these market surveys advised businessmen to take cognizance of the political tension produced by that country's system of racial inequality. [19]

The intensifying black struggle in South Africa that followed the suspension of the Defiance Campaign of 1952-53 necessitated the building of South Africa's military might by the US. A declassified memorandum from the Joint Chiefs of Staff to the Secretary of Defense dated December 11, 1956, urged the strengthening of South Africa's military capability.

> The United States does have an interest in developing a military capability in the South African Air Force which would be immediately available for use in collective defense, in the event of Communist aggression. Accordingly, it is recommended that the Union of South Africa be encouraged to purchase military aircraft, including fighter-bomber types, from the United States. [20]

In 1955 a visit of the U.S. carrier *Midway* to South Africa created domestic opposition to the growing military ties between the US and South Africa. The NAACP, supported by opinion makers such as *The New York Times* and *Commonweal*, argued that unless the US Navy could guarantee equal treatment of black and white sailors while on shore leave in South Africa, the *Midway* visit should be cancelled. The Navy rejected these demands. [21] The rationale for this snub to the black community was clear:

> If the United States government attempted to accede to the NAACP demand, it would have been put in the incongruous position of demanding of Cape Town, South Africa, something it could not demand of the Midway's home port of Norfolk, Virginia, or of other naval installations at Charleston, New Orleans, and other locations in the South. [21]

Professor Danaher discusses other links which solidify the US-South Africa relations in the 1960s and 1970s. But the examples we have noted above were sufficient to drive home to Afro-Americans that the devaluation of black freedom in South Africa only strengthened the hand of those forces that would do likewise in the United States. [23]

After 1960, when most African colonies became sovereign states, the US foreign policy toward Africa made several ideological adjustments. In 1958 the US cast its first UN vote in favor of a resolution critical of the apartheid regime—after making sure that the resolution had been sufficiently weakened. The US "opposition" to apartheid came with the Kennedy administration. In 1962 the Kennedy administration declared an embargo on the sale of weapons to the South African regime. In August 1963 US Ambassador to the UN Adlai Stevenson stated his government's intention to stop the sale of all weaponry to South Africa by the end of that year. Kennedy himself was the first US president to state publicly his "abhorrence" for apartheid. While the Kennedy administration was making these pompous declarations, US investors were at the same time underwriting apartheid, especially after the Sharpeville Massacre. The policy of effortless virtue was continued during the Johnson administration. But during the Nixon administration, as the armed struggles escalated in all of the white-dominated states, the Nixon administration commissioned the now famous National Security Memorandum No. 39, which outlined the situation in Southern Africa and advocated the "Tar Baby option" for US policy. This option declared that the white colonial regimes were in Southern Africa to stay and that a more friendly stance had to be cultivated between the US and the apartheid regime.

The reassuring estimate of the "Tar Baby option" was short-lived, as the coup in Portugal revealed that the colonial wars in Angola, Mozambique and Guinea had been lost. Desperately, the US tried to manage the rapid events that followed to salvage imperial political interests in Angola (Mozambique and Guinea Bissau were "conceded") by promoting the fortunes of FNLA and UNITA, the two Angolan groups that offered the prospects for a neo-colonial regime similar to the Mobutu regime in Zaire that the US had installed in 1965. To achieve this, the US gave a green light to South Africa to intervene.

The MPLA victory in Angola necessitated another major revision of US Africa policy. Not only had the self-serving assumptions of NSSM-39 been shattered, but a whole new set of political realities had emerged in Southern Africa with implications for a major shift in the strategic balance of forces in Africa and the world. The question which now faced the capitalist powers was how to safeguard their economic stakes in the region. The NSSM-39 had forthrightly stated in 1969: "The US has an especially critical interest in maintaining a stable supply of gold from South Africa, which has been the major gold supplier to the noncommunist world." U.S. officials pointed out "the contribution that orderly marketing of South African gold makes to the world financial system."

In the middle 1970s Washington faced many problems in formulating its policy for Africa. First, the US had suffered a humiliating defeat in Vietnam and at least for a while the traditional policy based on the military option involving American personnel was fraught with danger. Second, with almost 30 million blacks in the U.S. who identified with the struggles of blacks in Southern Africa against white racism, the domestic implications of sending American personnel to suppress African liberation movements were incalculable. The resistance to US intervention would go far beyond Afro-Americans as the Vietnam War had demonstrated.

Above I referred to a brief submitted by the US Justice Department to the Supreme Court to the 1954 school desegregation case. In 1976, Zbigniew Brzesinski made the point that open support of racist regimes would seriously undermine Washington's stance in the developing countries.[24] Cyrus Vance, Secretary of State in the Carter Administration, noted that Washington could not afford to ignore the growing political consciousness of the almost 30 million black Americans who were said to be particularly attentive to White House handling of problems connected with the African peoples' struggles for freedom. "The success or failure of the search for racial justice and peace in Southern Africa will have profound effects among American people."[25]

Whatever the ideological permutations in public policy, the US could not afford to abandon the South African regime. Today, the white minority regime is if anything, even more indispensable to the US and its capitalist allies in Western Europe.

The economic and strategic imperatives necessitated a re-packaging of the policy of support for South Africa. Hence the policy of "constructive engagement." The continued support of South Africa by various US administrations, and even more so by the Reagan Administration, has confronted Afro-Americans with their greatest foreign policy challenge. Having successfully destroyed apartheid in the US, can Afro-Americans help their kith and kin in South Africa do the same?

It is not the purpose of this chapter to discuss each and every campaign and/or intervention by Afro-Americans on behalf of the peoples of Southern Africa. We have seen that among the factors that forced the US foreign policy establishment to take Afro-American concerns seriously in formulating their policy toward white minority regimes were Malcolm X and Dr. King, who had made the appropriate connections between the Afro-American struggle and the struggles of the peoples of Southern Africa in the early 1960s. When the peoples of Southern Africa in Angola, Mozambique, Namibia, Zimbabwe and South Africa took up arms in the 1960s to free themselves from colonial and white minority rule, expressions of solidarity and cooperation proliferated in the black community. Professor Sylvia Hill recalls that:

> One of the earliest connections during this period between black people and the liberation movements occurred when Robert Van Lierop, a

young black lawyer, met Eduardo Mondlane, the first President of the Frente de Libertacao de Mocambique (Mozambican Liberation Front, FRELIMO), in 1967. As a result of Van Lierop's interests in the struggle waged by FRELIMO against Portuguese colonialism, he traveled to see for himself what it meant to wage a national liberation struggle and later produced the first American independent film by an African-American describing the armed struggle as a national liberation struggle, *A Luta Continua*. This film became one of the decisive tools in facilitating mass organization. In 1972 the political content and form of African identity was expressed specifically as international solidarity when a national black organization was formed to support African liberation movements. This organization, the African Liberation Support Committee, was able to mobilize twenty thousand people in a march on Washington, D.C., to protest U.S. foreign policy and later was able to organize dockworkers to refuse to unload "Rhodesian" chrome (Walters, 1980:89-101). During this period, another group of black activists was able to organize the Sixth Pan-African Congress in Dar es Salaam, Tanzania, and carry a delegation of close to three hundred African-Americans to participate in the international deliberations of African statesmen, Caribbean statesmen, liberation movements, and delegates from England and from the South Pacific. Opportunities to discuss with liberation movements and to hear how the African leadership defined their problems and their solutions profoundly influenced the conception of Pan-African thought. For one thing, the notion that Pan-Africanism meant that all black people had a common interest and must unite was challenged by the question of class interests. The conference also made it clear that the question of national liberation of colonized territories was the chief struggle of progressive African people, and that Africans scattered throughout the world, particularly in the United States, must join that struggle in solidarity.[26]

The true intentions of the policy of "constructive engagement" between the *apartheid* regime in South Africa and the government of the United States became clear in 1981. Press reports and subsequent developments, revealed that the two countries had formed an unholy alliance to reverse the gains achieved by the African liberation movements culminating in the independence of Zimbabwe in 1980.[27] If foreign policy, in a way, is the extension of domestic class relations to the international arena, then the attitude of the Reagan American administration toward Afro-Americans is a good guide to its foreign policy options. Just as Graham Hovey of *The*

New York Times had characterized the policy options of NSSM39 as an "expression of our own racism and lingering notions of White supremacy,"[28] so can we describe Reagan's policy of "constructive engagement" in the same terms.

Today, the basic outlines of America's imperialist and racist social order are being starkly revealed as the Reagan Administration announces its priorities. In a secret meeting in 1981, Under Secretary for African Affairs, Dr. Chester Crocker, told the Foreign Minister of the racist regime of South Africa, P.K. Botha, that the "US ability to develop full relations with SAG [South African Government] depends on the newness of Prime Minister Botha's [reform] program and the extent to which it is seen as broadening SAG's domestic support." Substantial change in apartheid itself was not a condition of the relations, but "credible" appearance of change was, Crocker added. The domestic side of "constructive engagement" was President Reagan's rhetoric emphasizing a new jingoist US patriotism. Monroe Anderson, one of the two black columnists at the *Chicago Tribune*, astutely observed that behind this thinly veiled patriotism was a racial message:

> Ronald Reagan is using this manufactured patriotism to give some very subtle codes to white America. The essence of his message is that it's okay again to be a racist. White superiority is "in" once again. How else can you explain why a white, blue-collar worker could be for Reagan? The only way to make sense of that is to understand that Reagan appeals to them on another level. This new patriotism is actually a code word for racism-as-usual.[29]

Meg Greenfield observed in 1984 that "respectable" racism was pervasive in private gatherings of even the highest circles of this country's white intellectuals and political leaders, where a double standard was displayed—whites snicker at the alleged incompetence of city governments headed by black mayors and self-righteously deride political violence in Africa. As Greenfield put it:

> Blacks, both here and abroad, are talked about in much more critical, unforgiving terms than anyone else. It seems to satisfy something quite unattractive in those who talk this way to give vent to their unfair appraisals of the competence and civility of blacks.[30]

All these developments raised the specter of the failure of the first Reconstruction. At the April 20, 1985, mobilization for peace, jobs and justice, held in Washington, D.C., Reverend Jesse Jackson presented *"A Moral Appeal to Resist Fascism."* Focusing on the links between President Reagan's visit to a German military cemetery in Bitburg, where soldiers of the Nazi SS are buried, and Reagan's embrace of South Africa's apartheid regime, Jackson made his indictment of fascism and called on the US people to resist:

> We learned in 1945 that the logical conclusion of the Third Reich was genocide. In 1985, South Africa is the Fourth Reich, built on race supremacy. The same ethical standards that applied to Hitler's Germany must apply to South Africa; South Africa cannot stand alone. South Africa needs US investment, strategic military planning, university and church credibility, diplomatic support and the conspiracy of Western democratic allies. For the record, South Africa is not standing based on Soviet investment and markets. The credibility of free democracy is jeopardized by the South African partnership. We must put ethics over expediency, and as a superpower, we should convene Great Britain, West Germany, Israel, Italy, France, Japan, Holland, and Belgium and together make a concerted move against apartheid and for the people, and maintain our self-respect.[31]

The widespread and escalating struggle in South Africa had reached new levels in the second half of 1984. This development together with the election of Ronald Reagan to a second term posed a new danger for the Afro-American community. On Thanksgiving eve in 1984, three prominent Afro-Americas—Dr. Mary Berry of the United States Civil Rights Commission, Congressperson Walter Fauntroy, delegate from the District of Columbia, and Randall Robinson, Executive Director of TransAfrica, staged a "sit-in" at the South African embassy which resulted in their arrest. This incident led to a series of demonstrations and arrests planned by the Free South Africa Movement all over the country. Hundreds of black folks, together with other Americans, picketed South Africa's diplomatic posts from New York City to San Francisco, from San Antonio, Texas to Chicago. Those arrested wanted to express moral outrage at the intensification of repression in South Africa and, in their words, to "arouse the American people to the true and universal meaning of human rights." The steadily worsening racial conflict in South Africa had come home to roost in the United States.

> More than 5,000 citizens have been arrested nationwide. Grassroots direct action campaigns now exist in more than 40 cities. It is the

longest running non-stop demonstration in US history and anti-apartheid actions have been continually taking place by countless black organizations having different political perspectives.[32]

After one year of daily demonstrations at the South African Embassy, the Free South Africa Movement (FSAM) has shifted its focus to the private sector, embarking upon a campaign against corporations conducting business in both the United States and South Africa. The new FSAM Corporate Campaign is an addition to previously launched anti-apartheid initiatives endorsed by FSAM, calling on corporations to terminate their business relationships in South Africa. These include: the Southern Christian Leadership Conference's boycott of the Winn Dixie Corporation, the Northern Virginia Coalition Against Apartheid's demonstrations against the Control Data Corporation, and the National Council of Church campaign against its list of "dirty dozen" corporations active in the US and South Africa.

Like the Embassy demonstrations, which heightened the American people's awareness of the unholy alliance between the Reagan Administration and the government of South Africa, the Free South Africa Movement's Corporate Campaign is designed to educate. The lesson which the Corporate Campaign will teach through nationwide protest activities is the pivotal role transnational corporations play in supporting the system of apartheid. The Free South Africa Movement private sector campaign aims to be a catalyst for generating popular support for complete corporate withdrawal from South Africa (unless the South African government negotiates with legitimate black leaders for a new political and economic order), much in the same way as the South African Embassy demonstrations helped achieve overwhelming support for the imposition of US sanctions against South Africa.[33]

The struggle and suffering of the people of South Africa and the indifference of the Reagan Administration had inspired anger and militant protest in the US and other imperialist countries. Because of the groundswell in the anti-apartheid campaign, President Reagan was forced to announce limited sanctions against South Africa. The sudden change in Reagan's position and the limited sanctions he imposed are important, less for what they contained (a watered-down version of the compromise agreed upon by the Senate and the House of Representatives Conference Committee) than for the political *volte face* involved. In August, the President had wholeheartedly rejected sanctions on the grounds that they would be harmful to South Africa and to surrounding African states. The executive order was issued to create the impression that the President was in charge of US foreign policy;

and the President wanted to avoid the humiliation that would have come from a congregational override of a veto. This *volte face* represented an ideological victory for TransAfrica, the Black Congressional Caucus and for the anti-apartheid movement.

Although "constructive engagement" to all intents and purposes is now completely discredited, the Reagan Administration continues to see the racist regime of South Africa as the bulwark against communism and a cornerstone of its anti-Soviet policy. Thus, the sanctions Reagan imposed in September 1985 were far from signaling Washington's abandonment of Pretoria. The Administration was only deflecting attention from its unconscionable policy, while searching for new ways to support the racist regime. From September onward the Reagan Administration launched its most sustained anti-Communist and anti-Soviet crusade in Angola. Both the White House and members of Congress initiated moves to provide covert and overt aid to South Africa's-backed UNITA mercenaries trying to overthrow the Angolan government. Finally, in January Jonas Savimbi, the leader of the bandits in Angola, was given a red-carpet treatment to the dismay of the anti-apartheid movement. Indeed, the invitation of Savimbi was a direct snub to the Black Caucus and to the black community.

In a prophetic article in 1972, J.K. Obatala reviewed the emerging Nixon Doctrine and observed that the rapid decline of British military power following World War II had thrust the US into a position of defender of imperialism:

> The U.S. now assumed the responsibility for protecting British interests in Africa and elsewhere. As a consequence in the very near future, the Afro-American Movement will be confronted with the Herculean challenge of devising a program of effective resistance to American military conquest of progressive states.[34]

The demise of the Carter Human Rights policy and the rise of Reaganism is an interesting commentary on the objectives of US imperialism. The right-wing attacks on Carter and Andy Young were based on the belief that human rights rhetoric was, to use *The New York Times'* phrase, "the policy of the self-righteous humbug" which paved the way for the upheavals in Iran, Nicaragua, Southern Africa and elsewhere that plagued the Carter administration. The dilemma of the US is that a final rejection of Carter's human rights rhetoric irrevocably sealed the fate of the United States as a historical force for "good" in world politics, and yet even a token commitment to the rhetoric of human rights made obvious its hypocrisy when it openly aligns and supports dictatorial regimes.

The greatest tragedy for the US and the world is that as long as it is wedded to an untrammeled rule of capital and the inequalities that are inherent in it, it will always be faced with the unwholesome duty of using its force to uphold the international system of property and privilege against the poor, the exploited and the oppressed. The capitalist civilization that the US is determined to uphold is a majestic social edifice which for 500 years was built on so iniquitous a base that it now cries out for rehabilitation if humanity itself is to be saved.

Notes

[1]*The Last Will and Testament of Cecil John Rhodes* (Ed.), W.T. Stead, "Review of Reviews" Office, Norfolk Street, London, 1902, p. 52.

[2]James P. Sheraton, "Imperialism and Race," in *Essays in American Historiography*, Paper Presented in Honor of Allan Nevins, Columbia University Press, New York, 1960, pp. 238-9.

[3]*Ibid.*

[4]This and the following are owed to Victor G. Kiernan, *America: The New Imperialism, From the White Settlement to World Hegemony*, Zed Press, London, 1978, pp. 104-05.

[5]*Ibid.*

[6]J.A. Hobson, *The Crisis of Liberalism: New Issues of Democracy*, with Introduction by P.F. Clarke, Harper and Row, New York, 1974, p. 246.

[7]Quoted in Shirley Graham DuBois, "The Liberation of Africa: Power, Peace, and Justice," *The Black Scholar, Journal of Black Studies*, Vol. 2, No. 6, 1971, p. 34.

[8]This and the following section owes a great deal to the tribute paid to Paul Robeson by His Excellency Sir Leslie Harriman (Nigeria), Chairman. United Nations Special Committee Against Apartheid, 1968, published by the African Heritage Studies Association in cooperation with the United Nations Centre against Apartheid.

[9]Quoted in Kevin Danaher, *The Political Economy of U.S. Policy Toward South Africa*, Westview Press, Boulder and London, 1985, p. 60.

[10]*Ibid.*

[11]*Ibid.*

[12]Pan Africanism and the Liberation of Southern Africa. International Tribute to William E.B. DuBois, United Nations Centre Against Apartheid, 1982, p. vvi.

[13]For an excellent discussion of U.S. voting record on racial and colonial question see Camille A. Bratton, "A Matter of Record: The History of the United States Voting Pattern in the United Nations (1946-76), *Freedomways*, Vol. 17, No. 3, 1977, pp. 155-163.

[14]Frederick Engels, *Anti-Duhring*, International Publishers, New York, 1939, p. 127.

[15]J.H. O'Dell, "Paradise Lost: Soviet Observations Directed Toward the Bicentennial of the U.S.," *Freedomways*, Vol. 15, No. 1, 1975, p. 7.

[16]Paul Robeson, *Here I Stand*, Othelo Associates, New York, 1958, pp. 115-116.

[17]Dr. King's speech is reprinted by the Bay Area Free South Africa Movement, December-January, 1985-1986, No. 2, p. 1.

[18]*Freedomways: A Quarterly Review of the Freedom Movement*, Vol. 17, No. 1, 1977, p. 1.

[19]Danaher, *op. cit.*, 1985, p. 69.

[20]*Ibid.*

[21]*Ibid.*

[22]*Ibid.*

[23]Al Mitchell, "Apartheid and the threat to Blacks Worldwide," *Ground Level Magazine*, 4, special edition, undated, p. 3.

[24]*Foreign Policy*, No. 23, 1978, p. 96.

[25]*The Department of State Bulletin*, Vol. LXXVII, No. 1989, August 8, 1977, p. 165.

[26]Sylvia Hill, "International Solidarity: Cabral's Legacy to the Afro-American Community," *Latin American Perspectives*, No. 41, Vol. 11, No. 2, Spring 1984, pp. 69-70.

[27]TransAfrica News Report, Special Edition, August 1981. The documents leaked to TransAfrica included: a briefing paper on US-South Africa relations written by Assistant Secretary of State for Africa, Chester Crocker to prepare Secretary of State Alexander Haig for a 14 May 1981 meeting with South African Foreign Minister Roelof Botha; a summary of an April meeting in Pretoria between Crocker, Botha, and South African Defense Minister Magnus Molan; and a short paper detailing South Africa's request for resumption of enriched uranium deliveries from the United States (the Carter Administraiton halted uranium shipments in 1977).

[28]*New York Times*, March 2, 1976.

[29]Quoted by Monte Piliawsky, "The 1984 Election's Message to Black Americans: Challenges, Choices and Prospects," *Freedomways*, Vol. 25, No. 1, 1985, p. 20.

[30]*Ibid.*, p. 21.

[31]Rev. Jesse Jackson, "A Moral Appeal to Resist Fascism," a speech delivered on April 20, at the Mobilization for Jobs, Peace, and Justice, Washington, D.C., 1985.

[32]Sanford Wright, "Constructive Disengagement: U.S. Sanctions Against South Africa," *Black Scholar*, Vol. 16, No. 6, 1985, p. 5.

[33]*Trans Africa News*, Vol. 5, No. 1, Winter 1986, p. 3.

[34]J.K. Obatala, "The 'Nixon Doctrine' and Africa," *Freedomways*, Vol. 12, No. 1, 1972, p. 55.

CHAPTER TEN
By Way of a Conclusion

History is the nightmare from which I am trying to awake.
　　　　　　　　　　　　　　　　　　—James Joyce

Ideas are seen through history as light through a prism: their various and brilliant colors are but broken reflections of a single concentrated ray. The fortunes of such ideas, like those of men, depend as much on accident as on their own worth and character. If the inward spiritual striving of the American black man eludes the sociologist, its outward and visible signs meet him at every turn in such movements as Ethiopianism of the late 19th century, Garveyism and Pan-Africanism of the early 20th century and in the ideas of the nation of Islam and black nationalism.

The black has striven by unceasing activity to exorcise a haunting demon asking *who he is* and where he belongs. In the effort to "find" himself in the historical drama of humankind, he set in motion in the United States movements which stimulated reciprocal movements in his original homeland—Africa. In his efforts to create from the ruins of slavery an acceptable image, he found that he could not escape the specter of his African past. The poet Roman gives particularly poignant testimony to this:

Africa I guard your memory Africa
You are in me as the shaft is in the wound
as the guardian fetish in the Center of the
Village make me the stone of your ship
of my mouth the lips of your sores
of my knees the broken columns of your
　　humiliation and yet

I wish to be only of your race
fellow worker of every land.

It was these sentiments which have worked themselves out into ideas which have grown up into what is now known as the Pan-African consciousness.

The Pan-African consciousness has always been a determined effort on the part of black peoples to rediscover their shrines from the wreckage of history. It was a revolt against the white man's ideological suzerainty in culture, politics and historiography. The meaningfulness of these ideas, I have maintained, cannot be assessed from the number of believers, but rather through the historical understanding which they provide for the blacks' strivings. The various manifestations of African consciousness among American blacks articulate an experience which goes beyond individual awareness. Pan-African consciousness which originated among black peoples in diaspora prepared a position in the African mind from which white hegemony was to be continually attacked. Pan-African consciousness proclaimed the idea of black emancipation as a necessary state for the full development of blacks everywhere. Black consciousness of Africa is truly the pre-history of African nationalism. The black man in his diaspora, rejected with almost physical horror the lies prevalent in the lands of his captivity about Africa and its past. The black could not accept their scorn and indifference, and his anguish was to be the spirit behind the development of Pan-African consciousness.

In a brief chapter of *Black Skin, White Masks*, entitled "The Negro and Hegel," Fanon grasped that colonial domination of African peoples meant not only economic domination, but also the destruction of the spirit and the personality of the oppressed people. What appears at first glance to be a summation of the "Lordship and Bondage" section of Hegel's phenomenology, is an exposition of the dialetical interrelationship of the independence and dependence of self-consciousness to the black situation in a racist society.

That is, Fanon stressed that self-consciousness of blacks has been sublated by oppression; and that the other, the white oppressors, do not regard black self-consciousness as real, but see in the black only their own self-consciousness. As long as black self-consciousness is not recognized by the other, "the other will remain the theme of his [the black's] actions." If there is no reciprocity between the real self-consciousness of Blacks and the other, the circuit is closed and ultimately Blacks are deprived of being for themselves.[1] The search for self-recognition necessarily led to a search for roots in Africa. Blacks had to rediscover their lost humanity and fashion it in their own image.

The recognition that Blacks are saddled with a false consciousness of self—or rather two consciousnesses of self—is not new. It is a theme that runs through the writings of W.E.B. DuBois, Richard Wright and others. In *American Hunger*, for instance, Wright reminisces about the lunch hours he spent on a bench in a park in Chicago, and about the white waitresses who would come and sit beside him:

> They lived on the surface of their days; their smiles were surface smiles, and their tears were surface tears. . . . The girls never talked of their feelings; none of them possessed the insight or the emotional equipment to understand themselves or others. How far apart in culture we stood! All my life I had done nothing but feel and cultivate my feelings; all their lives they had done nothing but strive for petty goals, the trivial material prizes of American life. We share a common tongue, but my language was a different language from theirs.

> *It was in the psychological distance that separated the races that the deepest meaning of the problem of the Negro lay for me.* For these poor, ignorant white girls to have understood my life would have meant nothing short of a vast revolution in theirs. And I was convinced that what they needed to make them complete and grown-up in their living was the inclusion in their personalities of a knowledge of lives such as I lived and suffered containedly.[2] (My emphasis)

In his study of American culture, Wright explores its two-sided character for black and white. The black personality is essentially a portrait of men and women made deficient; of a whole people instilled with fear, and degraded through the destruction of their natural means of sociability. On the emotional and psychological agony of being black in America Wright has this to say:

> As I, in memory, think back now upon those girls and their lives I feel that for white America to understand the significance of the problem of the Negro will take a bigger and tougher America than any we have yet known. I feel that America's past is too shallow, her national character too superficially optimistic, her very morality too suffused with color hate for her to accomplish so vast and complex a task. Culturally the Negro represents a paradox: Though he is an organic part of the nation, he is excluded by the entire tide and direction of American culture. Frankly, it is felt to be right to exclude him, and it is felt to be wrong to admit him freely. Therefore if, within the confines of its present culture,

the nation ever seeks to purge itself of its color hate, it will find itself at war with itself, convulsed by a spasm of emotional and moral confusion. If the nation ever finds itself examining its real relation to the Negro, it will find itself doing infinitely more than that; for the anti-Negro attitude of whites represents but a tiny part—though a symbolically significant one—of the moral attitude of the nation.[3]

To the Afro-American, the system of white domination is not only insidious, it was built on his total negation. The black, permanently an alien in his own country, lives in a state of permanent depersonalization. The whites accepted their "superiority" as self-evident and would only accept blacks on terms and standards they have set. As Fanon put it, "The whiteman is the master who has allowed his slaves to eat at his table."[4] Here lies the negative meaning of wishing to be accepted—there is absence of reciprocal recognition by the white. "The psycho-existential perception of race had become atrophied as each group approached the other through a haze of historically redundant stereotypes."[5]

The civil rights struggles of the 1950s and 60s changed all that. It was during the civil rights struggles that African consciousness among Afro-Americans reached new dimensions, as materials about Africa and its history were unearthed and made more readily available. African cultural forms—natural hair styles, dashikis, African names, African dances, etc., proliferated, as did the study of Swahili and other African languages.

African consciousness reached its apogee with the publication in 1976 of Alex Haley's *Roots* and its dramatization in a 13-hour series on television.[6] Never before had the history of black America, and especially its African connection, become an issue of national debate. For the first time Alex Haley had actually traced Afro-American history, not only through six generations in America, but to Africa. Haley, through Kunta Kinte had established real continuity between Africa and Afro-Americans, in actions and thoughts, through sorrows and tribulations, as no one had ever done. The publication of his book, exactly 200 years after the Declaration of Independence, was ironic and it did not escape James Baldwin:

> I cannot guess what Alex Haley's countrymen will make of his birthday present to us during this election and Bicentennial year. One is tempted to say that it could scarcely have come at a more awkward time—what with conventions, the exhibition of candidates, the dubious state of this particular and perhaps increasingly dubious union, and the American attempt hopelessly and predictably schizophrenic, of preventing total disaster, for white people and the West, in South Africa. There is a

carefully muffled pain and panic in the nation, which neither candidate, neither party, can coherently address, being themselves but vivid symptoms of it.[7]

Roots is about lineage and blood, history and suffering and the need to know about these things. The particular pain of not knowing is the fate of all Afro-Americans whose history was so curiously mislaid in America, cast aside as a first sacrifice to survival on the plantations of the New World. According to reviewer Willie Lee Rose, "Omoro and Binta Kinte could possibly become the African proto-parents of millions of Americans who are going to admire their dignity and grace."[8]

The world of Alex Haley's *Roots* is Gambia, West Africa, around 1750, where one of his ancestors, Kunta Kinte, born of Omoro and Binta Kinte of the Mandinka people and of the Muslim faith, lived. In the recreation of this time and place, the ancestral village is brought to life with all its beauty and dignity. The public ceremonies of the beautiful Mandinka people are revealed as precise and coherent mirrors of their private and yet connected imaginations. Baldwin noted that these ceremonies, imaginations, however removed in time, are yet, for the black man anyway, naggingly familiar and present, I say, for the black man, but these ceremonies, those imaginations are really universal, finally inescapably as old and deep as the human race. The tragedy of the people doomed to think of themselves as white lies in their denial of these origins: they became incoherent because they can never stammer from whence they came.[9]

Afro-American consciousness of Africa thus reflects the experience of a people, their aims, their struggles and their goals as they continued to live in hostile climes. As *Roots* indicated, the American black's interest in Africa was not nostalgia. It was produced from the deep layers of their tormented lives in the New World. "The American Negro has a definable and legitimate historical tradition, no matter how painful, in America, but it is the only place such a tradition exists, simply because America is the only place the American Negro exists ... He is an American capable of identifying with the fantastic cultural ingredients of this society, but he is also forever outside that culture, an invisible strength within it, an observer."[10] Whether Black Americans tried to identify or attempted to evade identification with things African, the specter of Africa continued to haunt them; and in one way or another, they had to come to peace with it. Haley's saga is a magnificent attempt to re-establish the *ties* that bind Afro-Americans to their ancestral home. As Chuck Stone put it: "Alex Haley is the Thucydides of our day, interpreting the Black Diaspora as majestically as the Greek historian catalogued the Peloponnesian War ... The quest from Tennessee succeeded, painstakingly unraveling the umbilical cord that had stretched to a tortured distance from Africa and America." [12]

Now that the roots have been re-established and the mental anguish of not knowing are at least partially solved, what next? The real roots of alienation in capitalist society still remain. *Roots*, as Robert Staples pointed out, tells little about how black folks were used as human capital to shore up a fledgling industrial order during the so-called triangular trade, nor does it explain how black folks continue to be used as a scapegoat for all America's problems. [13]

Important as it is to establish ones cultural roots, if no revolution takes place in the productive forces that alienates black labor power, culture will lack substance. Re-establishing Afro-America's cultural roots must not be mere "folklore" but must be something that validates itself through revolutionary struggles to emancipate human labor from the shackles of capital. Bringing to life the culture of an oppressed people is not just a question of looking back to the past, but in understanding the past in order to transcend it. In *The Eighteenth Brumaire*, Karl Marx wrote:

> The social revolution . . . cannot draw its poetry from the past but only from the future. It cannot begin with itself before it has stripped itself of all its superstitions concerning the past. Earlier revolutions relied on memories out of world history in order to drug themselves against their own content. In order to find their own content, the revolutions of the 19th century have to let the dead bury the dead. Before, the expression exceeded the content; now, the content exceeds the expression. [13]

Afro-Americans have made large contributions to the struggle for emancipation of peoples under colonial and imperial domination, and in the process have paid a supreme price. Dr. DuBois was charged (and acquitted) for being a foreign agent; Mr. Robeson's career as an actor and musician was ruined; Malcolm X and Dr. Martin Luther King were assassinated.

When Malcolm X attempted to tie together the meaning of our public movements in America with the worldwide struggle for self-determination, and with the internal black struggle for integrity and self-discipline, he was assassinated. Three years later, as Martin King sought to bring the power of the black movement to bear against America's racist imperialism in Vietnam, and threatened to call for black draft resistance, he was gunned down. Then on the night of King's death, in 1968, the federal and state military forces put more troops and equipment out on the streets (and in the skies) of America than we had ever known since the Civil War, effectively blunting and cordoning off the terrified and painful anger of black America. These deaths, and the display of raw military power that we saw before and after them, hit hard against us. Along with the brutal harassment and killing of the Panthers and other forces, they presented the black community with a stunning, sometimes numbing reality—and we were unprepared for it.[14]

The blows stunned the movement: "For some the answer was now to be found in various forms of religion, from astrology to the nation of Islam. The talk of our real struggle 'being in Africa' became another sign of despair."[15]

The deepening crisis now facing the Black community, even as the number of Afro-Americans at local, state and national levels has increased, has forced new understandings. As Harding puts it: "The roots we had in Africa continue to be important, necessary, life-affirming sources. But roots are ultimately for trees; and we must become new trees, striking out, reaching out, seeking new levels, new possibilities, here on these new shores."[16]

The American black's African consciousness from its earliest manifestations made sense when understood in terms of the logic of the black's status in American society. It was and continues to be a "natural" yet highly idiosyncratic and personal version of the black's life. It indeed spells out his movements from African slave to American slave, from a freedman to a citizen. The history of the black's perception of Africa provides insights into his dilemma as an American citizen. Black leaders who attempt to formalize their anguish (like Garvey and Malcolm X) and to give it political direction are always castigated by both white and black middle classes as preaching race hatred or race chauvinism.

There is no doubt that anti-white feelings exist among blacks, implicitly or explicitly. But as Frank Kofsky pointed out: "anti-white sensibilities among black nationalists operate to supply a unifying ideology which transcends the experience of any single individual." Kofsky quotes Malcolm X as saying that:

Unless we call one white man by name a "devil," we are not speaking of any individual whiteman. We are speaking of the white man's historical record. We are speaking of the collective white man's cruelties, and evil, and greed, which have seen him act like a devil toward the non-white man. Any intelligent, honest, objective person cannot fail to realize that this white man's slave trade, and his subsequent devilish actions are directly *responsible* for not only the presence of this blackman in America, but also for the condition in which we find this black man here.[17]

Such an assumption on the part of the black nationalists should not be difficult to comprehend because it is a sentiment closely analogous to class solidarity. Unlike the civil rights leaders, the nationalists do not couch their demands in terms of love, brotherhood, and gratefulness. According to I.F. Stone, "the basic emotion is hatred of 'whitey' and this is why Black Nationalism of one variety or another strikes so deeply into the apathetic, and despairing black masses."[18] Professions of love may be soothing to the black's oppressors, but have nothing to do with his human conditions and his historical experience in America. Typical civil rights agitation becomes an easy way of gaining prestige in the white world—hence its ideology, if any, must be acceptable to the white middle classes who derive satisfaction in feeling that their way of life is both eternal and ultimately desirable to everyone. Hankering after middle-class goals limited the programs of the civil rights movements to futile and spiritually deadening aims, such as integration and what is called equality. The Afro-American is black and because of his color, he stands out and cannot melt into a crowd—which is what I understand by integration. Socially he occupies the lowest rung and although he may be equal (which, of course, he is) his equality would not affect his socio-political status. Stanley Burch, writing from Washington in the *Daily Mail* of August 13, 1965 observed that: "The American Negro has run into a terrible paradox. He wins his triumphs in Congress, enlists the President as an ally and breaks down barricade after barricade. But when he goes home at night, things are worse than ever."

Hans J. Morgenthau has made an observation which I think is extremely significant for the Afro-American's struggle for what is called equality:

The two great domestic changes testing again the purpose of America— equality in freedom for the American Negro and the restoration of a meaningful economic and social order—are interconnected. The former cannot be fully achieved, and might even be ultimately jeopardized, without the latter. For even if the Negro were to come into full possession of legal and social equality, he would still be exposed to the disabilities of a contracting labor market: As an unskilled laborer, discriminated against as a Negro, he is likely to be permanently unemployed. But as a skilled worker competing without discrimination for ever scarcer jobs, he would still be threatened with unemployment. The resentment of Negroes whose new equality reveals itself as meaningless in economic terms would be a source of alienation from America. The resentment of the ever-swelling mass of white unemployed would be a source of alienation from the political and social status quo. And in all probability one resentment would be pitted against the other, fanning anew the enmity of races.[19]

It is submitted here that no progress will be made in reference to what is called the Negro problem without an appropriate perception of what the problem is. Existentially the black is poor, poor almost beyond enduring because of historical circumstances. The slavery experience and the post-slavery history of oppression for better or for worse give the black a different reality. Even though the blacks in America have long been the most substantial minority group they have lacked the power to determine their own needs. It has been said that:

> Poverty, differential poverty, has the structure of slavery. There is the primary insult, with all that it entails of lack of command over events, so that the children of the poor die when (under a mere redistribution of means) they need not. There is the secondary insult of involvement in a productive process that gives the non-poor the means to increase, maintain, command. There is the third and final insult that causes the poor to become willing poor—happy slaves—who support the system of poverty whether or not anyone tries to struggle out of it.[20]

Integration and equality as schemes for improving the black position are mere abstractions for the mass of blacks. They do not confront the issues of lack of power, of self-determination and the existential poverty which afflicts the black masses. The present movement toward accepting blacks into the American life is predicated on a maintenance of the status quo, an attitude that implicitly assumes its values to be supremely desirable: it is "a movement that will—in a moment of boundless magnanimity—allow the Negro to elevate himself ... if he proves himself worthy enough."[21] The implications of this attitude are two-fold. The ultimate objective of integration is to identify the black with a prosperity that perpetually reflects his humiliation. Integration if perfected means that certain types of blacks would join the white community and be willing participants in the oppression of the rest that cannot be integrated. This has been the tragedy and the triumph of integration, the tragedy being that "it has no relevance to the Harlem wino or to the cotton picker making three dollars a day. As a lady I know in Alabama once said, 'the food that Ralph Bunche eats doesn't fill my stomach.' "[22]

The second implication of the integrationist attitude is that it embodies the very essence of white supremacy—the self-righteous condescension of the whites who have convinced themselves that the black is passionately striving to be lost in white society. William Stringfellow in his book, *My People is the Enemy*, reached the conclusion through his years of work in Harlem as legal counsel for the poor that "the political recognition" which Negroes have so far received ... "has been purchased by the surrender of their identity and integrity as Negroes." Although Stringfellow is " . . . as much in favor of social change in the urban ghettoes as the next, perhaps more," he remains " . . . by no means persuaded that the standard should be that of the great American bourgeoisie."[23]

Any serious attack on poverty, then, is an attack on the discrepancies among men in their power to command events and, more particularly, one another. Besides the black church, it has been in the "nationalist movements" of the so-called lower-class blacks that elementary conditions have been fulfilled for genuine political action from the bottom, in contrast to attempts to "give freedom" to the masses from above. The Garvey Movement, the Muslin movement, the Student Nonviolent Coordinating Committee and the Congress of Racial Equality have made efforts at black self-determination. At the heart of their attempts, with all their limitations, was the belief that freedom can be realized through the self-emancipation of activized masses in motion. The problem of being black in America has demoralizing psychological factors. African consciousness and "Black Power" can appeal directly and instinctively to the masses, giving them pride and a sense of direction. By acknowledging their African past, the oneness of their struggle with their African kith and kin, they have strengthened their cause. The beginning of the Afro-American's calamity was the sequel to the African's calamity. Therefore the emancipation of Africa will signal the emancipation of the blacks wherever they may be.

I have tried here to construct a picture with perceivable patterns into which parts can be fitted to make an organic whole. The Muslims and Malcolm X, CORE and SNCC in the 1960s have all in one way or the other identified earlier movements with black nationalism and with the independence movement in Africa. These movements attest to an objective, social historical reality. They disclose the actual conditions of life of the American black—all the problems of day-to-day living which lead up to an historical crisis. I have shown why the crisis arose, and for what reason the black was made to feel alien and a pariah. It is not by psychological explanations of individual feelings that we can familiarize ourselves with the peculiar historical qualities of the inner life, but by the broad portrayal of a people's being; by showing how thoughts, feelings, and modes of behavior grow out of this base.

Why must "Black Power" and black nationalism be such insistent cries among American blacks? Following the achievement of juridical equality the black might be expected to at least identify more closely with American society and push harder for integration. But the concept of black nationalism goes beyond formal juridical equality. To participate in power on the present terms would be to ignore those blacks who are poorest and to betray the Third World countries which the white Western nations have always exploited. The "internationalism" which was part and parcel of Pan-Africanism still informs the leadership of the nationalist movements.

This study has attempted in a limited way to unravel those feelings which seem always latently present in people; and which with every disturbance of social or even of personal life emerge suddenly with colossal force. We saw how this happened after World War I and after the Italo-Ethiopian conflict, and we see it now in the era of colonial emancipation from white rule. The upsurge of national consciousness in times of crisis shows that such forces are lying dormant in people, requiring only the occasion to appear on the surface. The influence on blacks of a movement like that of Garvey or Elijah Muhammad, whether it is positive or pervasive or indirect, stirs all classes in the black community. The intellectual hostility and criticism directed toward these movements are usually motivated by resentment that the amazing energy and genius shown by the leaders were not harnessed to practical and constructive ends. That is why it is so difficult to assess the pervasiveness of these ideas. Let us not forget that an endless number of people live their lives quietly, without any awareness because no opportunity has come their way to evoke such an exertion of their powers. The present upsurge of black consciousness operates in a changing world situation[24] in which bridges long broken by the curtain of ignorance are being rebuilt; in which blacks' relations to Africa are much clearer and accessible without extensive learning. For a long time the conditions did not exist for this kind of awareness, but the ideological appeal of Africanism was always unconsciously and instinctively present.

Notes

[1]Franz Fanon, *Black Skin, White Masks*, trans. C.L. Markman, McGibbon and Kee, London, 1968, p. 223.

[2]Richard Wright, *American Hunger*, Harper and Row, New York, 1977, pp. 12-13.

[3]*Ibid.*

[4]Fanon, *op. cit.*, p. 219.

[5]Jack McCulloch, *Black Soul, White Artifact: Fanon's Clinical Psychology and Social Theory*, Cambridge University Press, New York, 1983, p. 56.

[6]For a critique of the *Roots* TV series, see "Forum: A Symposium on Roots," *The Black Scholar*, Vol. 8, No. 7, May, 1977, pp. 36-42.

[7]James Baldwin, Review, "Roots: The Saga of an American Family," *The New York Times Book Review*, September 26, 1976, p. 3.

[8]Cf. Willie Lee Rose, Review of "An American Family, Roots," in *New York Review of Books*, Vol. 23, No. 11.

[9]Baldwin, *op. cit.*, p. 3.

[10]Chuck Stone, "Roots: An Electronic Orgy in White Guilt," *The Black Scholar*, Vol. 8, No. 7, 1977, p. 40.

[12]Robert Staples, "Roots: Melodrama of the Black Experience," *The Black Scholar*, Vol. 8, No. 2, 1977, p. 37.

[13]Karl Marx, *The Eighteenth Brumaire of Louis Bonaparte*, Foreign Publishing House, Moscow, 1852, p. 18.

[14]Vincent Harding, *The Other American Revolution*, Center for Afro-American Studies, University of California Press, Los Angeles, 1980, p. 202.

[15]*Ibid.*, p. 203.

[16]*Ibid.*, p. 209.

[17]Frank Kofsky, "Malcolm X," *Monthly Review*, Vol. 18, No. 4, September, 1966, p. 45.

[18]I.F. Stone, *op. cit.*, p. 8.

[19]Hans J. Morgenthau, *The Purpose of American Politics*, Vintage Books, New York, 1963, p. vii.

[20]John R. Seeley, "Progress from Poverty," *Liberation*, Vol. 11, No. 4, August, 1966, p. 9.

[21]*Negro Digest*, Vol. 25, No. 11, September 1966, pp. 10-11.

[22]Stokely Carmichael, "What We Want," *New York Review of Books*, September 22, 1966, p. 6.

[23]Quoted in *Negro Digest*, Vol. 25, No. 11, September, 1966, p. 11.

[24]Malcolm X recognized this great historical transformation and said about it: "We are living in an era of revolution, and the revolt of the American Negro is part of the rebellion against the oppression and colonialism which has characterized this era . . . It is incorrect to classify the revolt of the Negro as simply a racial conflict against white, or as purely an American problem. Rather, we are today seeing a global rebellion of the oppressed against the oppressor, the exploited against the exploiter." *Malcolm X Speaks*, edited by George Breiman, Merit Publishers, New York, 1965, p. 133.

Index

Adam, 50, 52

Addis Ababa, 112, 162, 210

Africa, vii, viii, ix, 3, 4, 5, 6, 10, 12, 21, 22, 23, 24, 25, 27, 28, 31, 34, 35, 36, 37, 43, 51, 52, 53, 60, 65, 67, 73, 75, 76, 77, 78, 80, 81, 82, 85, 96, 97, 99, 119, 120, 130, 133, 134, 139, 142, 143, 161, 172, 173

African Aid Association, 140

African Community League, 113

African consciousness, 10, 33, 65, 66, 71, 82, 83, 109, 117, 129, 165

African culture, 22

African Emigration Association, 80, 81

African Methodist Episcopal Church (AME), 75, 76, 210

African National Congress of South Africa, 108, 174, 210

African past, 2, 4

African states, 4

Africanize, 132

Afro-American, vii, viii, ix, x, 1, 2, 3, 5, 10, 11, 35, 36, 49, 50, 66, 80, 99

Afro-American league, 80

Age of Enlightenment, 215

Alienation, 9, 44, 84, 123, 138, 183, 234, 236

Allen, Rev. Richard, 76, 218

America, 22, 28, 29, 33

American attitude to history, 17

American, Black, 1, 2, 3, 4, 5, 7, 34, 43, 65, 66, 67, 71, 80, 119, 130, 134, 160, 162

American civilization, 20, 30

American Colonization Society, 69, 70, 72, 109

American creed, 9, 60, 66, 86, 102

American Indian, 20

American Republic, 80

Amistad, xi

Anderson, Perry, 21, 45, 46, 109, 122

Anglo-American, 18, 69

Anglo-Saxon, 5, 6, 9, 26, 33, 44, 48, 53, 58, 77, 80, 84, 113, 208, 210

Anti-colonization movement, 69

Apartheid, 214, 219, 220, 221

Aptheker, Herbert, 161